Lecture Notes in Computer Science 9208

Commenced Publication in 1973
Founding and Former Series Editors:
Gerhard Goos, Juris Hartmanis, and Jan van Leeuwen

More information about this series at http://www.springer.com/series/7409

Chengqi Zhang · Wei Huang
Yong Shi · Philip S. Yu
Yangyong Zhu · Yingjie Tian
Peng Zhang · Jing He (Eds.)

Data Science

Second International Conference, ICDS 2015
Sydney, Australia, August 8–9, 2015
Proceedings

 Springer

Editors
Chengqi Zhang
University of Technology
Sydney
Australia

Wei Huang
Xi'an Jiaotong University
Xi'an Jiaotong
China

Yong Shi
Chinese Academy of Sciences
Beijing
China

Philip S. Yu
University of Illinois at Chicago
Chicago, IL
USA

Yangyong Zhu
Fudan University
Shanghai
China

Yingjie Tian
Research Center on Fictitious Econo
Chinese Academy of Sciences
Beijing
China

Peng Zhang
University of Technology
Sydney
Australia

Jing He
Victoria University
Melbourne, VIC
Australia

ISSN 0302-9743   ISSN 1611-3349   (electronic)
Lecture Notes in Computer Science
ISBN 978-3-319-24473-0   ISBN 978-3-319-24474-7   (eBook)
DOI 10.1007/978-3-319-24474-7

Library of Congress Control Number: 2015949284

LNCS Sublibrary: SL3 – Information Systems and Applications, incl. Internet/Web, and HCI

Springer Cham Heidelberg New York Dordrecht London

Printed on acid-free paper

Springer International Publishing AG Switzerland is part of Springer Science+Business Media
(www.springer.com)

Preface

The 2015 International Conference on Data Science, ICDS 2015, held its 2nd meeting at the University of Technology Sydney on August 8–9, 2015, in co-location with the 21st ACM SIGKDD Conference on Knowledge Discovery and Data Mining, held on August 10–13 in Sydney. The 24 papers accepted in this year's ICDS conference covering a wide variety of topics within the field of big data science were divided into five oral sessions and one poster and reception session. We are particularly indebted to our 12 keynote speakers: Yixin Chen, Huan Liu, Ramamohanarao Kotagiri, Jian Pei, Yong Shi, Geoff Webb, Wei Wang, Hui Xiong, Philip Yu, Albert Zomaya, Yangyong Zhu, and Zhi-Hua Zhou. The keynote speakers are world-renowned researchers in big data analytics. The keynote talk title and abstract can be found online at http://ic-datascience.org/icds2015/.

The editors would like to thank all of the presenters who made this conference so interesting and enjoyable. A special thanks should also be extended to the session chairs and to the over 50 reviewers, who gave of their time to evaluate the record number of submissions. We are grateful to all of the faculty, staff, and volunteer students of the Research Centre on Quantum Computation and Intelligent Systems (QCIS), University of Technology Sydney (UTS), especially to the committee chair, Chengqi Zhang, and QCIS staff, Dr. Jing Jiang and Ms. Li Liu. They have contributed much time in coordinating the conference. Special thanks also go to Dr. Ling Chen, the general chair of the 13th Australian Data Mining conference, AusDM 2015. We owe all these people a great debt as this conference would not have been possible without their constant efforts. Finally, we would like to especially thank the Research Center on Fictitious Economy and Data Science, and the CAS Key Laboratory on Big Data Mining and Knowledge Management, of the Chinese Academy of Sciences, China; the University of the Chinese Academy of Sciences, China; the Shanghai Key Laboratory of Data Science, Fudan University, China; the School of Management, Xi'an Jiaotong University, China; and the Centre for Quantum Computation & Intelligent Systems (QCIS), Australia. We hope that all of you reading this enjoy these selections as much as we enjoyed the conference.

July 2015

Chengqi Zhang
Jing He
Peng Zhang

Organization

Program Committee members

Chengqi Zhang	University of Technology Sydney, Australia
Wei Huang	Xi'an Jiaotong University, China
Yong Shi	Chinese Academy of Sciences, China
Philip S. Yu	University of Illinois at Chicago, USA
Yangyong Zhu	Fudan University, China
Yingjie Tian	Chinese Academy of Sciences, China
Peng Zhang	University of Technology Sydney, Australia
Jing He	Victoria University, Australia

Sponsors

The Centre for Quantum Computation & Intelligent Systems, University of Technology Sydney, Australia
Research Center on Fictitious Economy and Data Science, the Chinese Academy of Sciences, China and the CAS Key Laboratory on Big Data Mining and Knowledge Management, University of the Chinese Academy of Sciences, China
Shanghai Key Laboratory of Data Science, Fudan University, China
School of Management, Xi'an Jiaotong University, China

Contents

Design of Personalized News Comments Recommendation System

Mingnan Zhou[4], Ruisheng Shi[1,2(✉)], Zhaozhen Xu[4], Yuan He[4],
Yiyi Zhou[4], and Lina Lan[3]

[1] Key Laboratory of Trustworthy Distributed Computing and Service (BUPT),
Ministry of Education, Beijing, China
shiruisheng@bupt.edu.cn
[2] School of Humanities, Beijing University of Posts and Telecommunications,
Beijing, China
[3] School of Network Education,
Beijing University of Posts and Telecommunications, Beijing, China
lanlina@bupt.edu.cn
[4] International School, Beijing University of Posts and Telecommunications,
Beijing, China

Abstract. Nowadays people spend lots of time on browsing news on the Internet. News comment as one of the most common things that people find on the website, is earning more attention than before. News comments have significant impacts on people's decision and behavior as news itself. People find that they are always overwhelmed by massive comments and valuable comments are drowned in large amounts of uninteresting comments. This paper presents a multi-dimensional classification system and the personalized recommendation system of news comments, which aims to provide comments classification and personalized recommendation services. With this system, users will get a better users experience and get a comprehensive view of the news and comments with cheaper time cost.

Keywords: Multi-dimensional classification · Personalized recommendation · Comments

1 Introduction

Nowadays people are facing a growing number of information. News is one of the most important parts of the information that people read every day. According the research, users even pay more attention to the news comments, some of which contain more

Supported by National Grand Fundamental Research 973 Program of China under Grant No. 2013CB329605; Key Project of Science and Technology in Henan Province (2014) under Grant No. 144300510001; Transformation Project of Scientific and Technological Achievements in Henan Province (2014) under Grant No. 142201210009; Chinese Universities Scientific Fund (BUPT2014RC0701); BUPT (Beijing University of Posts and Telecommunications) Undergraduate Innovation Research Fund.

C. Zhang et al. (Eds.): ICDS 2015, LNCS 9208, pp. 1–5, 2015.
DOI: 10.1007/978-3-319-24474-7_1

useful information, but some not. Reading the valuable comments can let users have a good habit of calm thinking. Many comments on the websites are valid and repeated, which means the comments should be screened, classified and recommended. So this system is designed to produce a better and more efficient way for users to read the news comments on the Internet.

2   Related Works

It is extraordinarily important for the news website to give a special and scientific order for the news comments. This paper has made an investigation of the most popular news website, and found the following standard to give the order of the comments: (a) Posted time: Its disadvantage is the latest comment may not be the most valid one and could not give more meaningful information. (b) The number of "hearts": At present there is usually an icon of heart just under each piece of the comments. If someone like some comment, he could just lick the button to show his opinion or attitude. Its disadvantage is that the most popular comments may not fit you. Everyone has his own view and standard of judgment, so it is not so scientific to order with only one dimension. (c) The counts of the discussion: The number of discussion under a comment reflects the fact that it attracts more attention from the Internet. Some website manager puts the most attracted one in the front of the comments queue [1]. Its disadvantage is sometimes the number of discussions under some comment may not tell the true popularity. Two users can have a long conversation that is unrelated with the news.

3   System Architecture

The system contains three main parts: the comments collecting and filtering system, the multi-dimension classification system and the personalized recommendation system (Fig. 1).

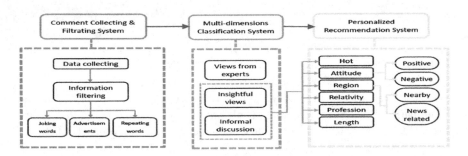

Fig. 1. System architecture

Data Collecting. The system uses crawler to collect data from the website Sina (www. sina.com.cn), which is one of the biggest websites of the news with comments coming from a large variety of people. The layout of the comments of the Sina is more complex than other website. We use ICTCLAS [2] to do Chinese word segmentation for news and comments, where a piece of news or a comments is seen as a sequence of words and weights which valued with the word frequency.

Information Filtering. The initial comments collected from the websites contain much repeat and unrelated information 78.3 % of the news has similar comments that provides less information for users, and 37.3 % of the news contains meaningless information. So the initial filtering is important for the system and it contains joking words, advertisements and repeating words.

The Multi-dimensions Classification. This is the most important part of the system. There is a multi-dimensional standard including attitude aspects, relativity, length of comments, hottest comment, region aspects, and profession of the comments. SVM (support vector machine) algorithm [3, 4] is used to do the emotion classification.

The Personalized Recommendation. The recommendation system evaluates the value of the comments based on the classification and the habits of the users. And to present objective and meaningful comments, the system will mix different kinds of information to do recommend.

4 Multi-dimensional Classification

1. **Profession Dimension:** This dimension is used to get 'views from experts'. It will be classified through the source of information. The comments in this category are collect from the 'expert comments' area on the websites.
2. **Length of the Comment:** The length of the comments is used to distinguish 'insightful views' and 'informal discussion'. We found comments of below 20 words are 35 %, 20–30 words are 17 %, 30–40 words are 9 %, 40–50 words are 8 %, 50–60 are 10 %, 60 words and over are 21 %. According to the statistics, 60 % of the comments are under 39 words (include 39). So that the comments which over 39 words are defined as 'long comment' and classified in 'insightful view'. The comments that are under 39 words (include 39) are classified in 'informal discussion'.
3. **Relativity:** Relativity between the news and a comment is used to further distinguish 'insightful views' and 'informal discussion'. The cosine similarity metric is used to calculate the relativity between the news and a comment, following the Eq. (1) $\vec{C}_i$ and $\vec{N}$ are the comment and the news vector weighted with word frequency. After the calculation, some comments are classified as 'insightful views'.

$$Sim(\vec{C}_i, \vec{N}) = \cos < \vec{C}_i, \vec{N} > = \frac{\vec{C}_i \cdot \vec{N}}{|\vec{C}_i| * |\vec{N}|} \tag{1}$$

4. **Attitude Consideration:** The comments of the news contain both rational and emotional information. For emotion, the comments of specific news often have lots of comments that show similar attitude. In our system, the comments are simply classified into two categories: positive and negative (Table 1).

Table 1. The attitude of news comments (sample numbers: 500 source: news.sina.com)

	Political news	Social news	Military news	Processed news
Positive	74 %	61 %	34 %	45 %
Negative	20 %	25 %	40 %	45 %
Neural	6 %	14 %	26 %	10 %

The training dataset is labeled with 3500 comments of 100 news posts, which form a dataset containing over 5800 features. The trained model can be used to make classification. Comments are put into the model to make prediction.

5. **Region:** The authenticity is important. Some news writers come to the place of the incident themselves to observe what happened, but some may not. The later groups of people may only judge and analysis the property from others, but not the fact. The people live locally may know more information and details, so their critics have stronger voice than others.

5 Personalized Recommendation

The recommendation system is used to provide a better user experience, let the users get what they interested in rapidly and help them understand the news in detail.

- **Collecting user information**
  This system uses an implicit way to collect user information that mainly comes from users' personal records. Users will leave their respective log data on Web servers when visiting these sites. These log data are usually stored in servers in the form of document files [5]. Every user will have their own log, which contains their record of liking and the comment they wrote before.
- **The standard of recommendation**
  Three aspects are designed to present the information for each user.

(a) Attitude collocation: The system gives each comment a label. And the habit of users is collected and it can be used to predict which kind of comment they prefer and present the information.

(b) Region based recommendation: Sometimes only the local people know the truth. So the comments written by indigenes will get marks and are recommended firstly.

(c) The valuable comments recommendation with our classification algorithm:

'Views from experts' collects the professional comments from the experts.
'Insightful views' collects the insightful and useful comments from the users.
'Informal discussion' collects some low-value comments from the users.

6 Conclusion

By using this system, users can read the comments more convenient, which means they can get the valuable and expected information effectively and broaden their horizon through reading. The classification and recommendation of the comments will bring a totally new user experience. Next we're trying to build a recommendation model, to score each comment and to rank the comments for recommendation.

Acknowledgements. Thanks for the valuable comments from Ruifang Liu and technical discussion with Yongjiang Zhao, Qinlong Wang.

References

1. By the counts of discussion. Tecent coral news. http://www.qq.com/coral/coralindex/indexCoral_new.htm
2. ICTCLAS. http://ictclas.org. Accessed 10 September 2009
3. Jakkula, V.: Tutorial on Support Vector
4. Yu, H., Kim, S.: SVM Tutorial: Classification, Regression, and Ranking. Handbook of Natural Computing. Springer, Berlin (2009)
5. Fan, Y., Shen, Y., Mai, J.: Study of the model of e-commerce personalized recommendation system based on data mining

Minimizing the Social Influence from a Topic Modeling Perspective

Qipeng Yao[1,2]([✉]) and Li Guo[1]

[1] Institute of Information Engineering, Chinese Academy of Sciences,
Beijing 100093, China
yaoqipeng0706@gmail.com, guoli@iie.ac.cn
[2] School of Computer Science, Beijing University of Posts
and Telecommunications, Beijing 100876, China

Abstract. In this paper, we address the problem of minimizing the negative influence of undesirable things in a network by blocking a limited number of nodes from a topic modeling perspective. When undesirable thing such as a rumor or an infection emerges in a social network and part of users have already been infected, our goal is to minimize the size of ultimately infected users by blocking k nodes outside the infected set. We first employ the HDP-LDA and KL divergence to analysis the influence and relevance from a topic modeling perspective. Then two topic-aware heuristics based on betweenness and out-degree for finding approximate solutions to this problem are proposed. Using two real networks, we demonstrate experimentally the high performance of the proposed models and learning schemes.

Keywords: Influence minimization · Blocking nodes · Social networks

1 Introduction

In the past decade, the online social networks are providing convenient platforms for information dissemination and marketing campaign, allowing ideas and behaviors to flow along the social relationships in the effective word-of-mouth manner [1,2]. From the functional point of perspective, networks can mediate diffusion including not only positive information such as innovations, hot topics, and novel ideas, but also negative information like malicious rumors and disinformation [3]. Take the rumor for example, even with a small number of its initial adopters, the quantity of the ultimately infected users can be large due to triggering a word-of-mouth cascade in the network. Therefore, it is an urgent research issue to design effective strategies for reducing the influence coverage of the negative information and minimizing the spread of the undesirable things.

This problem has received a good deal of attention by the data mining research community in the last decade [4,5], but quite surprisingly, the characteristics of the item being the subject of the influence minimization has been left out of the picture.

© Springer International Publishing Switzerland 2015
C. Zhang et al. (Eds.): ICDS 2015, LNCS 9208, pp. 6–15, 2015.
DOI: 10.1007/978-3-319-24474-7_2

In this paper, we aim to minimize the spread of an existing undesirable thing by blocking a limited number of nodes in a network from a topic modeling perspective. More specifically, when some undesirable thing starts with some initial nodes and diffuses through the network under the topic-aware independent cascade (TIC) model, we consider finding a set of k nodes such that the resulting network by blocking those nodes can minimize the expected contamination area of the undesirable thing, where k is a given positive integer. We refer to this combinatorial optimization problem as the *influence minimization problem*. For this problem, we first employ the HDP-LDA and KL divergence to analysis the authoritativeness, influence and relevance from a topic modeling perspective. Then we propose two topic-aware heuristics based on betweenness and out-degree for finding approximate solutions to the problem. With two large real networks including Sina microblog and Facebook, we experimentally demonstrate that the proposed topic-aware node-removal heuristics outperform the well-studied notions of centrality measures.

2   Related Works

The research on finding influential nodes that are effective for the spread of information through a social network, namely Influence Maximization Problem, has attracted remarkable attention recently due to its novel idea of leveraging some social network users to propagate the awareness of products [2,6]. To improve the efficiency of seed selection, many heuristics and optimized greedy algorithms have been proposed, *e.g.*, DegreeDiscount [2], MIA [7], DAG [8], SIMPATH [9], ShortestPath [10], SPIN [11], CELF [12], CELF++ [13] and UBLF [14–16]. Besides, Guo et al. [17] investigated the influence maximization problem from the item-based data. Rodriguez et al. [18] studied the influence maximization problem in continuous time diffusion networks. Goyal et al. [19] proposed an alternative approach to influence maximization which, instead of assuming influence probabilities are given as input, directly uses the past available data. In the works [20,21] the authors discussed the integral influence maximization problem when repeated activations are involved. Zhou and Guo [22] established a constraint influence maximization framework for special targeted users. As a reverse problem, the source detection in a social network was discussed by Zang et al. [23,24]. However, the problem of minimizing the negative influence of undesirable things gets less attention, although it is an important research issue.

Some related research work has been made on minimizing the influence of negative information by removing nodes or links from a network [25,26]. It has been shown in particular that the strategies of removing nodes in decreasing order of out-degree can often be effective [5,27,28]. Kimura et al. proposed a links blocking method to minimize the expected contamination area of the network [4]. However, the fact of part nodes infected is not considered. Yu et al. addressed the problem of finding spread blockers are simply those nodes with high degree [29]. Budak et al. investigated the problem of influence limitation where a bad campaign starts propagation from a certain node in the network and use the notion of limiting campaigns to counteract the effect of misinformation [3]. Different from previous work, our research cares more about a specific contamination scenario in the social network, and how to minimize the negative influence by blocking a small set of nodes from a topic modeling perspective.

3   Problem Formulation

To model the topic-aware social influence, we adopt the *Topic-aware Independent Cascade (TIC) Model* [30], where the user-to-user influence probabilities depend on the topic. Therefore, for each arc $(v, u) \in E$ and each topic $z \in [1, K]$ we are given a probability $p_{v,u}^z$, representing the strength of the influence exerted by user v on user u on topic z. Moreover for each item $i \in \mathcal{I}$ that propagates in the network, we have a distribution over the topics, that is for each topic $z \in [1, K]$ we are given $\gamma_i^z = P(Z = z|i)$, with $\sum_{z=1}^{K} \gamma_i^z = 1$. In this model a propagation happens like in the IC model: when a node v first becomes active on item i, has one chance of influencing each inactive neighbor u, independently of the history thus far. The tentative succeeds with a probability that is the weighted average of the link probability w.r.t. the topic distribution of the item i:

$$p_{v,u}^i = \sum_{z=1}^{K} \gamma_i^z p_{v,u}^z. \tag{1}$$

Under the directed graph $G = (V, E)$, the *influence spread* of the initially infected set S, which is the ultimately expected number of infected nodes, is denoted as $\sigma(S|V)$.

Now we present a mathematical definition for the *influence minimization problem*. Assume the negative information spreads in the network $G = (V, E)$ with initially infected nodes $S \subseteq V$, our goal here is to minimize the number of ultimately infected nodes by blocking k nodes (or vertices) of set $D \in V$, where k ($\ll |V|$) is a given const. It can be formulated as the following optimization problem:

$$D^* = \arg \min_{D \subseteq V, |D| \leq k} \sigma(S|V \backslash D) \tag{2}$$

where $\sigma(S|V \backslash D)$ denotes the influence (number of ultimately infected nodes) of S when the node set D is blocked.

4   Topic Model Analysis

Before we solve this problem above, we should introduce the Latent Dirichlet Allocation based on Hierarchical Dirichlet Process (HDP-LDA) method first.

In the first step, we adopt the hierarchical Dirichlet processes to learn the topic distribution $\theta_{e_{u,v}}$ for each link $e_{u,v}$. HDP-LDA is non-parametric topic model which can automatically determine the proper number of topic K based on

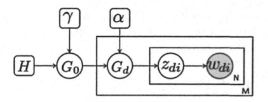

Fig. 1. Graphical Model for HDP. γ, α_0 and H are hyper parameters. G_d denotes random measure at the document level while G_0 at the corpus level. z_{di} denotes the topic of word w_{di} while w_{di} denotes the ith word in document d.

the data at hand. It has been proved that HDP outperforms other unsupervised topic models, e.g. *LDA* [31] and *LSI* [32], on modeling large scale web texts.

This step contains three sub-steps. First, we collect all the messages on the links, which forms a document set $D = \{d_{e_{u,v},i} | e_{u,v} \in E, i = 1, \cdots, N_{e_{u,v}}\}$, where $N_{e_{u,v}}$ is the number of messages on link $e_{u,v}$. Second, we adopt HDP-LDA to learn the number of topic K and the topic distribution $\theta_{e_{u,v},i}$ for each message. Third, the topic distribution for link $\theta_{e_{u,v}}$ is calculated by averaging the topic distribution $\theta_{e_{u,v},i}$ and the topic distribution of the target information $\theta_{d'}$ is predicted (Fig. 1).

4.1   Model Description

HDP defines a set of random measures G_d, one for each document, and a global random measure G_0. G_d models the topic distributions at the document level while G_0 at the corpus level. Each word w_{di} is associated with a topic z_{di} sampled from G_d. To share the topics across documents, the document-specific random measures G_d are drawn from the global measure with Dirichlet process $DP(\alpha, G_0)$, where α is a concentration factor. The global measure G_0 is also sampled from a corpus-level DP with a concentration parameter γ and a base probability measure H. In summary, we define the generative process of HDP as follows.

$$G_0 | \gamma, H \sim DP(\gamma, H), \quad G_d | \alpha, G_0 \sim DP(\alpha, G_0)$$
$$z_{di} | G_d \sim G_d, \quad w_{di} | z_{di} \sim F(z_{di}) \tag{3}$$

HDP can be constructed with the Chinese Restaurant Franchise processes (CRF). In the metaphor of CRF, a restaurant franchise corresponds to a corpus, and each restaurant corresponds to a document. A global menu of dishes in the restaurant corresponds to a topic $\phi_1, \cdots, \phi_K$. A customer corresponds to a word in a document. And the process of a customer picking a table corresponds to generating a word with a topic. In particular, we need to maintain the counts of customers and tables. Here, n_{dbk} denotes the number of customers in the restaurant d at table b eating dish k and m_{dk} denotes the number of tables in the restaurant d serving dish k. In this paper, marginal counts are represented with dots. Thus, $n_{db.}$ represents the number of customers in the restaurant d

at table b, and so on. In metaphor of CRF, for a word w_{id}, the conditional distribution for the word's topic selection z_{di} given $z_{d1}, \cdots, z_{d,i-1}$ and G_0 as in Eq. (4), where G_d is integrated out.

$$z_{di}|z_{d,1:i-1}, \alpha, G_0 \sim \sum_{b=1}^{m_{d \cdot}} \frac{n_{db \cdot}}{i-1+\alpha} \delta_{\psi_{db}} + \frac{\alpha}{i-1+\alpha} G_0 \qquad (4)$$

And the conditional distribution of $\psi_{db^{new}}$ is given in Eq. (5).

$$\psi_{db^{new}}|\psi_{1:d-1}, \cdot, \psi_{d,1:m_{d\cdot}-1}, \gamma, H \sim \sum_{k \in K} \frac{m_{\cdot k}}{m_{\cdot\cdot}+\gamma} \delta_{\phi_k} + \frac{\gamma}{m_{\cdot\cdot}+\gamma} H \qquad (5)$$

Equations (3), (4) and (5) together describe the CRF construction of HDP.

4.2   Model Inference

We adopted the Gibbs sampling algorithm to infer the latent state of HDP. In Gibbs sampling scheme [33], the state of one variable is sampled with all the other states fixed. We sample the latent variables in sequence until convergence. In HDP, the latent variables of interests are the corpus-level topic distribution β, the topic for each word z_{di}, and the number of tables for each topic in document m_{kj}.

– **Sampling G_0.** Given CRF construction of HDP, the corpus-level topic distribution G_0 can be instantiated as $G_0 = \sum_k \beta_k \delta_{\phi_k} + \beta_u H$. And it is distributed as in Eq. (6):

$$\beta = (\beta_1, ..., \beta_K, \beta_u)|m_{\cdot, P\cdot}, \gamma \sim Dir(m_{\cdot 1}, ..., m_{\cdot K}, \gamma) \qquad (6)$$

– **Sampling z_{ji}.** Given CRF construction of HDP, It can be realized by grouping together terms associated with each k.

$$p(z_{ji} = k|z^{-ji}, m, \beta) = \begin{cases} (n_{j \cdot k}^{-ji} + \alpha_0 \beta_k) f_k^{-x_{ji}}(x_{ji}, w_{ji}) & \text{for existing } k\,, \\ \alpha_0 \beta_u f_{k^{new}}^{-x_{ji}}(x_{ji}) & \text{for new topic } k = k^{new}. \end{cases} \qquad (7)$$

– **Sampling m.** Given the CRF construction of HDP, the number of tables is determined by the scaling factors as well as the number of words in the documents. Antoniak(1974) [34] has shown that m_{jk} is distributed as in Eq. (8):

$$p(m_{jk} = m|z, m^{-jk} = k, \beta) = \frac{\Gamma(\alpha_0 \beta_k)}{\Gamma(\alpha_0 \beta_k + n_{j \cdot k})} s(n_{j \cdot k}, m) \alpha_0 \beta_k{}^m \qquad (8)$$

where $s(n, m)$ are unsigned Stirling number of the first kind.

Given the samples, the posterior of topic distribution of message j can be calculated as in Eq. (9)

$$\theta_j = (\theta_{j1}, \theta_{j2}, \cdots, \theta_{jK}) \sim Dir(n_{j \cdot 1} + \alpha_0 \beta_1, n_{j \cdot 2} + \alpha_0 \beta_2, \cdots, n_{j \cdot K} + \alpha_0 \beta_K) \qquad (9)$$

And the distributions of the link can be computed by averaging the distribution of messages on that link:

$$\theta_{e_{u,v}} = \frac{\sum_{i \in d_{e_{u,v}}} \theta_i}{N_{e_{u,v}}} \qquad (10)$$

4.3   Prediction

We have trained the model on a fully observed data of social network $G = (V, E)$ at hand, and get the word distribution for each topic denoted as ϕ_k, where $k = 1, 2, ..., K$ and K is the number of topics. We will use the ϕ_k to predict the topic distribution $\theta_{d'}$ for the new message d' with EM algorithm. In the E-step, given fixed ϕ_k and random topic distribution $\theta_{d'}$, we can compute the topic of every word z_{ji}. And in the M-step, we will compute the new $\theta_{d'}$ with the result from E step. The E-step and M-step is conducted iteratively until convergence.

5   Analysis and Solution for Influence Minimization

The problem of learning the parameters of the TIC models takes in input the social graph $G = (V, E)$, a log of past propagations $\mathbb{D}$, and an integer K, which can be learnt by the Latent Dirichlet Allocation based on Hierarchical Dirichlet Process (HDP-LDA) method. The propagation log is a relation (User, Item, Time) where a tuple $(u, i, t) \in \mathbb{D}$ indicates that user u adopted item i at time t. The output of the learning problem is the set of all parameters of the TIC propagation model, which we denote Θ: these are γ_i^z and $p_{v,u}^z$ for all $i \in \mathcal{I}$, $(v, u) \in E$, and $z \in [1, K]$. Assuming that each propagation trace is independent from the others, the likelihood of the data given the model parameters Θ, can be expressed as: $\mathcal{L}(\Theta; D) = \sum_{i \in \mathcal{I}} \log \mathcal{L}(\Theta; D_i)$. We then adopt the standard EM inference of parameters Θ for TIC. We calculate the topic distributions of each uninfected node w and negative information i via HDP-LDA, then calculate the KL divergences $d(w, i)$ between node w and information i from the topic perspective.

Now we are back to the optimal problem (2), any straightforward method for exact solution suffers from combinatorial explosion for a large network. Therefore, we consider approximately solving the problem, while a natural idea is to block the nodes in the neighborhood of infected set. Specifically, given the initially infected set S and the negative information i, define the neighborhood set $N(S)$ like

$$N(S) := \big\{ v \in V \backslash S : \ \exists u \in S, \ s.\ t.\ (u, v) \in E \big\}.$$

We want to block k susceptible nodes in the set $N(S)$ to minimize the negative influence. Since the set $N(S)$ is usually very large (i.e. $|N(S)| \gg k$), a natural question arises, *how to select k susceptible nodes from the set $N(S)$ to block in order to make the ultimate influence as small as possible?* In this paper, given the negative information $i \in \mathcal{I}$, we introduce two scoring methods for the nodes in $N(S)$, and then select k nodes with the highest scores as the objectives to block.

Topic-aware Betweenness Scoring Method. Given the initially infected nodes S, the betweenness score $b(w)$ of a node $w \in N(S)$ is defined as follows:

$$b(w) = \sum_{u \in S, v \in V \backslash S} \frac{n(w; u, v)}{N(u, v)} \tag{11}$$

where $N(u,v)$ denotes the number of the shortest paths from node u to node v in G, and $n(w;u,v)$ denotes the number of those paths that pass w. Here we set $n(w;u,v)/N(u,v) = 0$ if $N(u,v) = 0$. We defined the topic-aware betweenness as

$$tb(w) = \frac{b(w)}{d(w,i)}. \tag{12}$$

Topic-aware Out-degree Scoring Method. Previous work has shown that simply removing nodes in order of decreasing out-degrees works well for preventing the spread of contamination in most real networks [5]. Here we focus on the contaminated set S and the corresponding $i \in \mathcal{I}$. We define the out-degree score $o(w)$ of node $w \in N(S)$ as the number of non-contaminative nodes around w. We defined the topic-aware out-degree as

$$to(w) = \frac{o(w)}{d(w,i)}. \tag{13}$$

Equations (12) and (13) are reasonable, since we can find that the smaller $d(w,i)$ is, the more susceptible the node w is; and the bigger $b(w)$ or $o(w)$ is, the more pivotal the node w is. Hence blocking the nodes with the highest topic-aware betweenness and outdegree score should be effective for preventing the spread of contamination in the network.

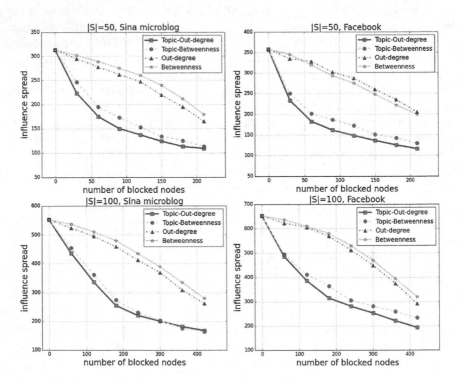

Fig. 2. Experiment result on two data sets.

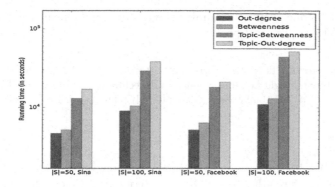

Fig. 3. The time comparison among the four methods.

6   Experiment Results

We experimentally evaluate the performance of our proposed approaches on two networks. One is crawled from Sina microblog containing 2,000 nodes, 14,426 edges and the propagation log. The other is Facebook data acquired from Stanford Network Analysis Project containing 4,039 nodes and 88,234 edges, where the topic probability for each user is created by the HDP-LDA model. We use the Gibbs sampling method to estimate the hyper parameters γ, α_0 and H in HDP-LDA. We employ the Monte-Carlo simulation of TIC model to estimate the influence spread.

From the results in Fig. 2, we can observe that the ultimate influence spreads by Topic-aware heuristics are significantly reduced compared to that by Out-degree and Betweenness centralities, especially in the early stage. For the infected set S with $|S| = 50$ on Sina microblog, we can observe that the proposed method can reduce the negative spread from 320 to 180 by blocking 60 nodes. Here the blocked 60 nodes only accounts to 15 % of the nodes that are connected to infected nodes. From the running results in Fig. 3, we can draw a conclusion that, although the performance is improved greatly, the time cost of topic-aware heuristics are still in the same magnitude with centrality measures.

7   Conclusion

In this paper we investigate the problem of minimizing the spread of negative things by blocking nodes in social networks from a topic modeling perspective. We use the HDP-LDA and KL divergence to analysis the influence and relevance, then two topic-aware heuristics based on betweenness and out-degree for finding approximate solutions are proposed. Using two real networks Sina Microblog and Facebook, we demonstrate experimentally the high performance of the proposed algorithms.

There are several interesting future directions. First, how to extend it to a dynamic network when the network structure changes over time is an interesting question [35]. Second, how to minimize the negative influence with the real cascade data is also a practical problem.

Acknowledgements. This work was supported by the 973 project (No. 2013CB 329606), and the Strategic Leading Science and Technology Projects of Chinese Academy of Sciences (No. XDA06030200), Australia ARC Discovery Project (DP1402206).

References

1. Domingos, P., Richardson, M.: Mining the network value of customers. In: Proceedings of the Seventh ACM SIGKDD International Conference on Knowledge Discovery and Data Mining, pp. 57–66. ACM (2001)
2. Chen, W., Wang, Y., Yang, S.: Efficient influence maximization in social networks. In: Proceedings of the 15th ACM SIGKDD International Conference on Knowledge Discovery and Data Mining, pp. 199–208. ACM (2009)
3. Budak, C., Agrawal, D., El Abbadi, A.: Limiting the spread of misinformation in social networks. In: Proceedings of the WWW 2011, pp. 665–674. ACM (2011)
4. Kimura, M., Saito, K., Motoda, H.: Minimizing the spread of contamination by blocking links in a network. In: AAAI, vol. 8, pp. 1175–1180 (2008)
5. Wang, S., Zhao, X., Chen, Y., Li, Z., Zhang, K., Xia, J.: Negative influence minimizing by blocking nodes in social networks. In: AAAI (Late-Breaking Developments) (2013)
6. Kempe, D., Kleinberg, J., Tardos, É.: Maximizing the spread of influence through a social network. In: Proceedings of the Ninth ACM SIGKDD International Conference on Knowledge Discovery and Data Mining, pp. 137–146. ACM (2003)
7. Chen, W., Wang, C., Wang, Y.: Scalable influence maximization for prevalent viral marketing in large-scale social networks. In: Proceedings of the 16th ACM SIGKDD International Conference on Knowledge Discovery and Data Mining, pp. 1029–1038. ACM (2010)
8. Chen, W., Yuan, Y., Zhang, L.: Scalable influence maximization in social networks under the linear threshold model. In: ICDM 2010 (2010)
9. Goyal, A., Lu, W., Lakshmanan, L.V.: Simpath: an efficient algorithm for influence maximization under the linear threshold model. In: IEEE 11th International Conference on Data Mining (ICDM), pp. 211–220. IEEE (2011)
10. Kimura, M., Saito, K.: Tractable models for information diffusion in social networks. In: Fürnkranz, J., Scheffer, T., Spiliopoulou, M. (eds.) PKDD 2006. LNCS (LNAI), vol. 4213, pp. 259–271. Springer, Heidelberg (2006)
11. Narayanam, R., Narahari, Y.: A shapley value-based approach to discover influential nodes in social networks. IEEE Trans. Autom. Sci. Eng. **99**, 1–18 (2010)
12. Leskovec, J., Krause, A., Guestrin, C., Faloutsos, C., VanBriesen, J., Glance, N.: Cost-effective outbreak detection in networks. In: KDD 2007 (2007)
13. Goyal, A., Lu, W., Lakshmanan, L.V.: Celf++: optimizing the greedy algorithm for influence maximization in social networks. In: WWW 2011 (2011)
14. Zhou, C., Zhang, P., Guo, J., Zhu, X., Guo, L.: Ublf: an upper bound based approach to discover influential nodes in social networks. In: IEEE 13th International Conference on Data Mining (ICDM), pp. 907–916. IEEE (2013)
15. Zhou, C., Zhang, P., Guo, J., Guo, L.: An upper bound based greedy algorithm for mining top-k influential nodes in social networks. In: 23rd International World Wide Web Conference (WWW), pp. 421–422. ACM (2014)

16. Zhou, C., Zhang, P., Zang, W., Guo, L.: On the upper bounds of spread for greedy algorithms in social network influence maximization. IEEE Trans. Knowl. Data Eng

17. Guo, J., Zhang, P., Zhou, C., Cao, Y., Guo, L.: Item-based top-k influential user discovery in social networks. In: IEEE 13th International Conference on Data Mining Workshops (ICDMW), pp. 780–787. IEEE (2013)

18. Rodriguez, M.G., Schölkopf, B.: Influence maximization in continuous time diffusion networks, arXiv preprint arXiv:1205.1682

19. Goyal, A., Bonchi, F., Lakshmanan, L.V.: A data-based approach to social influence maximization. Proc. VLDB Endowment **5**(1), 73–84 (2011)

20. Zhou, C., Zhang, P., Zang, W., Guo, L.: Maximizing the long-term integral influence in social networks under the voter model. In: 23rd International World Wide Web Conference (WWW), pp. 423–424. ACM (2014)

21. Zhou, C., Zhang, P., Zang, W., Guo, L.: Maximizing the cumulative influence through a social network when repeat activation exists. In: ICCS 2014 (2014)

22. Zhou, C., Guo, L.: A note on influence maximization in social networks from local to global and beyond. Procedia Comput. Sci. **30**, 81–87 (2014)

23. Zang, W., Zhang, P., Zhou, C., Guo, L.: Discovering multiple diffusion source nodes in social networks. Procedia Comput. Sci. **29**, 443–452 (2014)

24. Zang, W., Wang, P., Zhou, C., Guo, L.: Topic-aware source locating in social networks. In: 24th International World Wide Web Conference. ACM (2015)

25. Yao, Q., Zhou, C., Xiang, L., Cao, Y., Guo, L.: Minimizing the negative influence by blocking links in social networks. In: 2014 International Standard Conference on Trustworthy Computing and Services (2014)

26. Yao, Q., Zhou, C., Shi, R., Wang, P., Guo, L.: Topic-aware social influence minimization. In: 24th International World Wide Web Conference. ACM (2015)

27. Albert, R., Jeong, H., Barabási, A.-L.: Error and attack tolerance of complex networks. Nature **406**(6794), 378–382 (2000)

28. Newman, M.E., Forrest, S., Balthrop, J.: Email networks and the spread of computer viruses. Phys. Rev. E **66**(3), 035101 (2002)

29. Habiba, Yu, Y., Berger-Wolf, T.Y., Saia, J.: Finding spread blockers in dynamic networks. In: Giles, L., Smith, M., Yen, J., Zhang, H. (eds.) SNAKDD 2008. LNCS, vol. 5498, pp. 55–76. Springer, Heidelberg (2010)

30. Barbieri, N., Bonchi, F., Manco, G.: Topic-aware social influence propagation models. In: Proceedings of the ICDM 2012, pp. 81–90. IEEE Computer Society (2012)

31. Blei, D.M., Ng, A.Y., Jordan, M.I.: Latent dirichlet allocation. J. Mach. Learn. Res. **3**, 993–1022 (2003)

32. Dumais, S.T.: Latent semantic analysis. Ann. Rev. Inf. Sci. Technol. **38**(1), 188–230 (2004)

33. Casella, G., George, E.I.: Explaining the gibbs sampler. Am. Stat. **46**(3), 167–174 (1992)

34. Antoniak, C.E.: Mixtures of dirichlet processes with applications to bayesian nonparametric problems. Ann. Stat. **2**, 1152–1174 (1974)

35. Zhang, P., Zhou, C., Wang, P., Gao, B.J., Zhu, X., Guo, L.: E-tree: an efficient indexing structure for ensemble models on data streams. IEEE Trans. Knowl. Data Eng. **27**(2), 461–474 (2015)

A Study on Optimal Policy for Purchase Data Updating in ERP Systems

Wei Zong[1,2], Feng Wu[1,2(✉)], Zhengrui Jiang[3], and Yi Qu[1,2]

[1] School of Management, Xi'an Jiaotong University, 28 Xianning West Road, Xi'an 710049, People's Republic of China
wei.zong@stu.xjtu.edu.cn, fengwu@mail.xjtu.edu.cn
[2] The Key Lab of the Ministry of Education for Process Control & Efficiency Engineering, Xi'an Jiaotong University, 28 Xianning West Road, Xi'an 710049, People's Republic of China
[3] Department of Supply Chain and Information Systems, Iowa State University, 2340 Gerdin Business Building, Ames, IA 50011, USA
zjiang@iastate.edu

Abstract. In the age of big data, it is a challenging task for ERP systems to maintain data timeliness over changing data sources. Purchase data is an important dynamic data and its timeliness directly affects the accuracy of inventory data and purchase plans. According to the characteristics of Markov decision process, we design a dynamic programming algorithm to obtain the optimal purchase data updating policy. Its effectiveness is tested by comparing with traditional fixed interval policies with real-life enterprise data. The comparison results show the proposed updating policy outperforms the fixed interval policies and can be applied to enterprises when updating ERP systems.

1 Introduction

Implementing enterprise resource planning (ERP) systems is the most pervasive organizational change [1, 2]. In the era of big data, data is changing at an alarming velocity [3]. This requires ERP systems react to data changes rapidly. For inventory data, if a new purchase order has arrived and the ERP system is not updated in time, the staleness cost for making decisions on inaccurate inventory data will occur. An obvious solution is to update the ERP system once there is a change in data source, but it is costly because personnel cost in updating process is higher than the equipment and computational cost [4]. Therefore, this necessitates the analysis when and how to update the ERP data to optimize the staleness cost and updating cost.

2 Literature Review

2.1 Data Timeliness

Timeliness is an important data quality dimension. A general definition comes from [5] which referred timeliness to whether the data was out of date. They employed currency

C. Zhang et al. (Eds.): ICDS 2015, LNCS 9208, pp. 16–24, 2015.
DOI: 10.1007/978-3-319-24474-7_3

and volatility to measure timeliness. Currency is the time difference between data changes in the real-world and users use it. Volatility is the time interval that data remains valid and s is a sensitivity factor of timeliness.

$$Data\, timeliness = \left[max\left(0; 1 - {Currency}/{Volatility} \right) \right]^s \qquad (1)$$

Equation (1) denotes data timeliness is a time-related concept. The literature on data timeliness is classified into two categories. The first stream stresses when to extract data changes in the real-world into information systems. The second stream stresses how to quickly deliver data changes to users. Our research problem is when to update ERP systems with changing data, belonging to the first research stream. We need to review the related literature in the first research field.

2.2 Updating Policy

The process of determining the optimal updating policies is called synchronization or materialized view maintenance. Segev and Fang [6] proposed a stochastic model to obtain the optimal time-based and query-based updating policies. Adelberg et al. [7] discussed four updating strategies to balance the transaction deadlines with database currency. Ling and Mi [8], Dey et al. [9] formulated the synchronization process as a stochastic model to determine the optimal updating frequency by minimizing the staleness cost and synchronization cost. However, the optimal polices in these studies are mainly based on fixed intervals. In this paper, we propose an aperiodic purchase data updating policy in ERP systems and validate its optimality by comparing with the results obtained by fixed interval policies.

3 Research Model

For ease of illustration, we only consider inventory request. We model the purchase data updating problem in ERP systems as a Markov decision process [10, 11] and the updating process is elaborated in Fig. 1. The symbols used are listed in Table 1.

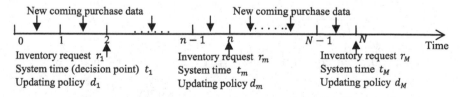

Fig. 1. The updating process for purchase data in ERP systems

The requests and updates in a database are approximated as Poisson processes [8, 9, 12]. We also assume the arrival of purchase data and inventory request is a

Table 1. The symbols used in the research model

Parameter	Description
N	The time horizon in purchase data updating problem
M	The average total number of inventory requests in a time horizon
r_m	The mth inventory request arriving at an ERP, $m = 1, \ldots, M$, $m \in Z^+$
t_m	The time when the mth inventory request arrives at an ERP system
s_m	The system state at time t_m. $s_m \in Z^+$
d_m	The decision at time t_m, $d_m = \{0, 1\}$
$P_{s_m, d_m, s_{m+1}}$	State transition probability
λ_u	The arrival rate of new purchase data in an ERP system
λ_r	The arrival rate of an inventory request in an ERP system
c_u	The updating cost at time t_m
$c_s(s_m)$	The staleness cost for inventory request r at time t_m
δ_m^*	The optimal updating policy from time t_m to t_M, $\delta_m^* = (d_m^*, d_{m+1}^*, \ldots, d_M^*)$
l_m^*	The optimal control limit at time t_m. $l_m^* \in Z^+$

Poisson distribution with intensity rate λ_u and λ_r. $d_m = 0$ indicates not updating the ERP system with new arriving purchase data. Then the accumulated purchase data at t_m will be carried to t_{m+1}. $d_m = 1$ means updating the ERP system at t_m. Then the accumulated purchase data will be input into the ERP system and will not be carried to t_{m+1}. The system state s_{m+1} can be represented as:

$$s_{m+1} = \begin{cases} s_m + I_{m,m+1} d_m = 0 \\ I_{m,m+1} d_m = 1 \end{cases} \tag{2}$$

where $I_{m,m+1}$ is the quantity of accumulated purchase data from t_m to t_{m+1}. The system transition from s_m to s_{m+1} is controlled by the transition probability. By the Poisson distribution assumption, we know the time interval between two continuous inventory requests follows the exponential distribution. Therefore we can obtain the probability of the data quantity accumulated from t_m to t_{m+1}, i.e. $P(I_{m,m+1} = h)$.

$$P(I_{m,m+1} = h) = \int_0^\infty P(I_{m,m+1} = h | (t_{m+1} - t_m)) \cdot f(t_{m+1} - t_m) d(t_{m+1} - t_m)$$

$$= \frac{(\lambda_u)^h \cdot \lambda_r}{(\lambda_u + \lambda_r)^{h+1}} \tag{3}$$

When $d_m = 0$, from Eq. (2) we know $I_{m,m+1} = s_{m+1} - s_m$ and therefore:

$$P_{s_m, d_m=0, s_{m+1}} = P(I_{m,m+1} = s_{m+1} - s_m) = \frac{(\lambda_u)^{(s_{m+1} - s_m)} \cdot \lambda_r}{(\lambda_u + \lambda_r)^{(s_{m+1} - s_m + 1)}} \tag{4}$$

When $d_m = 1$, from Eq. (2) we know $s_{m+1} = I_{m,m+1}$ and we can get:

$$P_{s_m, d_m = 1, s_{m+1}} = P\big(I_{m,m+1} = s_{m+1}\big) = \frac{(\lambda_u)^{s_{m+1}} \cdot \lambda_r}{(\lambda_u + \lambda_r)^{(s_{m+1}+1)}} \tag{5}$$

For system cost $c_m(s_m, d_m)$, if $d_m = 0$, the inventory request r_m will receive stale data and the staleness cost is generated. If $d_m = 1$, the staleness cost is avoided but the updating cost occurs. The updating cost is a constant, not depending on the number of new arriving data [9]. The system cost can be represented by Eq. (6).

$$c_m(s_m, d_m) = \begin{cases} c_s(s_m) & d_m = 0 \\ c_u & d_m = 1 \end{cases} \tag{6}$$

We define $c_s(s_m)$ as Eq. (7) shows,

$$c_s(s_m) = (c_p + c_l) \cdot F(s_m) \tag{7}$$

where purchase cost c_p and inventory cost c_l are constant, $F(s_m)$ is data staleness function. The more the purchase data is accumulated, the more likely it is to make wrong purchase decisions, thus the higher the staleness cost is. Therefore $c_s(s_m)$ is a monotone increasing function in s_m. We define $F(s_m) = 0$ when $s_m = 0$. The objective function of the purchase data updating problem is as Eq. (8) shows,

$$C = minE(c_1(s_1, d_1) + c_2(s_2, d_2) + \cdots + c_M(s_M, d_M)) \tag{8}$$

The objective function is to minimize the expected total cost in a time horizon by finding the optimal updating decision δ^* where $\delta^* = (d_1^*, d_2^*, \ldots, d_M^*)$.

4   Computation Method for the Optimal Updating Policy

From Eq. (2) we can see s_m is only affected by s_{m-1}, not dependent on the state before s_{m-1}. Define V_m as the expected total system cost from t_m to t_M,

$$V_m = c_m(s_m, d_m) + \sum\nolimits_{s_{m+1} \in S} P_{s_m, d_m, s_{m+1}} \cdot V_{m+1} \tag{9}$$

Then the minimal expected total system cost V_m^* can be written as:

$$V_m^* = min\left(c_m(s_m, d_m) + \sum\nolimits_{s_{m+1} \in S} P_{s_m, d_m, s_{m+1}} \cdot V_{m+1}^*\right) \tag{10}$$

Especially when $m = M$, due to $V_{M+1} = 0$, we have $V_m^* = c_M(s_M, d_M)$. Based on Eq. (10), we define Eq. (11),

$$R(s_m, d_m) = c_m(s_m, d_m) + \sum\nolimits_{s_{m+1} \in S} P_{s_m, d_m, s_{m+1}} \cdot V_{m+1}^* \tag{11}$$

From Eqs. (10) and (11), the minimal expected total cost V_m^* can be interpreted as the comparison result between $R(s_m, d_m = 1)$ and $R(s_m, d_m = 0)$. If $R(s_m, d_m = 0) \geq R(s_m, d_m = 1)$, it is better to update the ERP system with the new arriving purchase data. Otherwise, not updating the ERP system is better. Therefore, there is a control limit l_m^* for s_m at each decision point, as Eq. (12) shows.

$$d_m^* = \begin{cases} 0 & s_m < l_m^* \\ 1 & s_m \geq l_m^* \end{cases} \tag{12}$$

Now, finding optimal policy δ^* is reduced to determining the control limit l^*, where $l^* = (l_1^*, \ldots, l_m^*, \ldots, l_M^*)$. For the ease of calculation for infinite value of s_{m+1}, we can record the values $R(s_m, d_m = 0)$ and $R(s_m, d_m = 1)$ where s_m gradually increases from zero until the minimal s_m makes $R(s_m, d_m = 0) \geq R(s_m, d_m = 1)$. In this way, we can get the control limit l_m^* instead of directly solving $R(s_m, d_m = 0) \geq R(s_m, d_m = 1)$. We first compute l_M^* by getting the minimal quantity of accumulated purchase data by solving Eq. (13),

$$R(s_M, d_M = 0) \geq R(s_M, d_M = 1) \tag{13}$$

Next for $m = M - 1, \ldots, 1$, we judge whether $R(s_m, d_m = 0) \geq R(s_m, d_m = 1)$ where s_m gradually increases from zero to get l_m^* at each decision point. The whole computation algorithm and its sub-functions are shown in Fig. 2.

```
m = M;
compute l*_M by solving ceil (c_s(s_M) ≥ c_u);
for m = M − 1 to 1
    if m = M − 1
        compute R(s_m = 0, d_m = 0) by equation (11);
    end
    R(s_m, d_m = 1) = R(s_m = 0, d_m = 0) + c_u;
    s_m = 0;
    s_n = s_m + 1;
    while s_n > 0
        compute R(s_m, d_m = 0);
        if R(s_m, d_m = 0) ≥ R(s_m, d_m = 1)
            V*_m = R(s_m, d_m = 1);
            l*_m = s_m;
            break;
        else
            V*_m = R(s_m, d_m = 0);
            s_m = s_m + 1;
            s_n = s_n + 1;
        end
    end
    compute R(s_m = 0, d_m = 0) for m = M − 2, ..., 1;
end
```

Fig. 2. The computation algorithm for the optimal purchase data updating policy

5 Empirical Analysis

To examine the performance and effectiveness of the optimal purchase data updating policy in ERP systems, experimental tests are conducted using a real-life data from the Hua Heng Company in China (http://www.shxhh.cn/). The Hua Heng Company has a history of more than 30 years, and it is located in the Shaanxi province. It specializes in developing, designing and producing over 40 automotive part types such as radiators, expansion tanks for cars and heavy trucks. It implemented a Kingdee ERP system in March 2011. The various types of products in this company result in various kinds of materials need to be purchased and managed, which brings a big challenge to maintain the data timeliness in ERP system.

5.1 Parameter Settings

At first, the unit of time is assumed to be one day and the entire time horizon is set to be 365 days, i.e. one year in this research. According to the arriving characteristics of new purchase data and inventory requests to the ERP system in Hua Heng Company, the arrival rate of new purchase data λ_u is set to 113, representing the average number of purchase records arriving to the ERP system in one day. The arrival rate of inventory requests λ_r is 1/7, indicating that the inventory state is checked every seven days. The updating cost c_u is constituted by computation cost and personnel cost. Computation cost referred to the hardware and software cost when updating the ERP system with new data. According to the ERP system manager in Hua Heng Company, the computation cost and personal cost when updating the ERP system is 274 RMB and 150 RMB respectively. Therefore the updating cost c_u is 424 RMB. As for the staleness cost, based on Eq. (7) and the previous analysis, we know that $F(s_m)$ is a monotone increasing function. In fact, $F(s_m)$ can be interpreted as the cumulative distribution function (*CDF*) of a certain distribution [10]. Based on the calculation from the ERP database in the Hua Heng Company, the purchase cost and inventory cost due to stale and invalid purchase data is 800 RMB and 750 RMB respectively. Therefore the staleness cost can be rewritten as $c_s(s_m) = 1550 \cdot F(s_m)$.

5.2 Effectiveness Analysis

The effectiveness of the optimal purchase data updating policy proposed in this paper is tested by comparing with traditional fixed interval updating policies. The fixed interval updating policies are mainly classified into three categories [9]:

(1) Fixed time interval policy, which means that the information system is updated after a fixed time interval.
(2) Fixed requests interval policy, which means that the information system is updated after a fixed number of requests have been received.
(3) Fixed updates interval policy, which means that the information system is updated after the accumulation of a fixed number of data updates arriving at the system.

Define C as the optimal expected total cost obtained by implementing the aperiodic data updating policy proposed in this paper, C_{time} as the optimal expected total cost obtained by implementing the fixed time interval policy, $C_{request}$ as the optimal expected total cost obtained by implementing the fixed requests interval policy, and C_{update} as the optimal expected total cost obtained by implementing the fixed updates interval policy. In the first experiment, we apply the *CDF* of exponential distribution (represented by $F_{exponential}$) to $F(s_m)$ as Eq. (14) shows, where λ is a parameter. To validate the effectiveness and robustness of the new data updating policy, we conduct a set of experiments when the parameter λ changes. A comparison of the results for the four data updating policies is shown in Table 2. An obvious result in Table 2 is that even though the optimal total cost C is increasing with the growth of λ value, none of the three fixed interval updating policies appears to outperform the proposed aperiodic data updating policy. Therefore, the new data updating policy is effective and robust.

$$F(s_m) = F_{exponential}(s_m) = 1 - e^{-\lambda \cdot s_m} \tag{14}$$

Table 2. Comparisons of optimal total cost under different data updating policies (RMB)

	C	C_{time}	$C_{request}$	C_{update}
$\lambda = 0.001$	19317	44197	66286	44169
$\lambda = 0.0$	22045	59769	100160	59718
$\lambda = 0.1$	22414	59780	100190	59729
$\lambda = 1$	22444	59780	100190	59729
$\lambda = 10$	22444	59780	100190	59729

Furthermore, we examine the effect of different forms of staleness functions on the results of optimal expected total system cost. Besides the *CDF* of exponential distribution, we choose a logistic function (represented by $F_{logistic}$) which is a monotone increasing S curve shown in Eq. (15).

$$F(s_m) = F_{logistic}(s_m) = \frac{1}{1 + e^{(\alpha - \beta \cdot s_m)}} \tag{15}$$

As defined before, $F(s_m) = 0$ when $s_m = 0$, therefore in Eq. (15), the value of α should be or more than 8. The comparison results for the optimal costs among four data updating policies with changing parameters in different staleness functions are shown in Table 3.

Table 3. Comparisons of optimal total cost with different forms of staleness functions (RMB)

	Parameters	C	C_{time}	$C_{request}$	C_{update}
$F_{logistic}$	$\alpha = 8, \beta = 0.001$	623.3	1597.9	1626.8	1597.9
	$\alpha = 8, \beta = 0.01$	13404	41309	60605	41285
	$\alpha = 8, \beta = 0.1$	20927	59780	100190	59729
	$\alpha = 8, \beta = 1$	22294	59780	100190	59729
	$\alpha = 8, \beta = 10$	22444	59780	100190	59729

The experimental results in Table 3 denote that all the costs under different policies are increasing with the growth of parameters. The data updating policy proposed in this paper significantly outperforms other three fixed interval updating polices even though the staleness function and parameter changes. That is to say, the new data updating policy is robust.

6 Conclusion

In the age of big data, how to maintain the data timeliness in ERP systems has become a challenging and significant operational issue in enterprises. This paper mainly studies when and how to update the ERP system with the purchase data so as to optimize the staleness cost and updating cost. We apply Markov decision process to the purchase data updating process and design an algorithm to find the optimal updating policy based on backward induction method. A series of experiments conducted on a real-life practical data from the Hua Heng Company show that the new updating policy proposed in this paper is effective and robust in saving enterprise cost compared with traditional fixed interval updating policies.

This study has implications for both researchers and practitioners. First for researchers, the purchase data updating process modeled as a Markov decision process increases the understanding of the data timeliness issue. It is also helpful in analyzing the properties of the optimal updating policy and further designing the algorithm. Second for practitioners, the new data updating policy can be directly applied in managing the operational issue of purchase data updating in ERP systems.

Acknowledgments. This work was supported by the National Natural Science Foundation under Grant No. 71428003,71471144, 71071126.

References

1. Zach, O., Munkvold, B.E., Olsen, D.H.: ERP system implementation in SMEs: exploring the influences of the SME context. Enterp. Inf. Syst. **1**, 1–27 (2012)
2. Huang, Y.-Y., Handfield, R.B.: Measuring the benefits of ERP on supply management maturity model: a "Big Data" method. Int. J. Oper. Prod. Manage. **35**, 2–25 (2015)
3. Manyika, J., Chui, M., Brown, B., Bughin, J., Dobbs, R., Roxburgh, C., Byers, A.H.: Big Data: The Next Frontier for Innovation, Competition, and Productivity. McKinsey Global Institute (2011)
4. Fang, X., Rachamadugu, R.: Policies for knowledge refreshing in databases. Omega **37**, 16–28 (2009)
5. Ballou, D.P., Pazer, H.L.: Modeling data and process quality in multi-input. Multi-output Inf. Syst. Manage. Sci. **31**, 150–162 (1985)
6. Segev, A., Fang, W.P.: Optimal update policies for distributed materialized views. Manage. Sci. **37**, 851–870 (1991)

7. Adelberg, B., Garcia-Molina, H., Kao, B.: Applying update streams in a soft real-time database system. In: Proceedings of the 1995 ACM SIGMOD International Conference on Management of Data, vol. 24, pp. 245–256. ACM, New York (1995)
8. Ling, Y.B., Mi, J.: An optimal trade-off between content freshness and refresh cost. J. Appl. Probab. **41**, 721–734 (2004)
9. Dey, D., Zhang, Z., De, P.: Optimal synchronization policies for data warehouses. INFORMS J. Comput. **18**, 229–242 (2006)
10. Fang, X., Sheng, O.R.L., Goes, P.: When is the right time to refresh knowledge discovered from data? Oper. Res. **61**, 32–44 (2013)
11. Abdellatif, A., Ammar, A.B., Mazlout, C.: Markov chain for the recommendation of materialized views in real-time data warehouse. Int. J. Comput. Sci. Eng. Appl. **4**, 13–25 (2014)
12. Paxson, V., Floyd, S.: Wide area traffic - the failure of Poisson modeling. IEEE-ACM Trans. Netw. **3**, 226–244 (1995)

Research of Community Partition Based on the Modularity in Signed Network

Jingfeng Guo[1,2], Xiao Chen[1,2,3]($\boxtimes$), Junli Yu[3], Chaozhi Fan[1,2],
and Miaomiao Liu[1,2]

[1] College of Information Science and Engineering,
Yanshan University, 438 Hebei Ave., Qinhuangdao 066004, China
jfguo@ysu.edu.cn, chenxiao0604@163.com,
{1053799686,58558607}@qq.com
[2] The Key Laboratory for Computer Virtual Technology and System Integration
of Hebei Province, 438 Hebei Ave., Qinhuangdao 066004, China
[3] Qianan College, North China University of Science and Technology,
5096 YanShan Road, Qian'an 064000, China
404941670@qq.com

Abstract. For the characteristics of topology structure attributes and edges' signed attributes in signed networks, a novel method of Signed Network Community Partition is proposed. Firstly, based on signed attributes, the initial center vertex is selected as random walk starting vertex. Secondly, according to the theory of metastable, confirm random walk step length L. Finally, achieve community partition of signed network on the basis of the maximum network modularity. Experiments show that the effect of community partition of this method is better than existing methods.

1 Introduction

The overall goal of community partition in signed network [1] is to make positive links within community and negative links among community dense, while make negative links within community and positive links among community sparse. Now signed network community partition methods are divided into two types. (1) Improving metric function that traditional community partition [2]. (2) Adopt the two-step operation [3, 4]. However, both have their own defects. According to the characteristics of signed networks, this paper considers the attributes of structure and signed (positive and negative links) directly, and then proposes a novel and effective method of signed network community partition (SNCP). Firstly, in order to distinguish the importance of the vertex in signed networks, the concept of the vertex center influence is proposed; and chooses the vertex with large influence as the starting point of random walk. Secondly, for considering the negative links' influence upon random walk, the weight transition matrix is put forward. Thirdly, according to the theory of metastable, confirm the step length L of random walk, and calculate tightness between community initial center vertex and other vertex. Finally, confirm the scope of community partition on the basis of the maximum network modularity and check the correctness and effectiveness of the algorithm through experiments.

© Springer International Publishing Switzerland 2015
C. Zhang et al. (Eds.): ICDS 2015, LNCS 9208, pp. 25–29, 2015.
DOI: 10.1007/978-3-319-24474-7_4

2 Algorithm of Signed Network Community Partition

Definition 1. Given signed network $G = (V, E)$, for any $v_i \in V$, the center influence of v_i as show in formula (1), that is $F(v_i)$. Where $DP(v_i)$ is the number of positive links, DN (v_i) is the number of negative links, $D(v_i) = DP(v_i) + DN(v_i)$ is the degree of vertex v_i.

$$F(v_i) = e^{DP(vi)} \Big/ e^{DN(vi)} \qquad (1)$$

Definition 2. Given signed network $G = (V, E)$, adjacency matrix A corresponds to weight transition matrix W as shown in formula (2).

$$W = (w_{ij})_{|V| \times |V|} = \begin{cases} \frac{1}{D(v_i)} & a_{ij} = +1 \\ \frac{1}{D(v_i)} \times \frac{-1}{DN(v_i)} & a_{ij} = -1 \\ 0 & a_{ij} = 0 \end{cases} \qquad (2)$$

Definition 3. Given signed network $G = (V, E)$, if there is at least one path L between vertex v_i and v_j, then the value w_{ij}^L of markova random walk is the product of weight that coming from v_i to v_j in L-steps, as shown in formula (3). where v_k is the reached vertex through random walk L-1 steps, w_{ik}^l is the transition weight of v_i reaching v_k, w_{kj} is the transition weight of v_k reaching v_j by one step.

$$w_{ij}^L = \prod_{l=1}^{L-1} w_{ik}^l \times w_{kj} \qquad (3)$$

Definition 4. Given signed network $G = (V, E)$, for any $v_i, v_j \in V$, tightness between vertex v_i and v_j is the sum of weight from v_i random walk to v_j in L-steps, that is $d(v_i, v_j)$, as show in formula (4). Where l is path length. For any vertex, distance from themselves to 1.

$$d(v_i, v_j) = \begin{cases} \sum_{l=1}^{L} w_{ij}^l & i \neq j \\ 1 & i = j \end{cases} \qquad (4)$$

As can be seen from formula (4), L is the only parameter. Considering the differences of the network size and density, we need to set up the different optimal steps parameter. Thus, choose walking steps L when the initial center vertex reaches metastable state at the first time as the random walk of the whole network.

Definition 5. The improved modularity based on signed network as shown in formula (5), that is Q. Where $2DP = \sum_i \sum_j a_{ij}^+$ is the sum of the number of positive edges, $2DN = \sum_i \sum_j a_{ij}^-$ is the sum of the number of negative edges; $\delta(C_i, C_j) = 1$ shows that vertex v_i and v_j belong to the same community, $\delta(C_i, C_j) = -1$ shows that vertex v_i and v_j belong to the different communities.

$$Q = \frac{1}{2DP + 2DN} \sum_i \sum_j [a_{ij} - (\frac{DP(v_i)DP(v_j)}{2DP} - \frac{DN(v_i)DN(v_j)}{2DN})] \times \delta(C_i, C_j) \quad (5)$$

The detailed algorithm description of signed network partition based on the meta-stability of random walk and the modularity is following.

Algorithm: SNCP (A, Community)
```
   Input: Adjacency matrix A
   Output: Community set {C₁, C₂,…, C_K}
   Begin
    Partition Position=0
    While (Partition Position ≠ dim(A))
      1) According to formula(1), calculate F(vᵢ), choose
      vᵢ with Max{F(vᵢ)} as community's initial center.
      2) According to formula(3), calculate L-step with-
      in the d(vᵢ,vⱼ) between vᵢ and the other vertices.
      3) A in descending order according to the d(vᵢ,vⱼ).
      4) According the descending order list, adjust the
      order of element Q in matrix.
      5) According to formula(5), calculate the Q of
      different Partition Position in Signed Network.
      6) Select the partition position with the Max{Q},
      partition into two parts, A=[A₁₁, A₁₂, A₂₁, A₂₂].
      7) SNCP (A₁₁, Community)
      8) SNCP (A₂₂, Community)
    End
   End
```

3 Experiments

In this section, we performed extensive experiments to evaluate the performance on both illustrative signed network and Gahuku-Gama Subtribes Network. The experiments are done on a 2.9 GHZ Intel Pentium G2020 PC with 4G main memory, Windows 7 Professional SP1. All algorithms were implemented in Matlab R2012.

To measure the partitioning quality, we define the error ratio [5] C of a signed network as shown in formula (6). The smaller the value of *error(C)* is the better the partitioning quality becomes. The algorithms of SNCP, CRA [4] and FEC [3] have the same error rate, as shown in Table 1.

$$error(C) = P(C) \Big/ \sum_i \sum_j |a_{ij}| \times 100\% \qquad (6)$$

We have applied three different algorithms to signed network, the relationship between run time and vertices number as shown in Fig. 1. We can see through the data curves: (1) the running time of the SCPN algorithm is low when the number is high; (2) the running time is approximately linear with respect to the network size; (3) with the increasing of the vertex number, the efficiency of the SCPN algorithm is superior to the algorithms of CRA and FEC.

Table 1. The error ratio of signed network partition.

Signed social network	SNCP	CRA	FEC
Illustrative signed network(A) [3]	0	0	0
Illustrative signed network(B) [3]	0	0	0
Gahuku-Gama subtribes network [3]	3.45	3.45	3.45

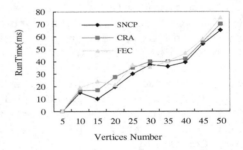

Fig. 1. Relationships between vertices and time for different.

4   Conclusion and Future Work

Based on the characteristics of structure attributes and signed attributes in signed networks, the novel method of signed network community partition (SNCP) is proposed. Because this method combines both local optimizations in metastable and global optimization in modularity, the SNCP is not only improving the algorithm efficiency but also guarantying the quality of community partition. At present, this paper only simply considers the effect of signed attribute to the community partition. How to handle complex signed social networks is the focus of future work.

Acknowledgments. This work is supported by the National Science Foundation of China, (No. 61472340), National Science Foundation of Hebei (No. F2012209019) and Science and technology condition construction project of Hebei (No. 14960112D).

References

1. Cheng, S.-Q., Shen, S.-H., Zhang, G.-Q., Cheng, X.-Q.: Survey of signed network research. J. Softw. **25**(1), 1–15 (2014)
2. Gómez, S., Jensen, P., Arenas, A.: Analysis of community structure in networks of correlated data. Phys. Rev. E **80**(1), 016114-1–016114-5 (2009)
3. Yang, B., Cheung, W.K., Jiming, J.: Community mining from signed social networks. IEEE Trans. Knowl. Data Eng. **19**(10), 1333–1348 (2007)
4. Sharma, T., Charls, A., Singh, P.K.: Community mining in signed social networks - an automated approach, vol. 2, pp. 152–157. IPCSIT © IACSIT Press, Singapore (2011)
5. Huang, J., Sun, H., Han, J.: Density-based shrinkage for revealing hierarchical and overlapping community structure in networks. Phys. A Stat. Mech. Appl. **390**(11), 2160–2171 (2011)

LDA Based Event Extraction: Detecting Influenza Epidemics Using Microblog

Jingwei Li[1(✉)], Wayne Huang[1], and Ping Chen[2]

[1] School of Management, Xi'an Jiaotong University,
No. 28 Xianning West Road, Xi'an 710049, China
li.jing.wei123@stu.xjtu.edu.cn
[2] Department of Computer Science, University of Massachusetts Boston,
A100 Morrissey Blvd, Boston 02125, USA

Abstract. As a major public health concern, influenza epidemics causes tens of millions respiratory illnesses worldwide each year. With the development of social network, interaction platform like microblog, is generating massive data providing us a faster and more accurate way to predict the trends in the spread of influenza, which can help us reduce the impact cause by the influenza. The problem of influenza epidemics prediction through Chinese microblog cannot be easily addressed by applying existing approaches and methods, some of which have been used for English documents. Besides, different from traditional text, the microblog is big in volume, update velocity, noise and small in the individual text volume, which cause that traditional deeper semantic analysis method like SVM is inefficient and easy to be over-fitting. To address this problem, we present a deeper semantic analysis to Chinese microblog using a LDA based event extraction framework. Our experiment using 332,886 microblogs from south and north China showed that our method achieved more detailed information extraction about the flu and an earlier flu prediction than the Chinese official ILI data.

1 Introduction

Microblog is increasingly being used as a tool for real-time knowledge discovery relating to emerging threats, social events, product trends and epidemics. For instance, real time analysis of Twitter users' tweet content can be or is being used to detect earthquakes and provide warnings (Sakaki et al. 2010), to identify needs during recovery from natural disasters such as the Haiti Earthquake (Caragea et al. 2011), to track emergence of specific characteristics of influenza-like illness (Paul and Dredze 2012), and to collect epidemic-related tweets (Aramaki et al. 2011).

We present a deeper semantic analysis to Chinese microblog using topic modeling algorithm LDA (Blei et al. 2003), with a time series analysis of the flu medicine related information, which has been proved to be a good way to investigate the flu trend (Magruder 2003). Our experiment using 332,886 microblogs showed that our methods achieved more detailed information extraction about the flu and an earlier flu prediction than the Chinese official ILI data.

C. Zhang et al. (Eds.): ICDS 2015, LNCS 9208, pp. 30–33, 2015.
DOI: 10.1007/978-3-319-24474-7_5

The remainder of this paper is organized as follows. We present a review of literature on flu prediction, LDA, and text mining on microblog. Next, we report on our experiments and discuss the results. Finally, we conclude this paper.

2 Related Work

We discuss works closely related to our research from two aspect: (1) influenza epidemic detection, (2) text mining on microblog.

Magruder used the amount of over-the-counter drug sales. Because an influenza patient usually requires anti-influenza drugs, this approach is reasonable. However, in most countries, anti-influenza drugs are not available at the drug store (Magruder 2003). Ginsberg et al. demonstrated that a regression model of influenza like illness can be estimated using the proportion of flu-related Google search queries over the same period. They classified the query logs by detecting the presence of flu-related keywords. Their method was implemented in Google Flu Trends, a Google based service providing almost real-time estimates of flu activity for a number of countries around the world (Ginsberg et al. 2008).

Sriram et al. show the limitation of bag-of-word in tweet classification, and propose 8F features, which capture the information about authors and reply-to users (Sriram et al. 2010). Silvescu et al. propose the system EMERSE for classifying and aggregating tweets and text messages about the Haiti earthquake disaster. They train a SVM classifier with the combination of 4 feature sets: unigrams, unigrams with Relief feature selection, abstractions, and topic words generated by LDA (Silvescu et al. 2009).

3 Experiment

3.1 Data Collection

Two dataset are collected during the experiment: a microblog dataset and an ILI dataset from the official website. The microblog dataset is mainly used in the experiment and test the ability of new generated model. The ILI dataset is used as the baseline to test the result of our experiment and modify the generated model accordingly.

We created four dataset according to the data we collected, like the Table 1 showed below.

3.2 Data Processing

We normalized the vaccine related data in south and north part of China by dividing the count for each query in a particular week by the total number of online search queries submitted in that location during the week. From the result we can see that, for each peak in the ILI data, our normalized microblog number with medicine related information will have a corresponding peak of wave ten days before. This show a great potential in the earlier flu prediction.

Table 1. Dataset summary

Dataset	Dataset 1	Dataset 2	Dataset 3	Dataset 4
Source	Radom from microblog	Microblog of south China with medicine related information from Dataset 1	Microblog of north China with medicine related information from Dataset 1	ILI from Chinese National Influenza Center
Time range	11/5/2013– 11/5/2014	11/5/2013– 11/5/2014	11/5/2013– 11/5/2014	11/5/2013– 11/5/2014
Time granularity	Every day	Every day	Every day	Every week
Number	332,886	39,361	40,521	52

3.3 Deeper Semantic Analysis

We use the topic modeling algorithm LDA to get a deeper understanding of the flu related microblog through R 3.1.3 and the topic model package. We focus on the days around the peak of the wave in the vaccine related curve. More specifically, we focus on the context of microblog from 50th, 51th, and 52th weeks in 2013 in both south and north part of China, which is also about ten days before the flu outbreak from the Chinese National Influenza Center. We set the number of topics being 11 and 15 separately in south and north China after the optimization of the perplexity. Flu related topic emerges in the results and showed more accurate and specific information of the flu. Like the Table 2 show below.

Table 2. Topic most related to flu generated by LDA in south China

Topic	15 components	Percentage %
7	注射 头疼 鼻塞 禁欲 感染 治疗 板蓝根 风寒 营养 广东 婴儿 水温 宝宝 医生 流感 (Injection, headache, nasal, infection, treatment, abstinence, Radix, Guangdong, baby, infant, nutrition, cold, temperature, doctor, flu)	16.23

The results also shows that flu related topic may emerge or ratio rise when there is or will be a flu outbreak. Furthermore, Table 2 shows that not only south part of China emerges flu, but also Guangdong and infants from south China may suffer a lot from the flu.

4 Conclusion

In this study, we propose a LDA based framework for detecting influenza epidemics using Chinese microblog. This framework includes four stages: data collection, data processing, LDA-based model running, and event extraction. Our experiments using real data show that our methods achieved more detailed information extraction about the flu and an earlier flu prediction than the Chinese official ILI data.

One limitation of our model is that flu detection based on topic modelling is kind of rough till now, especially when the ILI rate is low, there may not emerge a flu related topic. The reason may be that the flu related topic is not people's major concern when there is not a flu outbreak, which lead to the ignorance of the flu related topic. And the real time news have a great influence on the microblog too.

Our future work will be done in two directions: (a) try to find the quantitative relations between the percentage of the flu related topic and the ILI rate; (b) extend the use of the framework to other epidemic diseases and even other domains.

Acknowledgements. The research presented in this paper has been funded by grants from the Natural Science Foundation of China, No. 71331005.

References

Aramaki, E., Maskawa, S., Morita, M.: Twitter catches the flu: detecting influenza epidemics using twitter. Paper presented at the Proceedings of the Conference on Empirical Methods in Natural Language Processing (2011)

Blei, D.M., Ng, A.Y., Jordan, M.I.: Latent dirichlet allocation. J. Mach. Learning Res. **3**, 993–1022 (2003)

Caragea, C., McNeese, N., Jaiswal, A., Traylor, G., Kim, H.-W., Mitra, P., Jansen, B.J.: Classifying text messages for the haiti earthquake. Paper presented at the Proceedings of the 8th International Conference on Information Systems for Crisis Response and Management (ISCRAM 2011) (2011)

Ginsberg, J., Mohebbi, M.H., Patel, R.S., Brammer, L., Smolinski, M.S., Brilliant, L.: Detecting influenza epidemics using search engine query data. Nature **457**(7232), 1012–1014 (2008)

Magruder, S.: Evaluation of over-the-counter pharmaceutical sales as a possible early warning indicator of human disease. Johns Hopkins APL Tech. Digest **24**(4), 349–353 (2003)

Sakaki, T., Okazaki, M., Matsuo, Y.: Earthquake shakes twitter users: real-time event detection by social sensors. Paper presented at the Proceedings of the 19th International Conference on World Wide Web (2010)

Silvescu, A., Caragea, C., Honavar, V.: Combining super-structuring and abstraction on sequence classification. Paper presented at the Ninth IEEE International Conference on Data Mining, 2009, ICDM 2009 (2009)

Sriram, B., Fuhry, D., Demir, E., Ferhatosmanoglu, H., Demirbas, M.: Short text classification in twitter to improve information filtering. Paper presented at the Proceedings of the 33rd International ACM SIGIR Conference on Research and Development in Information Retrieval (2010)

A Friend Recommendation System Using Users' Information of Total Attributes

Zhou Zhang[1], Yuewen Liu[1], Wei Ding[2], and Wei Wayne Huang[1(✉)]

[1] Department of Management, Xi'an Jiaotong University, Xi'an 710049, China
zhouzhang@stu.xjtu.edu.cn,
{liuyuewen, whuang}@mail.xjtu.edu.cn
[2] Department of Computer Science, University of Massachusetts Boston,
Boston, MA 02125, USA
ding@cs.umb.edu

Abstract. Social network services, such as Facebook and Twitter in U.S.A., RenRen, QQ and Weibo in China, have grown substantially in recent years. Friend recommendation is an important emerging social network service component, which expands the networks by actively recommending new potential friends to users. We introduce a new friend recommendation system using a user's information of total attributes and based on the Law of total probability. The proposed method can be easily extended according to the number of user's attributes in different social networks. Our experimental results have demonstrated that superior performance the proposed method. In our empirical studies, we have observed that the performance of our algorithm is related with the number of user's friends. Our findings have important and practical applications in social network design and performance.

1 Introduction

Social network services, such as Facebook and Twitter in U.S.A., RenRen, QQ and Weibo in China, have grown substantially in recent years. Friends recommendation is crucial for the growth of social networks. At the early stage of social networks, the network is small with only a few users, it is easy to browse over other users' profiles to make a friend request. Nowadays, the number of social network users reaches an unbelievable level. In October 2012, the number of users in Facebook reaches one billion. The RenRen also have more than 200 million users by the end of 2012. Now it is obviously impossible for the user to browse over millions of other users' homepages to look for someone can be his/her friend. Social network users need an efficient friend recommendation system. For example, "People You May Know" of Facebook and other similar recommendation service are provided by Twitter, QQ, Weibo, and RenRen.

Existing friend recommendation algorithms in principle are based on two different approaches including the Path-based method and the Friends-of-Friend method. The Path-based method uses friend linkage information using concept of the well-known PageRank algorithm. Due to the high computational cost, this type of algorithms is seldom used in commercial social network services. The Friend-of-Friend (FoF) is an

C. Zhang et al. (Eds.): ICDS 2015, LNCS 9208, pp. 34–41, 2015.
DOI: 10.1007/978-3-319-24474-7_6

efficient and widely used recommendation algorithm in social networks due to its low time complexity. The algorithm identifies potential but unlinked friends and makes recommendations. Existing FoF algorithms only focus on the relations between users, but overlook user attributes.

In this study, we systematically evaluate the state-of-the-art algorithms to discuss their strengths and weaknesses. We then propose a new friend recommendation with user's information of total attributes (FRUITA). This paper is the first study that presents a friend recommendation system integrating social network users' attributes with the law of total probability. FRUITA can be easily extended to accommodate new set of user attributes in different social networks. In our empirical study, we have extensively evaluated the FRUITA algorithm with other state-of-the-art FoF algorithms, including Common-Neighbors algorithm, Jaccard algorithm and Adamic/Adar algorithm using real-world data. We have collected 7 million users' public information and their friend relationships from one of China's dominant social network website. We have observed that the performance of our algorithm is related with the number of user's friends. In particular, when a user has a small number of friends, the proposed FRUITA algorithm performs much better than other algorithms; when a user has a large number of friends, the overall performance of FRUITA becomes less impressive but it is comparable with others and its precision rate is outstanding.

The rest of this paper is organized as follows. Section 2 gives a brief literature review of recommendation algorithms. Section 3 presents the methodology of the new algorithm. Section 4 discusses our real-world case study. Section 5 concludes the paper.

2 Related Literature

Recommending people is an important issue in social network. It has been shown that a recommendation service increases the connections between users, as well the user's loyalty to the social network. Different from recommending items, recommending people is relatively new in the research of social network, and there is less literature in this field. Friend-of-Friend and Path-based approaches are two basic methods.

2.1 Friend-of-Friend (FoF) Method

The FoF algorithm derives from the fact that if two users in the social network share many common friends, they may have a great chance to become friends in the future. This algorithm is also called as "Common-Neighbors". Newman designed an experiment and exploited the data of authors in two databases for a six-year period to provide evidence for the primary idea of FoF [4]. Their research also showed the proportional relation between the probability of the author having new co-authors and the number of the coauthors he or she already had. Jin et al. used the FoF algorithm as one of the three general principles to create a simple model that described the growth of social networks [5]. The friend recommendation system on Facebook, which gives a list of the "people you may know", is also based on the FoF algorithm.

As the continuous growth of social networks, the primary Common-Neighbors model proliferates into several improved algorithms, such as Jaccard coefficient and Adamic/Adar. In order to prove that some factors perform better in the link prediction problem, Adamic and Adar introduced a new algorithm to calculate the similarity of two actors by analyzing text, in-links, out-links and mailing lists on the homepages of the social networks [6]. The number of common friends between two actors can be used to evaluate the similarity.

Preferential attachment is one of well-known models to describe the expansion of social networks. Barabasi and Albert explained that a social network expanded when new actors joined in, and these new actors link preferentially to the old actors who have more links already [7]. Barabasi et al. (2001) studied the data with an 8-year period in a database of co-authorship information, and tried to find the evidence of preferential attachment in the evolution of social network [8].

2.2 Path-Based Method

Differing from the neighbor-based FoF approach, calculating the shortest path is the basic idea of the Path-based methods. Katz predicts the probability by the sum of all paths between two nodes. And the shorter paths have more contribution than the longer paths in the link prediction [9].

Brin and Page introduced the PageRank algorithm as a key component of Google search engine. It weighs every element within a set by the link-in and link-out numbers, and then gives a rank of all the elements [10]. There are several improved algorithms based on PageRank [11, 12].

Jeh and Widom proposed SimRank to measure similarity of elements using the information of their relations. SimRank combined the features of FoF and the Random Walk algorithms, and Random Walk is also used in PageRank [13].

Yin proposed and evaluated a framework of LINKREC, which used the information of the network structure and the actors' attributes, based on the Random Walk with Restart algorithm [14].

3   Methodology

For a friend recommendation system, an example of a candidate friend may be $\langle x_1, x_2, \cdots, x_i, \cdots, x_m \rangle$. $x_i (i \in \{1, \cdots, m\})$ stands for the attributes of the candidate, such as gender, age, location, interest and number of common-neighbours, these attributes may be independent or not. For example, young men may show strong interest in sports, so the gender and age will actually have influence on the attribute of interest. Even if some of the attributes are not independent, we still use Eq. (1) to calculate the total probability of friend recommendation under strong independence assumption. Because we don't use the calculated probability value to directly predicate the chance that the candidate will really become a friend of the user in the future, we just use the probability values to select potential strong candidates. Our friend recommendation system will give the user a list of candidate friends ranked by the probability values. The advantage of decoupling of the class attributes using the strong independence assumption is that we can independently calculate each user attribute distribution quickly. Similar as the theory behind naïve independence assumption used in the successful naïve Bayesian classifier [23], dependence among users' attributes may likely be canceled out, and the performance of our friend recommendation system can still be strong. Our empirical results have approved our argument.

For each attribute, we can calculate the prior probability by the data of the existing friends of the user. The relation between a candidate and the user can only be two types: friends or not. Let y indicates a binary variable which reflects the relation between the candidate and the user. If the candidate is a friend of the user, we define $y = 1$; else $y = 0$. Consider $x_i (i \in \{1, \cdots, m\})$ as the attributes of the user, then the probability that the user will collaborate with the candidate is:

$$P\left(y = 1 \middle| \bigcap_1^m x_i\right) = 1 - \prod_1^m (1 - P(y = 1|x_i)) \tag{1}$$

In Eq. (1), m denotes the number of user's attributes existing in the social network. $P(y = 1|x_i)$ denotes the prior probability for each attribute that the probability that this candidate will be friend of the user in the future. It can be calculated by the statistical result including the information of all the friends of the user's existing friends (friends-of-friend) and the number that how many of them are already friends of the user. $\prod_1^m (1 - P(y = 1|x_i))$ denotes the probability that the candidate will not be the user's friend based on all the m attributes.

Algorithm 1: FRUITA (Friend Recommendation with Users' Information of Total Attributes)

---

1. Input: The database of the friendship relations between users in the social network; the database of the users' m attributes.

2. Construct the social network graph for the user by the database of the relation. All the friends of the user's existing friend are V_t; the set of the persons in V_t who have already been friends of user is V_f; the set of the other n persons in V_t will be the candidates for the friend recommendation system and we mark it as V_c.

3. Estimate the probability $P(x_1)$ that V_t will be friend of the user for attribute i by the statistical result of V_t and V_f. For all m attributes, we will get $\{P (x_1), P (x_2), \ldots, P (x_m)\}$.

4. Calculate the probability P for each of the n candidates in V_c using Equation (5) and $\{P (x_1), P (x_2), \ldots, P (x_m)\}$.

5. Sort the n candidate by the value of probability P.

6. Return: Top k of the sorted n candidates as the list of friend recommendation result.

The pseudo-code of recommendation algorithm FRUITA is shown in Algorithm 1. In step 3, if calculating each P of the attribute costs time m and there are n attributes, the time complexity of step 3 is $O(mn)$; in step 4, if calculating each P of the candidates costs time m and there are n candidates, the time complexity of step 4 is $O(mn)$; in step 5, we use the function "Rank()" in SQL to sort the results and the time complexity of step 5 is $O(n \log n)$.

4   Empirical Study

In order to carry out the experiments, we use a web crawler to get the user data from RenRen (http://www.renren.com) and store it into a database. RenRen is one of the most popular social network websites in China and have more than 200 million users in total. First, we download the information of 240 users with different attributes and we defined them as D1 nodes. Second, we extend to the information of 51,340 D2 nodes which are the friends of these 240 users. Third, we keep on collecting the data of the D2 users' friends and we call them D3 nodes and there are 7,158,934 D3 in total. These nodes and the edges between them form a social network structure for our case study.

With the data we get from RenRen, we have evaluated FRUITA with other state-of-the art FoF algorithms. Specifically we split each user's friends to 10 partitions, and try to see how well one specific algorithm can predict 1 partition using the other 9 partitions. As depicted in Fig. 3. This method of handling the data collected in a time point is widely used in the field of friend recommendation in a social network. This method also has one significant limitation. The friend recommendation results that are not in the set of the 1 partition do not mean they are wrong, because some of them may be the potential friends of the user and will be added by the user as friends in the future. So we expect that the actual precision value of the algorithms should be higher than the value in the evaluation report.

The link prediction results are showed in Tables 1, 2, and 3.

Table 1 shows an overall result of the friend recommendation for the 240 D_1 users in RenRen. We can see that the FRUITA performs best in MAP (16.97 %), and some P@N (76.92 % precision at 1, 50.17 % precision at 2, and 10.83 % precision at 100). Common-Neighbors and Adamic/Adar perform well too. Their MRRs are 40.51 %/ 41.59 % and MAPs are 16.24 %/15.97 %, both comparable to FRUITA. The result of Jaccard's coefficient is acceptable, but worse than other three.

Table 1. Overall result of algorithms comparison

	P@1	P@2	P@5	P@10	P@50	P@100	MRR	MAP
FRUITA	**0.7692**	**0.5017**	0.3897	0.2823	0.1719	**0.1083**	0.4121	**0.1697**
CN	0.6581	0.4957	**0.3932**	**0.2908**	**0.1737**	**0.1083**	0.4051	0.1624
JAC	0.5000	0.4171	0.3436	0.2675	0.1649	0.1069	0.3736	0.1340
ADA	0.6154	0.4744	0.3782	0.2812	0.1679	0.1076	**0.4159**	0.1597

Then we divide the D_1 users by the number of their friends into two groups, and repeat the experiments. Table 2 shows the result of the D_1 users whose friends are less than 100, and Table 3 shows the result of the D_1 users whose friends are more than 100.

In Table 2, all the results are worse than Table 1 as expected. The FRUITA has the best MAP (20.69 %), P@50 (2.95 %). The Common-Neighbors has the best P@1 (40.68 %), P@2 (16.27 %), P@5 (10.51 %), and P@10 (6.36 %). The result of Adamic/Adar is not as good as Common-Neighbors and FRUITA, but still comparable. The result of Jaccard's coefficient is much worse than other two algorithms and unacceptable.

Table 2. Result of algorithms comparison (Friends < 100)

	P@1	P@2	P@5	P@10	P@50	P@100	MRR	MAP
FRUITA	0.3390	0.1593	0.1000	0.0627	**0.0295**	0.0164	0.3287	**0.2069**
CN	**0.4068**	**0.1627**	**0.1051**	**0.0636**	0.0281	0.0158	0.2963	0.1739
Jaccard	0.1186	0.0610	0.0492	0.0305	0.0183	0.0112	0.1901	0.0997
Ada	0.2373	0.1288	0.0847	0.0576	0.0281	**0.0169**	**0.3430**	0.1530

In Table 3, all the results are better than Table 1. The Common-Neighbors beat other three algorithms in most of the indices (MRR 44.17 %, P@5 49.03 %, P@10 36.74 %, P@50 22.29 %, and P@100 13.95 %). The result of FRUITA is impressively outstanding on P@1 91.43 % and P@2 61.71 %. Because the top recommended person is always the first one browsed by the user, P@1 is the most important one in P@k. The results of Adamic/Adar are comparable to FRUITA and Common-Neighbors. Jaccard's coefficient is still worse than the other three, but the gap is evidently narrowed than the value in Table 3.

Table 3. Result of algorithms comparison (Friends > 100)

	P@1	P@2	P@5	P@10	P@50	P@100	MRR	MAP
FRUITA	**0.9143**	**0.6171**	0.4874	0.3563	0.2199	0.1393	0.4402	0.1572
CN	0.7429	0.6080	**0.4903**	**0.3674**	**0.2229**	**0.1395**	**0.4417**	0.1586
Jaccard	0.6286	0.5371	0.4429	0.3474	0.2143	0.1391	0.4350	0.1456
Ada	0.7429	0.5909	0.4771	0.3566	0.2151	0.1382	0.4404	**0.1619**

Our extensive empirical studies have shown that (1) in total, FRUITA performs much better than other basis algorithms. The performances of Common-Neighbors and Adamic/Adar algorithms are better than Jaccard's coefficient; (2) When the user has relatively less friends (e.g., <100), FRUITA performs better than Adamic/Adar and Common-Neighbors, and much better than Jaccard's coefficient; (3) When the user has relatively more friends (e.g., >100), the performance of FRUITA, Common-Neighbors and Adamic/Adar performs are comparable, and Jaccard's coefficient is still the worst. The precision of FRUITA is impressively outstanding at top recommended results.

5 Conclusions

The FRUITA not only inherits the advantage of FoF but also has a flexible format which can be easily extend according to the number of user attributes. We evaluate the new algorithm with other FoF algorithms using real-world data. Our result shows that the FRUITA performs best of all in total. And our study also finds that performance of all these friend recommendation methods may depend on the number of users' existing friends. When the number of existing friends is falling down to less than 100, the result of Jaccard's coefficient may be unacceptable and Adamic/Adar also performs worse but still acceptable. By contrast, Common-Neighbors and FRUITA keep perform well. Furthermore, FRUITA still keep its strong performance when the number of existing friends increases, while other algorithms may not be able to do so.

We also observed that the way of utilizing information is very important for an algorithm. Adding extra information to an algorithm does not necessarily enhance the performance of the algorithm, unless the information is integrated properly. The Common-Neighbors algorithm utilizes only the number of common-neighbors; the Jaccard's coefficient utilizes more information, including the number of common-neighbors, the number of the user's and the candidate's friends, but ironically performs worse than the Common-Neighbors algorithm, because the three numbers are integrated arbitrarily rather than properly. The Adamic/Adar algorithm also utilizes more information, i.e., the number of friends of the common neighbors. However, when the number of common-friends is relatively low, introducing extra information to the algorithm may introduce too much noise, thus the Adamic/Adar algorithm performs not better than the Common-Neighbors algorithm. When the number of common-neighbors is relatively high, the noise brought by the number of friends of common-neighbors is weakened, thus the Adamic/Adar algorithm performs better than the Common-Neighbor algorithm. Compared to Adamic/Adar, FRUITA efficiently utilizes users' information. It can handle all the user attributes flexibly in a social network. And the recommendation results will be enhanced with the increase of the number of user's attributes.

References

1. Pazzani, M.J., Billsus, D.: Content-based recommendation systems. In: Brusilovsky, P., Kobsa, A., Nejdl, W. (eds.) Adaptive Web 2007. LNCS, vol. 4321, pp. 325–341. Springer, Heidelberg (2007)
2. Pazzani, M.J.: A framework for collaborative, content-based and demographic filtering. Artif. Intell. Rev. **13**, 393–408 (1999)
3. Adomavicius, G., Tuzhilin, A.: Toward the next generation of recommender systems: a survey of the state-of-the-art and possible extensions. IEEE Trans. Knowl. Data Eng. **17**, 734–749 (2005)
4. Newman, M.E.: Clustering and preferential attachment in growing networks. Phys. Rev. E **64**, 025102 (2001)
5. Jin, E.M., Girvan, M., Newman, M.E.: Structure of growing social networks. Phys. Rev. E **64**, 046132 (2001)

6. Adamic, L.A., Adar, E.: Friends and neighbors on the web. Soc. Netw. **25**, 211–230 (2003)
7. Barabási, A.-L., Albert, R.: Emergence of scaling in random networks. Science **286**, 509–512 (1999)
8. Barabâsi, A.-L., Jeong, H., Néda, Z., Ravasz, E., Schubert, A., Vicsek, T.: Evolution of the social network of scientific collaborations. Phys. A **311**, 590–614 (2002)
9. Katz, L.: A new status index derived from sociometric analysis. Psychometrika **18**, 39–43 (1953)
10. Brin, S., Page, L.: The anatomy of a large-scale hypertextual Web search engine. Comput. Netw. ISDN Syst. **30**, 107–117 (1998)
11. Haveliwala, T.H.: Topic-sensitive pagerank: a context-sensitive ranking algorithm for web search. IEEE Trans. Knowl. Data Eng. **15**, 784–796 (2003)
12. Haveliwala, T., Kamvar, S., Jeh, G.: An analytical comparison of approaches to personalizing pagerank (2003)
13. Jeh, G., Widom, J.: SimRank: a measure of structural-context similarity. In: Proceedings of the Eighth ACM SIGKDD International Conference on Knowledge Discovery and Data Mining, pp. 538–543 (2002)
14. Yin, Z., Gupta, M., Weninger, T., Han, J.: A unified framework for link recommendation using random walks. In: 2010 International Conference on Advances in Social Networks Analysis and Mining (ASONAM), pp. 152–159 (2010)
15. Salton, G., McGill, M.J.: Introduction to Modern Information Retrieval. McGraw-Hill Inc., New York (1986)
16. Huang, Z., Li, X., Chen, H.: Link prediction approach to collaborative filtering. In: Proceedings of the 5th ACM/IEEE-CS Joint Conference on Digital Libraries, pp. 141–142 (2005)
17. Liben-Nowell, D., Kleinberg, J.: The link-prediction problem for social networks. J. Am. Soc. Inform. Sci. Technol. **58**, 1019–1031 (2007)
18. Chen, J., Geyer, W., Dugan, C., Muller, M., Guy, I.: Make new friends, but keep the old: recommending people on social networking sites. In: Proceedings of the 27th International Conference on Human Factors in Computing Systems, pp. 201–210 (2009)
19. Breese, J.S., Heckerman, D., Kadie, C.: Empirical analysis of predictive algorithms for collaborative filtering. In: Proceedings of the Fourteenth Conference on Uncertainty in Artificial Intelligence, pp. 43–52 (1998)
20. Zhang, H., Su, J.: Naive bayesian classifiers for ranking. In: Boulicaut, J.-F., Esposito, F., Giannotti, F., Pedreschi, D. (eds.) ECML 2004. LNCS (LNAI), vol. 3201, pp. 501–512. Springer, Heidelberg (2004)
21. Claypool, M., Gokhale, A., Miranda, T., Murnikov, P., Netes, D., Sartin, M.: Combining content-based and collaborative filters in an online newspaper. In ACM SIGIR 1999 Workshop on Recommender Systems: Algorithms and Evaluation, August 1999
22. Soboroff, I., Nicholas, C.: Combining content and collaboration in text filtering. In: 43 IJCAI 1999 Workshop: Machine Learning for Information Filtering, August 1999
23. Zhang, H.: The optimality of naive Bayes. In: Proceedings of the Seventeenth International Florida Artificial Intelligence Research Society Conference, Miami Beach. AAAI Press (2004)

Discovering Sequential Rental Patterns by Fleet Tracking

Xinxin Jiang[✉], Xueping Peng, and Guodong Long

Quantum Computation and Intelligent Systems,
University of Technology Sydney, Ultimo, Australia
Xinxin.Jiang@student.uts.edu.au,
{Xueping.Peng,Guodong.Long}@uts.edu.au

Abstract. As one of the most well-known methods on customer analysis, sequential pattern mining generally focuses on customer business transactions to discover their behaviors. However in the real-world rental industry, behaviors are usually linked to other factors in terms of actual equipment circumstance. Fleet tracking factors, such as location and usage, have been widely considered as important features to improve work performance and predict customer preferences. In this paper, we propose an innovative sequential pattern mining method to discover rental patterns by combining business transactions with the fleet tracking factors. A novel sequential pattern mining framework is designed to detect the effective items by utilizing both business transactions and fleet tracking information. Experimental results on real datasets testify the effectiveness of our approach.

Keywords: Sequential pattern mining · Fleet tracking · Item detection;

1 Introduction

In the rental business, the quality of services and products depends on how successful we are in satisfying the customers need for service, and the ability to get the equipment to customer and where they need it (Rieser 1994 and Trimble et al. 2012). Business transactions and fleet tracking information, such as working location and operating hours, have been widely recognized as important features of improving work performance, predicting consumer preferences, and increasing business competition (Trimble et al. 2012 and Andriesson et al. 2013).

Sequential pattern mining, as one of the most well-known method on customer behavior analysis, finds out frequent subsequences as patterns in a given sequence database (Zaki 2001, Pinto et al. 2001, Mooney and Roddick 2013). For sequential pattern mining in rental industry, combining it with fleet tracking information can efficiently identify high utility items and focus on more relevant circumstance.

As shown in Fig. 1(a) General sequential pattern mining, which compose items into a sequence by different customer. The rental pattern discovered in

© Springer International Publishing Switzerland 2015
C. Zhang et al. (Eds.): ICDS 2015, LNCS 9208, pp. 42–49, 2015.
DOI: 10.1007/978-3-319-24474-7_7

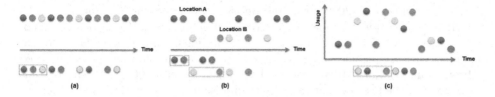

Fig. 1. Three sequential pattern mining approaches (a) General; (b) Location-based (c) Usage-based (Color figure online)

rectangle (red, grey, yellow) is the highest frequency, which has ignored the actual equipment circumstances in customer sites. For example, the rental fleets of one customer might be worked for two different work sites. It might decrease the pattern accuracy to put them into one sequence. (b) Location-based sequential pattern mining, describes this case. The sequence is divided into two different ones by location A and B. Two rental patterns of location A (red, grey) and location B (yellow, green) replace the previous traditional pattern with more accuracy. (c) Usage-based sequential pattern mining, analyzes equipment usage in time frequency, e.g. daily. Detecting high utility items in usage-time figure can help find out more accurate pattern (yellow, red, green) in rental behavior prediction.

To implement high efficient sequential pattern mining by fleet tracking in rental industry, we provide a novel framework to conduct rental pattern mining with proposed modeling algorithms. We propose two sequential rental pattern mining algorithms to identify frequent itemsets by utilizing fleet tracking information as location and usage. Further, our approach is demonstrated by real-world datasets in an rental industry case study. Specifically, we make the following contributions in this paper:

- Analyzed the problems of discovering sequential rental pattern by fleet tracking;
- Proposed sequential pattern mining framework to discover efficient rental pattern;
- Provided fleet tracking data and algorithms to compose location-based and usage-based sequences;
- Experiments on real-world industry dataset testify the effectiveness of the approach.

The paper is organized as follows. Section 2 reviews the related work. Section 3 proposes a sequential rental pattern mining framework. Section 4 details the approach and algorithm. Experimental results are presented in Sect. 5. Section 6 concludes the work.

2   Related Work

In the analyses of customer purchase behavior, sequential pattern mining with the algorithms such as SPADE by Zaki 2001, Prefixspan by Pei et al. 2001 and

SPAM by Ayres et al. 2002, proposed on the support/frequency sequences. The algorithms of frequent sequences often result in many patterns being mined; most of them may be hardly understood by business, while those related to real business with frequencies lower than the given minimum support are ignored (Mooney and Roddick 2013, Zhao et al. 2003 and Pei et al. 2007). Much work has been done in the area of sequential pattern discovery and periodicity detection, multiple minimum supports utilized to enhance the performance of sequential pattern mining by Kumar et al. 2012, DFSP in biological sequences analysis by Liao and Chen 2014, and utility measure to discover high utility patterns by Lan et al. 2014

In the rental industry, in terms of problem definition and utilizing other information such as fleet tracking by Trimble et al. 2012 and Andriesson et al. 2013 to discover high quality sequential rental patterns in the real-world cases, a major common shortcoming among previous work is losing the understanding of what customer actual needs to services and products.

3   Technical Preliminaries and Framework

3.1   Basic Concepts and Definitions

Sequential Pattern Mining. Given a sequence database and a min-support threshold, the problem of sequential rental pattern mining is to find the complete set of sequential rental patterns in the IoT data. Let $I = \{i_1, i_2, ..., i_n\}$ be a set of all items, An itemset is a subset of items. A sequence is an ordered list of itemsets. A sequence s is denoted by $< s_1 s_2 ... s_n >$, where is an itemset, i.e., $s_j \subseteq I$ for $1 \leq j \leq l$. s_j is also called an element of the sequence, and denoted as $(x_1 x_2 ... x_m)$, where x_k is an item, i.e., $x_k \subseteq I$ for $1 \leq k \leq m$. The number of instances of items in a sequence is called the length of the sequence. A sequence with length l is called an l-sequence.

A sequence database S is a set of tuples $< sid, s >$, where sid is a sequence-id and s is a sequence. A tuple $< sid, s >$ is said to contain a sequence α, if α is a subsequence of s, i.e., $\alpha \sqsubseteq s$. The support of a sequence α in a sequence database S is the number of tuples in the database containing α, i.e., $support_s(\alpha) = |< sid, s > |(< sid, s > \in S) \wedge (\alpha \sqsubseteq s)|$. Given a positive integer ξ as the support threshold, a sequence α is called a sequential pattern in database S if the sequence is contained by at least ξ tuples in the database, i.e., $support_s(\alpha) \geq \xi$. A sequential pattern with length l is called an l-pattern.

Fleet Tracking. With the integration of machines, sensors, information, software instruction, and communications technologies, fleet tracking creates connectivity between machines and business transactions (Andriesson et al. 2013). In the rental industry, fleet tracking has attracted considerable interest as a way to evaluate how they do business, optimize services and bring value to their customers. By knowing the location or usage of every vehicle in a fleet, a company can manage their vehicles in a more efficient and effective manner. The standard fleet tracking features include: equipment location with date and time, the current total operating hours of the equipment with date and time, the quantity of fuel that was used by the equipment during the 24-hour period that ended at the specific date and time (Trimble et al. 2012 and Andriesson et al. 2013).

3.2 Sequential Rental Pattern Mining Framework

The proposed framework combines sequential pattern mining techniques with fleet tracking information. A general framework is shown in the left of Fig. 2 with four following steps: Data Acquisition, Item Detection, Pattern Mining, and Prediction. With the evaluation and updated model parameters, these steps can be re-executed to peruse higher performance in future prediction. All components described on the right of the graph, give more specific design on how to make sequential pattern mining with fleet tracking data in rental industry.

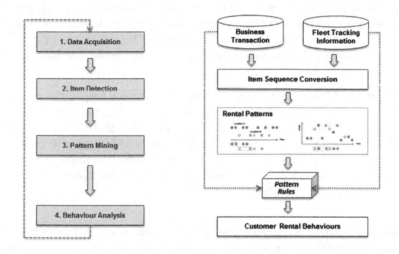

Fig. 2. Sequential rental pattern mining framework

In the framework above, the transaction dataset comes from business transaction and fleet tracking records. Item sequence conversion is designed to operate on business transaction with relevant tracking information. Each transaction is seen as a set of items (an itemset) with equipment tracking data. Given the threshold and parameters, the sequential rental pattern algorithms identify the itemsets which are subsets of the transactions in the database. The discovered rental patterns are stored as prediction rules in knowledgebase, which can be used to predict customer rental behaviors in future, with business transactions and fleet tracking information as inputting values.

4   Sequential Rental Pattern Mining

Sequential pattern mining, which discovers frequent subsequences as patterns in a sequence database, has proven to be a useful approach on handling order-based business problems as customer behavior analysis. The rental transactional data dealing with what the customers have bought in past will effectively reflects their behavior patterns around what they might rent in the future. To avoid the low efficient patterns from traditional sequential mining methods, our approach focusing on high performance events, utilizes both transactional data and fleet tracking information to get customer rental behaviors in real circumstance.

4.1   Data Acquisition and Item Detection

The data sources of data acquisition include two parts: Business Transaction and Fleet Tracking Information. It is the process of sampling and converting real-world business transactions and equipment information into series database tables that can be manipulated by following item detection phase. Data acquisition applications are controlled by Extract, Transform and Load (ETL) programs developed using various general purpose programming languages.

Item Sequence Detection by Location. Traditional sequential rental item detection focuses on the rental behaviors of a customer, however in practical, the customer rental behaviors depend on special characteristics of each project running in different locations. Detecting location-based items will capture the special features on different worksite and then will effective improve the prediction accuracy. The detecting results will be stored in a sequence database with customer id and project location.

Item Sequence Detection with Usage. Equipment utilization is the core of the equipment rental business. Usage information of the equipment is another important feature to identify high utility rental items. Analyzing customer behaviors on renting high utility equipment becomes hot requirements for many rental companies. Usage can be captured by fleet tracking that we described in Sect. 3.

4.2   Pattern Mining and Behavior Analysis

Objective of Discovering Rental Patterns. The aim of the approach is to discover high utility sequential rental patterns. We still need set up the detail objectives to define suitable parameter and fulfill the algorithm. In our case, by discussing with the equipment rental company, several objectives have been descripted for the project. The objectives are listed as follows: (1) To find out the products a customer prefers to hire sequentially and with high frequency, (2) To predict the product a customer might be interested to hire in the near future.

Sequential Pattern Mining Algorithm. Sequential pattern mining algorithm in sequential rental patterns discovering is described in the algorithm table. Given a sequence $s = < s_1 s_2 ... s_k >$, we denoted k-sequences as a sequence with k items. L_k is the set of frequent k-sequences, while C_k is the set of candidate k-sequences. Our goal is to generate a candidate set of all frequent k-sequences, given the set of all frequent $(k - 1)$-sequences.

Algorithm begin
1. Generate the candidate sequences in C_1
2. Save the frequent sequences in L_1
Iteratively find the sequences with kth pass:
3. Generate the candidate sequences in from the frequent sequences in L_{k-1}.
Join Phase: Join L_{k-1} with L_{k-1}.
if (s_1 first item) is the same as (s_2 last item), s_1 join with s_2.
Prune Phase: Delete candidate sequences C_k that have a contiguous $(k - 1)$ subsequence whose support count is less than the minimum support.
Terminated until
4. No more frequent sequences L_k are found. No candidate sequences C_k are generated.
End

Behavior Analysis. In the current setting learning is performed off-line. The result of learning is a set of Pattern Rules which give information what customer rental behavior might occur with some probability when certain preconditions are satisfied. On the other hand, Business Transaction and Fleet Tracking Information are used as input to the analysis algorithm as well. These rules and data sources are applied to analyze what future rental behaviors are likely to happen.

5   Testing and Results

We conduct intensive experiments on the real dataset from real-world rental industry, which holds 180,613 customer transactions with related fleet tracking from January 2014 to December 2014. The experiments evaluates the performance of Sequential Rental Pattern Mining in terms of computational cost, memory usage, number of patterns, and length of patterns on different item detection strategy from DS1 to DS4:

– DS1 focus on the rental transactions by customer only.
– DS2 uses the rental transactions by customer and fleet tracking with location.
– DS3 uses the rental transactions by customer and fleet tracking with usage.
– DS4 analyzes the patterns on the rental transactions by customer and fleet tracking with both location and usage.

The execution times of mining rental sequential patterns on DS1 to DS4 are shown in Fig. 3; the figure also since we can obtain many more sequential rental patterns. Especially for DS4, with the combination of fleet includes the number of patterns.

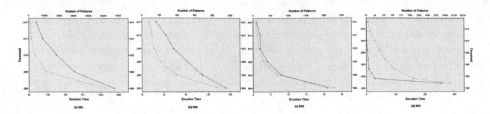

Fig. 3. Evaluation of Execution Time and Number of Patterns on the Four Item Detection Strategies

When the minimum threshold decreases, more execution time is required tracking with both location and usage, the results show that it can extract more sequential rental patterns with less execution cost. The results also show that compared with DS1 without fleet tracking, all the other three strategies with fleet tracking have taken less execution time under same threshold (for instance, 1719 for DS1 and 106 for DS2). Figure 4 (a) and (b) show the effectiveness of the approaches with the fleet tracking. The execution time has dramatically decreased with fleet tracking approaches as DS2 DS4, and the number of patterns under suitable threshold still can keep on a high level (for instance, 1719 with above 25000 patterns for DS1 and 258 with 24196 patterns for DS4). The results also show that utilizing multiple fleet tracking features has the better performance than the simple fleet tracking approaches. Compared with the simple fleet tracking DS2 and DS3, the complex fleet tracking DS4 with both location and usage has discovered much more rental patterns with the reasonable execution time (for instance, 258 with 24196 patterns). We validated the accuracy of discovering rental pat-

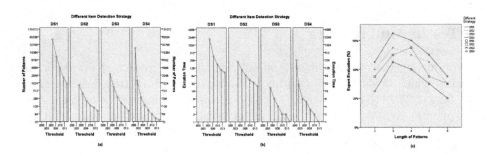

Fig. 4. Comparison of (a) Number of Patterns and (b) Execution Time on the Four Item Detection Strategy (c) Evaluation of Length of Patterns on the Four Item Detection Strategies

terns on different strategies through the evaluation from domain experts. The experts from rental industry randomly chose groups of the patterns of length (2 6) from different strategy (DS1 DS4) and evaluated the patterns with their domain knowledge. Then they picked up the qualified patterns from each group. The value of expert evaluation means the percentage of qualified patterns in each group. In Fig. 4(c), although the value of expert evaluation varied by length of patterns, the strategies with fleet tracking approaches show higher percentage of valuable patterns in every length group. The results show the effectiveness of the fleet tracking strategies.

6   Conclusion

Sequential rental pattern mining leads to patterns which discover the customers need for service and with the fleet tracking features we can know about the detail on when get the equipment to customer and where they need it. In this paper, we have proposed a novel framework on how to discover sequential rental patterns by fleet tracking and testified its performance with different fleet tracking strategies in the rental industry. The results demonstrate the effectiveness of our approach.

Acknowledgments. This work is funded by the Australian Research Council Linkage grant (LP120100566).

References

Rieser, C.: Service Success! Lessons from a Leader on How to Turn Around a Service Business. John Wiley & Sons (1994)

Trimble, T.E., Bowman, D.S.: Market Guide to Fleet Telematics Services: Creating a Consumer's Guide to Currently Available Aftermarket Solutions (2012)

Andriesson, J.E., Roe, R.A. (eds.): Telematics and work. Psychology Press (2013)

Zaki, M.J.: SPADE: an efficient algorithm for mining frequent sequences. Mach. Learn. **42**(1–2), 31–60 (2001)

Pinto, H., Han, J., Pei, J., Wang, K., Chen, Q., Dayal, U.: Multi-dimensional sequential pattern mining. In: Proceedings of the tenth international conference on Information and knowledge management, pp. 81–88. ACM (2001)

Mooney, C.H., Roddick, J.F.: Sequential pattern mining-approaches and algorithms. ACM Comput. Surv. (CSUR) **45**(2), 19 (2013)

Pei, J., Han, J., Mortazavi-Asl, B., Pinto, H., Chen, Q., Dayal, U., Hsu, M.C.: Prefixspan: Mining sequential patterns efficiently by prefix-projected pattern growth. In: 2013 IEEE 29th International Conference on Data Engineering (ICDE), pp. 0215–0215. IEEE Computer Society (2001)

Ayres, J., Flannick, J., Gehrke, J., Yiu, T. Sequential pattern mining using a bitmap representation. In: Proceedings of the eighth ACM SIGKDD international conference on Knowledge discovery and data mining, pp. 429–435. ACM (2002)

Zhao, Q., Bhowmick, S.S.: Sequential pattern mining: a survey.ITechnical Report CAIS Nayang Technological University Singapore, pp. 1–26 (2003)

Pei, J., Han, J., Wang, W.: Constraint-based sequential pattern mining: the pattern-growth methods. J. Intell. Inf. Syst. **28**(2), 133–160 (2007)

Kumar, K.M., Srinivas, P.V.S., Rao, C.R.: Sequential pattern mining with multiple minimum supports by MS-SPADE. Int. J. Comput. Sci. **9**(5), 61–73 (2012)

Liao, V.C.C., Chen, M.S.: DFSP: a Depth-First SPelling algorithm for sequential pattern mining of biological sequences. Knowl. Inf. Syst. **38**(3), 623–639 (2014)

Lan, G.C., Hong, T.P., Tseng, V.S., Wang, S.L.: Applying the maximum utility measure in high utility sequential pattern mining. Expert Syst. Appl. **41**(11), 5071–5081 (2014)

A Fast Climbing Approach for Diffusion Source Inference in Large Social Networks

Wenyu Zang[1], Xiao Wang[2]([✉]), Qipeng Yao[1,3], and Li Guo[1]

[1] Institute of Information Engineering, Chinese Academy of Sciences,
Beijing 100093, China
zangwenyu@nelmail.iie.ac.cn, yaoqipeng0706@gmail.com, guoli@iie.ac.cn
[2] National Computer Network Emergency Response Technical
Team/Coordination Center of China, Beijing 100029, China
wangxiao@cert.org.cn
[3] School of Computer Science, Beijing University of Posts
and Telecommunications, Beijing 100876, China

Abstract. In this era of information explosion, how to discover potential useful information in social networks and further locate the source has become of great importance. However, in front of the large scale social networks, the large calculation cost is the key difficulty in source locating algorithms. Aiming at this problem, we present a fast method based on climbing algorithms to locate the information source with less calculation cost in large scale social networks. Experimental results on both generated and real-world data sets show that our algorithm is more faster than existing algorithms, since it needs fewer iterations.

Keywords: Source locating · Fast algorithm · Large-scale social networks

1 Introduction

With the advent of big data era, magnanimity information are spreading quickly through social networks. Finding out the information source is essential for controlling and preventing rumor risks, which makes source locating an urgent problem to be solved.

Broadly speaking, there are several ways that can be used to solve this problem. The most intuitive approach [1] is centrality measurement on the network topology, the node with the highest centrality is regarded as the information source. On the other hand, this problem can be settled as a maximum likelihood problem [2]. Moreover, other methods like spectral analysis [3] and Monte Carlo [4] method can also be used in source locating problem. However, all these solutions exist some defects in large scale networks. First of all, all nodes or at least most of the nodes who have accepted and spread the information is required to be known in these methods. However, considering the query cost, picking out all the nodes (even most of the nodes) who have spread the information

© Springer International Publishing Switzerland 2015
C. Zhang et al. (Eds.): ICDS 2015, LNCS 9208, pp. 50–57, 2015.
DOI: 10.1007/978-3-319-24474-7_8

is impossible. Moreover, these solutions need complicated calculation over the whole networks, which cause the poor scalability.

Thus, in this paper we aim to developing a source locating algorithm for large-scale social networks with less calculation cost. The main challenges of the proposed problem are two aspects: (1) the sparsity of the observations; (2) the social network scale is too large to do the calculations on the whole network. Specifically, we proposed a fast source locating method for large-scale social networks. First, we chose k sensors strategically who monitoring the information spreading in social networks. And then, we proposed a time-based gradient descent algorithm to searching the information source with calculation cost as less as possible. If there is information we are interested in, we quickly locating the information source with our fast climbing algorithm.

Compared to exiting works the main contributions of our solution is as follows:

- We proposed several sensors selection strategies and we also compared these different sensors selection methods.
- We proposed a fast climbing method to locate the information source searching only a small subset of the whole network.
- Our algorithm achieves better scalability than other methods.

The remainder of the paper is organized as follows. Section 2 formulates the source locating problem. Section 3 introduces the proposed fast climbing algorithms. Section 4 reports experimental results. Section 5 discusses related work, and Sect. 6 concludes the paper.

2 Problem Formulation

Consider a network $G = (V, E)$, which contains a nodes set V and edges set E. Suppose a message m begin to spreading from $v_0 \in V$ in the network at some time t_0. After a period of time Δt, a set of nodes $V_I \subset V$ has infected by this message. Theoretically, we can identify the information source by monitoring all the nodes in the network. However, due to the huge scale of social networks, it is impossible to monitoring all the nodes. Thus, the key to solving this problem is minimizing the mathematical expectation of monitoring and querying cost in huge networks, as shown in Eq. (1)

$$E^{\Xi,\Psi}[T(\Xi(S,k),\Psi(S))] \tag{1}$$

where S is the set of sensors containing k sensors, Ξ is the strategy of sensors selection. And Ψ is the strategy of identifying the source based on the given S set.

3 Fast Climbing Algorithm

To locating the source, we use the intuition that the information source must be the earliest node publish the information. All we have to do is find out the earliest node with the minimum cost. First, we placed k sensors in the network monitoring the information we are interested in, here we present four sensors selection method. Then, we proposed a fast climbing Algorithm, as shown in Algorithm 1, to locating the information source if the sensors discovering some information we are interested in.

Algorithm 1. Fast Climbing Algorithm to Source Locating Problem

---

Initialization: the network $G = (V, E)$, and cascade of a typical item
$\quad\quad\quad\quad\quad \mathcal{D}_i = \{(u, t)\}$, set $STOP = 0$, infection time $t_u = N$ for every
$\quad\quad\quad\quad\quad u \in V$

for $(u, t_u) \in \mathcal{D}_i = \{(u, t)\}$ **do**
$\quad$∟ set $t_u = t$

Selected the sensors set $S = \{k \ nodes \ v \in V\}$
following the above sensor selection methods.

Update $S = \{v \in S | where \ t_v \ is \ minimum\}$
while $STOP == 0$ **do**
$\quad$**for** $v \in S$ **do**
$\quad\quad$**if** $\exists \ t_u < t_v \ for \ all \ u \in Neighbor(v)$ **then**
$\quad\quad\quad$∟ $S = S \cup u$
$\quad\quad$∟ Update $S = \{v \in S | where \ t_v \ is \ minimum\}$
$\quad$**if** $\nexists \ t_u < t_v \ for \ all \ u \in Neighbor(v \in S)$ **then**
$\quad\quad$∟ $STOP = 1$

return S *as the information source(s), when algorithm terminates.*

---

(1) **Random** Selected k sensors randomly in the whole networks. That is to say every node can be a sensor with the probability $\frac{k}{|V|}$, in a network containing $|V|$ nodes.

(2) **Degree** k nodes with the highest degree (largest count of incoming edges) in the whole networks are selected as sensors.

(3) **Distance** Selected k nodes that the distance between any two of them is greater than d (the distance d is given) as sensors. We can selected these k sensors as followings: first, we randomly selected a node as the sensor; then, we selected another node as a sensor only if it's minimum distance to all existing sensors is greater than d; repeated the step two until k sensors are selected.

(4) **Degree + Distance** Selected k nodes combines **Distance** and **Degree**. All k sensors should obey the distance rule, meanwhile, nodes with higher Degree are more likely chosen as the sensors.

Table 1. General situation of datasets

Dataset	Number of nodes	Number of edges
Facebook	4039	176468
Small-world	40,000	160,000

4   Experiments

We evaluate our algorithms on both synthetic and real-world datasets. More specifically, the synthetic dataset is a small-world network generated by *networkX* (software package for generating complete networks), and the real-world datasets is *Facebook*, a publicly available online social network dataset, which can be downloaded from http://snap.stanford.edu/data/. Each of these two datasets consists of both structure information of the network $G = (V, E)$ (as shown in Table 1) and the cascade information generated by SI propagation model with the infected probability equal to 0.9.

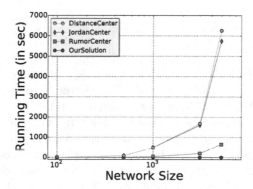

Fig. 1. Time cost of different source-locating algorithms.

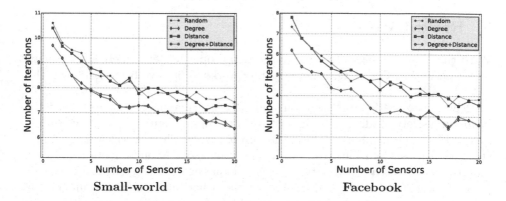

Fig. 2. Mathematical expectation of iterations.

Considering that we can query all nodes in networks for the time when them receiving a given information. The information must be find out as long as we have enough time. Thus, the number of iterations and calculate time is the major

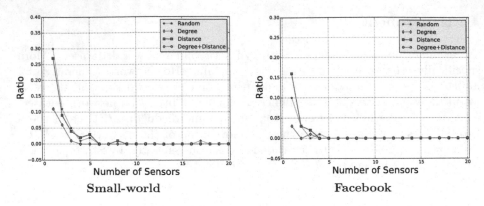

Fig. 3. Ratio of experiments in which no monitor receives the message.

concern in this problem. We first evaluate the time cost of our solution and other three representative algorithms, i.e., distance center, jordan center and rumor center, on generated differ-scale networks as shown in Fig. 1. Then, we compared the number of iterations and the calculation time vary with the number of sensors k for different sensor selection methods, as shown in Fig. 2. Furthermore, One of the important factors that affects the time cost is the number of positive sensors. Figure 3 shows the ratio of experiments in which no sensors received the specify item. All reported results are averaged over 100 independent runs on different sources. Experiment results show that we can monitoring the whole network with less than 10 sensors using the **Degree** sensors selection method, and then locate the information source with our fast climbing algorithm.

5   Related Works

With the advent of big data era, information propagates extremely fast through social networks. Therefore, a great deal of works [5,6] have been done over the past decade.

First, information propagation and influence maximization problem have been extensively studied over the last decade. On one hand, there are considerable works on modeling the information propagation. These works mainly model the information diffusion in networks, and the most popular models are SIR (susceptible-infected-recovered) model [7], SI (susceptible-infected) model [8] and IC (independent cascade) model [9]. On the other hand, influence maximization solutions are trying to find a small subset of nodes in a social network that could maximize the spread of the information. Domingos and Richardson [10,11] first formulated the influence maximization problem as an algorithmic problem in probabilistic methods. And, Kempe et al. [12] first modeled the problem as the discrete optimization problem. Later many heuristic algorithms [13–15] have been proposed to improve the efficiency of seed selection. In the works [16–18] the authors discussed the integral influence maximization problem when repeated activations are involved. Besides, Yao et al. [19,20] studied the problem of minimizing the negative influence by blocking links or vertexes in social networks.

Second, source locating problem has become a hot issue in recent years. Comin first proposed a heuristic topology center measurement [1] for source locating problems, but there is no theoretical analysis to support it. Next, pinto, etc. locating the source through infected time analysis [21]. Later, lots of works are based on sample path analysis, such as Rumor Center [2,22] and Jordan Center [23]. Besides, Luo proposed multiple sources locating algorithms [24], source locating based on limited observations [25] and identifying source on SIS model [26] through optimize a sample path. Unfortunately, these works are all based on tree like networks which greatly simplify the problem. Other methods, like spectral analysis [3,27] also be used to identifying the sources. Until 2013, Lokhov proposed a ML (maximum likelihood) estimator optimized by dynamic-message passing algorithms [28], the problem is addressed more systematically. Then, MAP (maximum a posteriori) algorithms [29] gave better solutions to the problems via considering the priori information. Moreover, multiple sources locating on SIR model [30] and topic-aware source locating [31] solutions also be discussed recently. However, few of these works considered the time cost in the source locating problem, which is particularly important in large scale social networks.

Compared with these approaches, we propose a solution to fast source locating problems based on climbing algorithm through only partially observed subsets of the whole social networks.

6 Conclusions

In this paper, we presented a fast climbing algorithm for source locating algorithm in huge social networks. Compared with existing source locating algorithms, our methods could locate the information source with less time cost. Moreover, few sensors were needed in our fast climbing algorithm, which would further save the observing cost. Experimental results on both generated and real-world data sets showed the effectiveness of our algorithm.

Acknowledgments. This work was supported by the NSFC (No. 61370025), 863 projects (No. 2011AA01A103 and 2012AA012502), 973 project (No. 2013CB329606), and the Strategic Leading Science and Technology Projects of Chinese Academy of Sciences (No. XDA06030200), Australia ARC Discovery Project (DP1402206).

References

1. Comin, C.H., da Fontoura Costa, L.: Identifying the starting point of a spreading process in complex networks. Phys. Rev. E **84**(5), 056105 (2011)
2. Shah, D., Zaman, T.: Rumors in a network: who's the culprit? IEEE Trans. Inf. Theory **57**(8), 5163–5181 (2011)

3. Fioriti, V., Chinnici, M.: Predicting the sources of an outbreak with a spectral technique, arXiv preprint arXiv:1211.2333

4. Agaskar, A., Lu, Y.M.: A fast monte carlo algorithm for source localization on graphs. In: SPIE Optical Engineering+ Applications, International Society for Optics and Photonics, p. 88581N (2013)

5. Zhang, P., Zhou, C., Wang, P., Gao, B.J., Zhu, X., Guo, L.: E-tree: an efficient indexing structure for ensemble models on data streams. IEEE Trans. Knowl. Data Eng. **27**(2), 461–474 (2015)

6. Zhou, C., Guo, L.: A note on influence maximization in social networks from local to global and beyond. Procedia Comput. Sci. **30**, 81–87 (2014)

7. Volz, E., Meyers, L.A.: Susceptible-infected-recovered epidemics in dynamic contact networks. Proc. Roy. Soc. B: Biol. Sci. **274**(1628), 2925–2934 (2007)

8. Anderson, R.M., May, R.M., Anderson, B.: Infectious Diseases of Humans: Dynamics and Control, vol. 28. Wiley Online Library (1992)

9. Kimura, M., Saito, K., Nakano, R.: Extracting influential nodes for information diffusion on a social network. In: AAAI, vol. 7, pp. 1371–1376 (2007)

10. Hulten, G., Spencer, L., Domingos, P.: Mining time-changing data streams. In: Proceedings of the Seventh ACM SIGKDD International Conference on Knowledge Discovery and Data Mining, pp. 97–106. ACM (2001)

11. Richardson, M., Domingos, P.: Mining knowledge-sharing sites for viral marketing. In: Proceedings of the Eighth ACM SIGKDD International Conference on Knowledge Discovery and Data Mining, pp. 61–70. ACM (2002)

12. Kempe, D., Kleinberg, J., Tardos, É.: Maximizing the spread of influence through a social network. In: Proceedings of the Ninth ACM SIGKDD International Conference on Knowledge Discovery and Data Mining, pp. 137–146. ACM (2003)

13. Zhou, C., Zhang, P., Guo, J., Zhu, X., Guo, L.: Ublf: an upper bound based approach to discover influential nodes in social networks. In: IEEE 13th International Conference on Data Mining (ICDM), pp. 907–916. IEEE (2013)

14. Guo, J., Zhang, P., Zhou, C., Cao, Y., Guo, L.: Personalized influence maximization on social networks. In: Proceedings of the 22nd ACM International Conference on Conference on Information & Knowledge Management, pp. 199–208. ACM (2013)

15. Zhou, C., Zhang, P., Guo, J., Guo, L.: An upper bound based greedy algorithm for mining top-k influential nodes in social networks. In: Proceedings of the 23rd International Conference on World Wide Web Companion, pp. 421–422. International World Wide Web Conferences Steering Committee (2014)

16. Zhou, C., Zhang, P., Zang, W., Guo, L.: Maximizing the cumulative influence through a social network when repeat activation exists. Procedia Comput. Sci. **29**, 422–431 (2014)

17. Zhou, C., Zhang, P., Zang, W., Guo, L.: Maximizing the long-term integral influence in social networks under the voter model. In: Proceedings of the Companion Publication of the 23rd International Conference on World Wide Web Companion, pp. 423–424. International World Wide Web Conferences Steering Committee (2014)

18. Zhou, C., Zhang, P., Zang, W., Guo, L.: On the upper bounds of spread for greedy algorithms in social network influence maximization. IEEE Trans. Knowl. Data Eng. **1**, p. 1 (PrePrints). doi:10.1109/TKDE.2015.2419659

19. Yao, Q., Zhou, C., Xiang, L., Cao, Y., Guo, L.: Minimizing the negative influence by blocking links in social networks. In: Lu, Y., Xu, W., Xi, Z. (eds.) ISCTCS 2014. CCIS, vol. 520, pp. 65–73. Springer, Heidelberg (2015)

20. Yao, Q., Zhou, C., Shi, R., Wang, P., Guo, L.: Topic-aware social influence minimization. In: 24th International World Wide Web Conference. ACM (2015)

21. Pinto, P.C., Thiran, P., Vetterli, M.: Locating the source of diffusion in large-scale networks. Phys. Rev. Lett. **109**(6), 068702 (2012)
22. Shah, D., Zaman, T.: Rumor centrality: a universal source detector. ACM SIG-METRICS Perform. Eval. Rev. **40**, 199–210 (2012). ACM
23. Zhu, K., Ying, L.: Information source detection in the sir model: a sample path based approach. In: Information Theory and Applications Workshop (ITA), pp. 1–9. IEEE (2013)
24. Luo, W., Tay, W.P., Leng, M.: Identifying infection sources and regions in large networks. IEEE Trans. Sig. Process. **61**(11), 2850–2865 (2013)
25. Luo, W., Tay, W.P., Leng, M.: How to identify an infection source with limited observations, arXiv preprint arXiv:1309.4161
26. Luo, W., Tay, W.P.: Finding an infection source under the sis model. In: 2013 IEEE International Conference on Acoustics, Speech and Signal Processing (ICASSP), pp. 2930–2934. IEEE (2013)
27. Prakash, B.A., Vreeken, J., Faloutsos, C.: Spotting culprits in epidemics: how many and which ones? In: 2012 IEEE 12th International Conference on Data Mining (ICDM), pp. 11–20. IEEE (2012)
28. Lokhov, A.Y., Mézard, M., Ohta, H., Zdeborová, L.: Inferring the origin of an epidemy with dynamic message-passing algorithm, arXiv preprint arXiv:1303.5315
29. Dong, W., Zhang, W., Tan, C.W.: Rooting out the rumor culprit from suspects, arXiv preprint arXiv:1301.6312
30. Zang, W., Zhang, P., Zhou, C., Guo, L.: Discovering multiple diffusion source nodes in social networks. Procedia Comput. Sci. **29**, 443–452 (2014)
31. Zang, W., Zhang, P., Zhou, C., Guo, L.: Topic-aware source locating in social networks. In: 24th International World Wide Web Conference. ACM (2015)

Satellite Data Science: A Case Study for Smog Disaster Prediction from Multiple Satellite Observations

Ming Wu$^{(\boxtimes)}$, Huajun Chen, and Jiaoyan Chen

College of Computer Science, Zhejiang University, Hangzhou, China

Abstract. Smog Disaster studies of $PM_{2.5}$ are limited by the lack of monitoring data, especially in developing countries. Satellite observations offer valuable global information about $PM_{2.5}$ concentrations, but have limited accuracy and completeness. In contrast to satellite domain-driven methods for $PM_{2.5}$ retrieval, our approach is satellite data-driven. Challenges and our proposed solutions discussed here in context of global scale $PM_{2.5}$ estimation include (i) $PM_{2.5}$ regression from Aerosol Optical Depth (AOD) data; (ii) training such a multi-view model for robust performance across multiple satellite measures; and (iii) the model for incomplete data avoids direct imputation of the missing elements. Experimental results on real-world data sets show that it significantly outperforms the existing approaches.

Keywords: Data science · Smog disaster · Multi-view learning

1 Introduction

$PM_{2.5}$ is tiny particulate matter less than $2.5\,\mu\text{m}$ in size. There are many attempts to gather air pollution information based on sources other than monitor stations. Zheng *et al.* [4] estimated the air quality in big cities by fusing monitor stations data with meteorological and traffic data. Chen *et al.* [1]. To have a better AOD estimate, Djuric *et al.* [2] aggregate both ground-based and satellite instruments in a semi-supervised learning manner.

In recent years, application of satellite observation in air quality studies has advanced greatly. Currently, many instruments aboard several Earth-observing satellites report their AOD estimates,such as MODIS instrument aboard Terra(MOD) and Aqua(MYD) satellites, MISR aboard Terra,OMI aboard Aura. Different spatial and temporal coverage, design, and specific mission objectives of the satellite instruments mean that they observe and measure differently. To have a better $PM_{2.5}$ estimate, one useful approach is to integrate measurements from multiple satellite measurements. It is expected that the performance can be significantly improved if information from different views can be properly integrated and leveraged. Multi-view learning refers to learning with multiple feature sets that reflect different characteristics or views of data, which is an vital research direction.

© Springer International Publishing Switzerland 2015
C. Zhang et al. (Eds.): ICDS 2015, LNCS 9208, pp. 58–61, 2015.
DOI: 10.1007/978-3-319-24474-7_9

2   Incomplete Multi-view Learning Model

In this section, we consider the more challenging and more realistic situation with general pattern of missing data. Xiang *et al.* [3] propose an Multi-Source Learning method with Block-wise Missing Data which avoids the direct imputation. Our intuition of designing such Incomplete multi-view learning (IMVL) model is illustrated in Fig. 1. First we learn different models for each data view and then combine these learned models properly integrated via extra regularizations/constraints.

Suppose we have S data views in total and each view has at least one data view available. For each sample, based on whether a certain data view is present, we just need to record a single decimal integer if we convert this binary vector to a binary number, called profile. All these profiles are stored in an n-dimensional vector $pf[1...N]$ where n is the number of samples. We are ready to give a concise description of our model. Following the aforementioned intuitions, we learn a consistent model (variable $\mathbf{w}$) across different view combinations, while within each combination, the function $\mathbf{h}(\mathbf{X})$ for different view are learned adaptively. Mathematically, the proposed model solves the following formulation:

$$\min_{w} \frac{1}{|\mathbf{pf}|} \sum_{m \in \mathbf{pf}} f(\mathbf{h}^m(\mathbf{X}^m), \mathbf{w}^m, \mathbf{Y}^m) + \lambda \mathbf{R_w}(\mathbf{w}) \tag{1}$$

where

$$f(\mathbf{h}(\mathbf{X}), \mathbf{w}, \mathbf{Y}) = \frac{1}{n} \mathbf{L}(\mathbf{Y}, \frac{\sum_{i=1}^{S^m} \mathbf{w}_i^m \mathbf{h}_i^m(\mathbf{X}_i^m)}{\sum_{i=1}^{S^m} \mathbf{w}_i^m}) \tag{2}$$

$$\mathbf{Y} = \mathbf{h}(\mathbf{X}) + \varepsilon \tag{3}$$

and $\mathbf{R}_w$ is regularizations on $\mathbf{w}$ respectively. The m superscript in (1) denotes the matrix/vector restricted to the samples that contain m in their profiles. $\mathbf{X}_i$ and

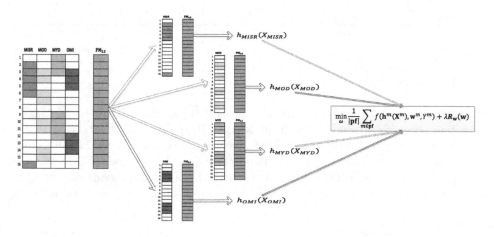

Fig. 1. Illustration of the proposed learning model.

$\mathbf{w}_i$ in (2) represent the data matrix and the weight of the ith view, respectively. S^m represent those views exist in the combination m. $\mathbf{h}_i(\mathbf{X}_i)$ represent linear regression model learning from ith view. $\mathbf{L}$ can be any convex loss function such as the least squares loss function or the logistic loss function and n is number of rows of $\mathbf{X}$.

When we learned prediction model in each view and seek the optimal $\mathbf{w}$, (1) becomes an unconstrained regularization problem:

$$\min_{w} g(\mathbf{w}) + \lambda \mathbf{R}_{\mathbf{w}}(\mathbf{w}) \tag{4}$$

where

$$g(\mathbf{w}) = \frac{1}{|\mathbf{pf}|} \sum_{m \in \mathbf{pf}} \frac{1}{2n_m} \| \mathbf{Y}^m - \frac{\sum_{i=1}^{S^m} \mathbf{w}_i^m \mathbf{h}_i^m(\mathbf{X}_i^m)}{\sum_{i=1}^{S^m} \mathbf{w}_i^m} \|_2^2 \tag{5}$$

and n_m is number of rows of $\boldsymbol{X}^m$. We can observe that $g(\boldsymbol{w})$ is a quadratic function of $\mathbf{w}$ and thus the overall formulation is to minimize the summation of a quadratic term and the regularization term ℓ_1-norm. In order to apply standard first-order lasso solvers, we only need to provide the gradient of $\mathbf{w}$ at any given point without knowing the explicit quadratic form. Algorithm 1 summarizes our alternating minimization scheme.

Algorithm 1. Iterative algorithm for solving (1)

Inpute: X,Y,λ
Output: solution $\mathbf{h}(\mathbf{X})$, $\mathbf{w}$ to (1)
  1: Compute each $\mathbf{h}_i(\mathbf{X}_i)$ via solving a linear regression problem (3) in ith view.
  2: Initialize $(\mathbf{w}^i)^0$ by fitting each view individually on the available data.
  3: **for all** $k = 1,2,...$ **do**
  4:    Update $(\mathbf{w})^k$ via solving a regularized lasso problem (4)
  5:    if the objective stops decreasing **then**
  6:       **return** $\mathbf{w} = (\mathbf{w})^k$
  7:    **end if**
  8: **end for**

---

3   Experiments

In this section, we perform experiments in three china citys(Guangzhou, Lanzhou, Hangzhou) using the ground-based PM$_{2.5}$ data[1] (16:00–17:00 local time) and four satellite measurements[2] (including two from Terra MODIS and MISR at 14:00–15:00 local time; and two from Aqua MODIS and OMI at 16:00–17:00 local time) from 2013–2014. After removing days with none of satellite data,we obtain 1,837 data points totally, where 49 % of satellite predictions were missing.

---

[1] http://www.pm25.in/.
[2] http://giovanni.gsfc.nasa.gov/mapss/.

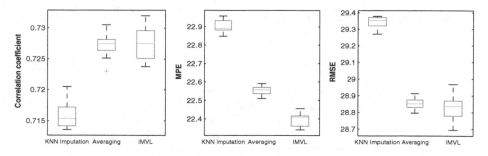

Fig. 2. Box plots of results on the real-world data set.

To reduce statistical variability, results are averaged over 10 repetitions. In each repetition, we randomly sample 20 % points as test set. 5-fold cross-validation is employed to evaluate the performance for each model. Although medians do not change significantly for Averaging and IMVL in Correlation coefficient and RMSE, IMVL has significantly lower MPE compared with the other methods in Fig. 2.

4 Conclusions

In this paper, we proposed a supervised method for aggregation of AOD predictions from incomplete noisy satellite-borne sensors into a single, more accurate estimate of $PM_{2.5}$. Our IMVL method is motivated by Multi-view Learning's principle of complementary, presenting a general optimization method. Results on real-world aerosol data comprising 4 satellite-borne sensors indicate the benefits of the proposed approach.

References

1. Chen, J., Chen, H., Zheng, G., Pan, J.Z., Wu, H., Zhang, N.: Big smog meets web science: smog disaster analysis based on social media and device data on the web. In: Proceedings of the Companion Publication of the 23rd International Conference on World Wide Web Companion, pp. 505–510. International World Wide Web Conferences Steering Committee (2014)
2. Djuric, N., Kansakar, L., Vucetic, S.: Semi-supervised learning for integration of aerosol predictions from multiple satellite instruments. In: Proceedings of the Twenty-Third international Joint Conference on Artificial Intelligence, pp. 2797–2803. AAAI Press (2013)
3. Xiang, S., Yuan, L., Fan, W., Wang, Y., Thompson, P.M., Ye, J.: Multi-source learning with block-wise missing data for alzheimer's disease prediction. In: Proceedings of the 19th ACM SIGKDD International Conference on Knowledge Discovery and Data Mining, pp. 185–193. ACM (2013)
4. Zheng, Y., Liu, F., Hsieh, H.-P.: U-air: when urban air quality inference meets big data. In: Proceedings of the 19th ACM SIGKDD International Conference on Knowledge Discovery and Data Mining, pp. 1436–1444. ACM (2013)

An Algebra Description for Hard Clustering

Bo Wang[1,2], Yong Shi[1,2(✉)], Zhuofan Yang[3], and Xuchan Ju[4]

[1] Research Center on Fictitious Economy and Data Science,
Chinese Academy of Sciences, Beijing, China
yshi@ucas.ac.cn
[2] Key Laboratory of Big Data Mining and Knowledge Management,
Chinese Academy of Sciences, Beijing, China
[3] School of Management, University of Chinese Academy of Sciences, Beijing, China
[4] School of Mathematical Sciences, University of Chinese Academy of Sciences,
Beijing, China

Abstract. Hard clustering algorithm partitions data set into several distinct regions. Clustering result offers a kind of characterization for the distribution of data relied on concentration. At the same time, the cluster structure can be regarded as a representation of knowledge in the form of data. However, as a sort of unsupervised learning task, due to a lack of overall criterion for evaluating the effect of clustering algorithms, different clustering algorithms lead to different results based on different considerations. Because of this uncertainty of single clustering result, by virtue of algebra tools, this paper tries to obtain a more reasonable cluster structure by combining various hard clustering results. Furthermore, based on the algebra representation and topological description of clustering, lattice theory and latticized topology can be employed, which allows us to define algebra operations and discuss topology property on clustering results.

Keywords: Hard clustering · Algebra description · Lattice theory · Latticized topology

1 Introduction

Different from goodness of fit based classification problem, as an unsupervised learning task, clustering algorithms offers the results based on several vague principles, which leads to the difficulty of evaluating for the cluster validity [1]. Traditionally, there are three different criteria for evaluating cluster validity, external criterion, internal criterion and relative criterion [2]. External criterion measures the difference between clustering result and predefined cluster structure. Based on similarity matrix, internal criterion compares clustering results under some test of statistical significance. Relative criterion selects the best parameter which is in accordance with the data set. At the same time, it can also tell whether the data set has a distinct cluster structure. However, because of the uncertainty of these criteria and the clustering analysis itself, we cannot ensure

© Springer International Publishing Switzerland 2015
C. Zhang et al. (Eds.): ICDS 2015, LNCS 9208, pp. 62–69, 2015.
DOI: 10.1007/978-3-319-24474-7_10

which result is the best one. Besides, according to the discussion in [3], clustering can be classified into hard clustering and soft clustering. Typical method in the former type is partition based clustering [4]. Soft clustering employs degree of membership to measure and define different clusters [5].

Lattice theory is an important topic of universal algebra, which mainly studies the algebra structure of arbitrary nonempty set [6]. Based on algebra operations on the set, equivalence relation can be developed to congruence relation, which keeps the equivalence under the corresponding algebra operations. Furthermore, all the congruence relations on the set construct a sublattice of the lattice formed by all the equivalence relations on the same set with respect to inclusion. It is clear that every single hard clustering is equivalent to some partitions on the data space. As a result, by means of defining proper operations on the same data space, we found the correspondence between the lattice of congruence relations and all the clustering results on the data set. In this way, the properties of congruence lattice can be extended to the clustering results.

In addition, latticized topology offers the topological structure on lattice. Based on the establishment of 8 different topological bases, the convergence properties can be discussed [7]. On one hand, hard clustering result can be viewed as a non-intersection subset of the power set of data set, which is a typical Boolean algebra. On the other hand, every single clustering result can be seen as an element in the power set of product space formed by data set. Based on algebraic closure operator, clustering result equals to closed set under the operator, which can build another cluster related lattice.

In this paper, we focus on algebra description for hard clustering and also discuss fundamental properties under specific latticized topology. Especially, congruence lattice of a certain algebra system will be used to describe results obtained by one single clustering algorithm or a class of clustering algorithms. By doing this, we will show the relation between clustering results and the congruence lattice on a specific algebra. Then, topological basis built by clustering results can be proposed.

2 Preliminaries

2.1 Algebraic Lattice and Congruence Lattice

Let $Eq(A)$ denote all the equivalence relations on A. It can be proved that poset $(Eq(A), \subseteq)$ is a complete lattice. In addition, if $\{\theta_i\}_{i \in I}$ is a subset of $Eq(A)$, we have $\bigwedge_{i \in I} \theta_i = \bigcap_{i \in I} \theta_i$ and $\bigvee_{i \in I} \theta_i = \cup\{\theta_{i_0} \circ \theta_{i_1} \circ \theta_{i_2} \circ \cdots \circ \theta_{i_k} : i_0, i_1, i_2, \cdots, i_k \in I, k < \infty\}$. Particularly, if θ_1 and θ_2 is permutable under the operation $\circ$, we have $\theta_1 \vee \theta_2 = \theta_1 \circ \theta_2$. All the partitions of set A is denoted by $\Pi(A)$. There is a bijection between $\Pi(A)$ and $Eq(A)$.

Definition 1 (Compact Element). *An element a in lattice L is compact if $\forall a \leqslant \bigvee A$, there is a finite subset B of A, such that $a \leqslant \bigvee B$. L is compactly generated iff every element in L is a supremum of compact elements.*

Definition 2 (Algebraic Lattice). *A lattice is an algebraic lattice iff it is complete and compactly generated.*

Definition 3 (Congruence Lattice). *Let A be an algebra of type $\mathcal{F}$ and $\theta \in Eq(A)$. Then θ is a congruence on A if θ satisfies the following compatibility property (CP): for each n-ary function symbol $f^A \in \mathcal{F}$ and $a_i, b_i \in A$, if $a_i \theta b_i, 1 \leqslant i \leqslant n$, then, $f^A(a_1, a_2, \cdots, a_n) \theta f^A(b_1, b_2, \cdots, b_n)$ holds.*

In Fig. 1, we show a sketch for congruence relation. The dotted lines subdivide A into the equivalence classes of θ. Then selecting a_1, b_1 and a_2, b_2 in the same equivalence class respectively. For binary operation f^A, compatibility property guarantees $f^A(a_1, a_2)$ and $f^A(b_1, b_2)$ to be in the same equivalence class. Denote the congruence lattice on A as **Con A**.

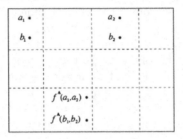

Fig. 1. Congruence relation

Theorem 1. Con A *is an algebraic lattice.*

2.2 General Latticized Topology

Let L be a complete lattice. We construct latticized topology on L, which can induce common topology on L.

Theorem 2. *Let $T_{10} = \{(\gamma] | \gamma \in \Gamma_u\} \cup \emptyset \subseteq P(L)$ and $P(L)$ be the power set of L. Then, T_{10} is a topological basis of L.*

Proof. Fist, $\bigcup T_{10} = L$. Next, let $(\gamma_1], (\gamma_2]$ be two arbitrary elements in T_{10}. Since $(\gamma_1] \cap (\gamma_2] = (\gamma_1 \wedge \gamma_2]$ and $\gamma_1 \wedge \gamma_2 \in \Gamma_u$, we have $\forall \alpha \in (\gamma_1] \cap (\gamma_2], \alpha \in (\gamma_1 \wedge \gamma_2] = (\gamma_1] \cap (\gamma_2]$. Now, let $\mathfrak{S} = \{U \subset L | \exists \{\gamma_t, t \in T\} \subseteq T_{10}, U = \bigcup_{t \in T} (\gamma_t]\}$.
It can be proved that $(L, \mathfrak{S})$ is the unique topology space with respect to T_{10} as its topological basis. $\qquad\square$

3 Algebra Characterization for Clustering Result

In this section, data set is denoted by X and the data space which X belongs to is denoted by X^∞. Specifically, each partition is equal to a certain equivalence relation on X^∞, denoted by R. And the clustering result can be denoted by P, which is also a partition on data set X. In the sense of restriction, we have $P = (X^\infty/R) \bigcap P(X)$. Here, $P(X)$ denotes the collection of all the power sets of X.

3.1 Description for Single Clustering Result

Let C be an operation which can assign every single data point to its corresponding center (or medoid), based on the nearest Euclidean distance. Define a mapping from the data space X^∞ to the collection of central points X_i, $\alpha_i : X^\infty \rightarrow X_i, \alpha_i(x) = C(x)$. Now, we need to construct languages on X^∞ and X_i, which can ensure the mapping α_i above to be a homomorphism. Here, we suppose X^∞ to be an Euclidean space.

Definition 4. *Define an n-ary on X^∞: $f^{X^\infty}(x_1, x_2, \cdots, x_n) = C(x_1) + C(x_2) + \cdots + C(x_n), \forall x_i \in X^\infty$. Define an n-ary on X_i: $f^{X_i}(c_1, c_2, \cdots, c_n) = C(c_1 + c_2 + \cdots + c_n)$. Here, $c_1, c_2, \cdots c_n \in X_i$.*

Proposition 1. *Based on the above definition of n-ary languages on X^∞ and X_i, α_i is a homomorphism.*

Proof. The proposition can be verified by the following:

$$
\begin{aligned}
\alpha_i(f^{X^\infty}(a_1, a_2, \cdots, a_n)) &= \alpha_i(C(a_1) + C(a_2) + \cdots + C(a_n)) \\
&= C(C(a_1) + C(a_2) + \cdots + C(a_n)) \qquad (1) \\
&= f^{X_i}(\alpha_i(a_1), \alpha_i(a_2), \cdots, \alpha_i(a_n)), \forall a_i \in X^\infty.
\end{aligned}
$$

Thus, α_i is a surjective homomorphism between X^∞ and X_i. □

According to fundamental homomorphism theorem, the kernel of the surjective homomorphism mapping $ker(\alpha_i)$ is an element in **Con X^∞**. Let X be the data set, which is a nonempty subset in the vector space. When restricting the universe in X, we obtain a relation between **Con X^∞** and partitions on X. Particularly, every partitions on X can be arranged with a class of elements in **Con X^∞**, which can induce an equivalence relation on **Con X^∞**. Consequently, $ker(\alpha_i)$ is a representative element in the equivalence class. In addition, the restriction of every coset under $ker(\alpha_i)$ in X is a cluster in the clustering result.

3.2 Description for a Class of Clustering Results

Here, we extend our algebra method to describe a class of clustering results. Without loss of generality, we consider two different Euclidean distance based clustering algorithms on X, whose collections of central points are denoted by X_i and X_j respectively.

Definition 5. *Let α_i be the homomorphism mapping from X^∞ to X_i. For arbitrary $\{x_1, x_2, \cdots, x_n\} \subseteq X^\infty$, define set $S_i(x_1, x_2, \cdots, x_n)$, which satisfies $\forall s \in S_i(x_1, x_2, \cdots, x_n)$: $\alpha_i s = f^{X_i}(\alpha_i x_1, \alpha_i x_2, \cdots, \alpha_i x_n)$.*
When $S_i(x_1, x_2, \cdots, x_n) \bigcap S_j(x_1, x_2, \cdots, x_n) \neq \emptyset$, for all $\{x_1, x_2, \cdots, x_n\} \subseteq X^\infty$, n-ary operation on X^∞ can be defined as follows: $f^{X^\infty}(x_1, x_2, \cdots, x_n) \in S_i(x_1, x_2, \cdots, x_n) \bigcap S_j(x_1, x_2, \cdots, x_n)$.

Remark 1. Suppose that there are two different Euclidean distance based clustering algorithms, whose collections of central points are denoted by X_i and X_j respectively. Consider f^{X_i} as the following: $f^{X_i}(c_1, c_2) = C^i(c_1 + c_2), i = 1, 2$, $S_1(x_1, x_2) \cap S_2(x_1, x_2) \neq \emptyset$ is equal to the intersection of the equivalence classes of the center corresponding to $C^1(x_1) + C^1(x_2)$ in X_1 and $C^2(x_1) + C^2(x_2)$ in X_2 is nonempty. Here, $C^i, i = 1, 2$ are the mappings arranging point to its nearest center according to two different clustering results respectively. In this case, we can define the value of $f^{X^\infty}(a_1, a_2)$ in the intersection. Here, α_1 and α_2 are the surjective homomorphisms from X^∞ to X_1 and X_2, respectively.

Definition 6. *Let f^{X_i} be an n-ary on X_i. If*

$$\bigcap_{i \in I} S_i(x_1, x_2, \cdots, x_n) \neq \emptyset, \forall \{x_1, x_2, \cdots, x_n\} \subseteq X^\infty, \tag{2}$$

then the algebra operation f^{X^∞} on X can be induced according to α_i and $f^{X_i}, i \in I$. Furthermore, the homomorphism from X^∞ to $\prod_{i \in I} X_i$ can be built, i.e., α satisfying $\alpha(a)(i) = \alpha_i(a), \forall a \in X^\infty$.

Remark 2. The kernel of homomorphism $ker(\alpha) = \bigcap_{i \in I} ker(\alpha_i)$ can build a new congruence on X^∞, in which elements in the same equivalence class restricted in data set X are also partitioned in the same cluster by every single algorithm. Particularly, when α is injective and homomorphic, we denote $ker(\alpha) = \Delta$, which leads to a trivial case.

Example 1. Here, we illustrate how the compatibility property can be satisfied. In Fig. 2, two clustering results are displayed. In the first one, data set is partitioned into two regions, i.e., inner layer and outer layer, which can be obtained by some density based algorithm. In the second one, data set is partitioned into four regions, which are indicated by the sectors. This result can be gained by Euclidean distance based algorithm, for example K-means. Consequently, two-tuples are used to mark the cluster labels of all the separated areas in two results respectively. For example, $(1, 2)$ represents that the corresponding area is in cluster 1 and cluster 2 according to two clustering results respectively. In Fig. 2, because every cluster obtained by one algorithm has a nonempty intersection with all the cluster obtained by the other algorithm, two clustering results satisfy the compatibility property naturally. In fact, if the congruences corresponding to two results are denoted by θ_1 and θ_2, we have $\theta_1 \bigcup \theta_2 = \nabla$, which means all the points are clustered in the same cluster. Additionally, as we have pointed out, $\theta_1 \bigcap \theta_2$ will induce a new congruence, containing 8 distinct clusters. Especially, when there is only one point in every single region, we have $\theta_1 \bigcap \theta_2 = \Delta$, i.e., different points in different regions. In this special case, we call θ_1 and θ_2 a pair of factor congruences on X^∞.

Remark 3. Now, we would like to discuss some properties on this algebra structure. Denote $\alpha|_X$ as α restricting in X. First of all, the homomorphism of every

Fig. 2. Compatibility property

single α_i guarantee the homomorphism of α, which also indicates the homomorphism of $\alpha|_X$. Secondly, for an infinite index of I and a finite data set X, $\alpha|_X$ cannot be a mapping from X onto $\prod_{i \in I} X_i$. In this case, we can only discuss when $\alpha|_X$ is an embedding. As is shown above, $\alpha|_X$ is an embedding iff α is an embedding iff $ker(\alpha) = \bigcap_{i \in I} ker(\alpha_i) = \Delta$.

Definition 7. *Mapping $\alpha_i : X^\infty \to X_i, i \in I$ separate points iff for any arbitrary pair $x_1, x_2 \in X^\infty$, exists α_i, $\alpha_i(a_1) \neq \alpha_i(a_2)$ holds.*

3.3 Relation Between Clustering Results and Congruences on Algebra

For data space constructed algebra X^∞, we point out when a class of clustering results, which are denoted by **Clu** X, satisfying compatibility property, they can be corresponded to a subset of all the congruences on X^∞, denoted by **Con** X^∞, by an injective mapping.

Here, any element in **Clu** X can be represented by a homomorphism mapping α_i or can be viewed as a quotient space $(X^\infty/ker(\alpha_i)) \cap P(X)$. For arbitrary $\theta_i \in$ **Con** X^∞ and $\alpha_i \in$ **Clu** X, there is a partition (equivalence relation) of data set X can be induced.

Next, $\forall \{x_1, x_2, \cdots, x_n\} \subseteq X^\infty$, define: $f^{X^\infty}(a_1, a_2, \cdots, a_n) \in \bigcap_{i \in I} \{s | \alpha_i s = f^{X_i}(\alpha_i a_1, \alpha_i a_2, \cdots, \alpha_i a_n)\}$. Obviously, $\forall i \in I, ker(\alpha_i) \in$ **Con** X^∞. Then, we have the following theorem.

Theorem 3. *For a class of clustering results on data set X, if they satisfy compatibility property, we can define algebra operation on X^∞. There is a bijective between* **Clu** X *and a subset of* **Con** X^∞. *The intersection of all the kernels under homomorphism with respect to every single clustering result products new congruence on X^∞.*

Remark 4. According to this theorem, we can construct the one-to-one correspondence between a class of clustering results and a subset of **Con** X^∞. Then, according to disjunction and conjunction operations on **Con** X^∞, we can study clustering result as congruence. Particularly, every clustering result can be viewed as compactly generated element.

4   Latticized Topology for Clustering Generated Lattice

4.1   Latticized Topology in Congruence Lattice

Firstly, according to *Theorem* 3, a correspondence can be built between clustering result in the data set and congruence relation on data space. Now, A is denoted an arbitrary algebra. According to algebraic closure operator Θ, all the congruence relations on A can be viewed as a closed set with respect to Θ. Every $\theta \in$ **Con** A is a closure of some subset of $A \times A$ with respect to Θ. Thus, we consider topological structure of lattice $(\Theta(P(A \times A)), \vee, \wedge)$. Denote $\Theta(P(A \times A))$ as L. $\tau_*(L)$ is the ideal of L, which is dual to filter $\tau^*(L)$ of L.

Notice that $T_{01} = \{[\gamma] | \gamma \in \Gamma_d\} \cup \emptyset \subseteq P(L)$. For every lower uniformly neighbor elements $\theta \in$ **Con** A with respect to n_*, we can define a new congruence on A/θ, which can be induced by an element ϕ in $[\theta, \nabla]$ as follows: $\phi/\theta = \{\langle a/\theta, b/\theta \rangle \in (A/\theta)^2 | \langle a, b \rangle \in \phi\}$.

Lemma 1. *For any pair* $\phi, \theta \in$ **Con** A*, if* $\theta \leq \phi$*, then* ϕ/θ *is a congruence relation on* A/θ*.*

4.2   Hierarchial Structure of Congruence Relations

Lemma 2. *For any pair* $\phi, \theta \in$ **Con** A*, if* $\theta \leq \phi$*, then* $(A/\theta)/(\phi/\theta) \cong A/\phi$*.*

Remark 5. According to *Lemma* 2, a hierarchial structure of clustering can be abstracted. Suppose θ_1 and θ_2 are two clustering results which satisfy compatibility property. If $\theta_1 \vee \theta_2 \neq \nabla$, then $\theta_1 \vee \theta_2 \in$ **Con** A. Because $\theta_1, \theta_2 \leq \theta_1 \vee \theta_2$ and $(A/\theta_i)/(\theta_1 \vee \theta_2/\theta_i) \cong A/(\theta_1 \vee \theta_2), i = 1, 2$, the clusters in $\theta_1 \vee \theta_2$ can be viewed as grouping on clusters in $\theta_i, i = 1, 2$.

Theorem 4. *For arbitrary element* θ *in congruence lattice* **Con** A*, sublattice* $[\theta, \nabla]$ *is isomorphic to* **Con** A/θ*.*

Remark 6. This theorem shows the rationality of clustering on equivalence classes, which is also the thought of granular computing. In *Fig.* 3, we indicate the total order hierarchial structure of congruence relations.

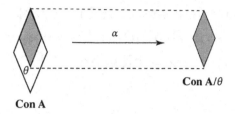

Fig. 3. Hierarchial structure of congruence

5 Conclusion

In this paper, we show the algebra structure of general hard clustering result. From single result to a class of results, homomorphic relation is built between data space and center points space, which can generate congruence of the algebra of data space. Furthermore, by virtue of fundamental homomorphism theorem, we describe single and a class of clustering results under algebra structure. Also, we prove the bijective correspondence between clustering results and the subset of congruences on data space. As a result, the property of algebraic lattice can be transfer onto clustering results, which will be one part of future work. Besides, we build topological basis on lattice to indicate the topological structure of clustering result. In the continued work, specific topology properties will be equipped in latticized topology based clustering analysis.

Acknowledgement. This work has been supported by Grants: No. 61472390, No. 11271361, Key Project (No. 71331005) and Major International Joint Research Project (No. 71110107026) from the National Natural Science Foundation of China.

References

1. Han, J.W., Kamber, M.: Data Mining Concepts and Techniques. Morgan Kaufmann publishers, San Francisco (2001)
2. Theodoridis, S., Koutroumbas, K.: Pattern Recognition, 4th edn. Academic Press, Boston (2008)
3. Jain, A.K., Murty, M.N., Flynn, P.J.: Data clustering: a review. ACM Comput. Surv. **31**(3), 264–323 (1999)
4. MacQueen, J.B.: Some methods for classification and analysis of multivariate observations. In: Proceedings of 5th Berkeley Symposium on Mathematical Statistics and Probability, vol. 1, pp. 281–297. University of California Press, Berkeley (1967)
5. Ruspini, E.R.: A new approach to clustering. Inf. Control **15**(1), 22–32 (1969)
6. Burris, S., Sankappanavar, H.P.: A Course in Universal Algebra. Springer, New York (1981)
7. Wang, P.Z.: Neighbor element structure of latticized topology and convergence ralation. J. Beijing Normal Univ. **2**, 19–34 (1984). (in Chinese)

Homeomorphism Between Fuzzy Number Space and the Space of Bounded Functions with Same Monotonicity on $[-1, 1]$

Huadong Wang[1,2,3], Sicong Guo[5], and Yong Shi[2,3,4]($\boxtimes$)

[1] College of Mathematical Sciences, University of Chinese Academy of Sciences,
Beijing 100190, China
[2] Research Center on Fictitious Economy & Data Science,
Chinese Academy of Sciences, Beijing 100190, China
yshi@ucas.ac.cn
[3] Key Laboratory of Big Data Mining and Knowledge Management,
Chinese Academy of Sciences, Beijing 100190, China
[4] School of Management, Chinese Academy of Science, Beijing 100190, China
[5] College of Sciences, Liaoning Technical University, Fuxin 123000, China

Abstract. In this paper, based on the fuzzy structured element, we prove that there is a bijection function between the fuzzy number space ε^1 and the space $B[-1, 1]$, which defined as a set of standard monotonic bounded functions with monotonicity on interval $[-1, 1]$. Furthermore, a new approach based upon the monotonic bounded functions has been proposed to create fuzzy numbers and represent them by suing fuzzy structured element. In order to make two different metrics based space in $B[-1, 1]$, Hausdorff metric and L_p metric, which both are classical functional metrics, is adopted and their topological properties is discussed. In addition, by the means of introducing fuzzy functional to space $B[-1, 1]$, we present two new fuzzy number's metrics. Finally, according to the proof of homeomorphism between fuzzy number space ε^1 and the space $B[-1, 1]$, it's argued that not only it gives a new way to study the fuzzy analysis theory, but also make the study of fuzzy number space easier.

Keywords: Fuzzy numbers · Fuzzy structured element · Standard monotonic bounded functions · Fuzzy functional · Homeomorphism

1 Introduction

Fuzzy numbers, which are a generalization of a real numbers, have been perfectly applied to model and shown the fuzzy data. Recently, application of fuzzy numbers in data mining algorithms has been an interesting topic to the researcher in this domain, for instance, clustering [13,15], classification [10] and regression [11,14]. Generally, the efforts have been done in study of fuzzy mathematical analysis and its application falls in to two main categories:

ⓒ Springer International Publishing Switzerland 2015
C. Zhang et al. (Eds.): ICDS 2015, LNCS 9208, pp. 70–77, 2015.
DOI: 10.1007/978-3-319-24474-7_11

First, studies on constructing fuzzy number metrics based on the fuzzy numbers and their topological properties. Many researchers proposed a different metrics and many discussion on them has been proposed. Here, Hausdorff metric [3], L_p metric [4] and sendograph metric [5], proposed as an examples of the most well-known widely used metrics.

The second category consist of those studies which address the relationship between the fuzzy number space and other topological spaces, study the properties of the fuzzy number space and develop some new methods in the proposed spaces. Among these studies, Goetschel and Voxman introduced a homeomorphic mapping from θ-crisp fuzzy number space to Hilbert space ℓ_2, which ranges in a convex cone (see [7]). Later, [6] generalized this mapping by extending the θ-crisp fuzzy number space to a more general one. In order to apply the functional analysis to the fuzzy-valued functions studies, in which variables are real numbers and function values are fuzzy numbers, Puri and Ralescu [12], proposed an embedding theorem in the sense that the fuzzy number space ε^1 can be embedded into a Banach space X, with the help of the Radstrom embedding theorem of compact convex set. This theorem establishes the theoretical link between the fuzzy number space and the Banach space. However, because of do not considering any specific structure of Banach space, it is not easy to implement (it is not applicable anymore). Thus, by adopting the mapping of Goetschel and Voxman, Wu and Ma [1,2] embedded fuzzy number can space into the concrete Banach space $C[0,1] \times C[0,1]$ ($C[0,1] = \{f : f$ is a bounded left-continuous function on $(0,1]$, and f has right limit on $(0,1]$, especially f is right-continuous at $0\}$), and present a specific isometrically isomorphic operator. Although the proposed embedding operator is proved to be as same as the embedding operator given by Puri and Ralescu [12] in the sense of isometrical isomorphism, the embedding operator has a specific form.

The research paper is organized in 6 sections: Sects. 2 and 3 provide some preliminaries, including the definitions of the extended set-valued function and fuzzy structured element. In Sect. 4, we introduce L_p metric and Hausdorff metric into $B[-1,1]$ and discuss some of its topological properties, such as completeness and separability. In Sect. 5, with the help of a fuzzy functional induced by the fuzzy structured element, two fuzzy number metrics induced by two given metrics of $B[-1,1]$ are presented. In this section, a significant conclusion that $B[-1,1]$ is homeomorphic to ε^1 will also be provided. In the end, we will conclude this paper in Sect. 6.

2   Preliminaries

2.1   Notions of the Extended Set-Valued Function and General Inverse Function

Definition 1. *Let f be a monotonic and bounded function on $[a,b]$ and $x_0 \in (a,b)$ be a discontinuous point in f. By considering f as a monotone increasing function, f can be a surjective function from $[a,b]$ to $(-\infty, +\infty)$ by the following* *formula;*

$$f(x_0) = [f(x_0-), f(x_0+)], f(a) = (-\infty, f(a+)], f(b) = [f(b-), +\infty),$$

Here, we denote a new function $\hat{f}$, which $\hat{f}$ is a monotonic set-valued function extended by f, it also called extensional set-valued function of f. Furthermore, we denote all the family of function f, which are bounded and have the same monotonicity on $[a, b]$, by $D[a, b]$.

Definition 2. *Suppose that f is a increasing and bounded function on $[-1, 1]$. $\hat{f}$ is the extensional set-valued function of f. Define inverse function of $\hat{f}$ as*

$$\hat{f}^{-1}(x) = \begin{cases} \sup\{t : \hat{f}(t) = x, -1 \leqslant t < 0\}, & -\infty < x \leqslant f(0-) \\ 0, & f(0-) \leqslant x \leqslant f(0+) \\ \inf\{t : \hat{f}(t) = x, 0 < t \leqslant 1\}, & f(0+) \leqslant x < +\infty \end{cases} \tag{1}$$

2.2 Notion of the Fuzzy Numbers

Fuzzy numbers are the natural generalization of real,crisp numbers. A fuzzy number is a normal fuzzy subset of a real line with the upper semi-continuous and quasi-concave membership function. The definition implies that α-cut A_α of such a fuzzy subset A is a closed interval A_l^α, A_r^α for any $\alpha \in (0, 1]$. The support of a fuzzy number A is a crisp set $\text{supp}A = \text{cl}(\{x : A(x) > 0\}) = [A_l^0, A_r^0]$,where cl is the closure. When $\text{supp}A$ is a bounded closed interval, A is called as a bounded fuzzy number. Denote all bounded fuzzy numbers on real line R as $\tilde{N}_c(\mathbb{R})$(or ε^1).

Theorem 1. *[1] If $u \in \tilde{N}_c(R)$, let*

$$\underline{u}(\alpha) = \inf\{x : x \in u_\alpha\}, \quad \overline{u}(\alpha) = \sup\{x : x \in u_\alpha\},$$

then $\underline{u}(\alpha)$ and $\overline{u}(\alpha)$ are two functions on $[0, 1]$ satisfying the following conditions (1)–(4):
(1) $\underline{u}(\alpha)$ is a bounded left continuous nondecreasing function on $(0, 1]$;
(2) $\overline{u}(\alpha)$ is a bounded left continuous nonincreasing function on $(0, 1]$;
(3) $\underline{u}(\alpha)$ and $\overline{u}(\alpha)$ are right continuous at $\alpha = 0$;
(4) $\underline{u}(\alpha) \leq \overline{u}(\alpha)$.
Conversely, if functions $\underline{u}(\alpha)$ and $\overline{u}(\alpha)$ on $[0, 1]$ satisfy the conditions (1)–(4), then there exists a unique $u \in \tilde{N}_c(R)$ such that $u_\alpha = [\underline{u}(\alpha), \overline{u}(\alpha)]$ for each $\alpha \in [0, 1]$.

3 Fuzzy Structured Element and Transformation

Definition 3. *[9] Let E be a fuzzy set on real numbers field $\mathbb{R}$,$E(x)$ is the membership function of E. Then, E is called a fuzzy structured element. If $E(x)$ satisfies the following properties: (1) $E(0) = 1$; (2) $E(x)$ is monotonic increasing and right-continuous on $[-1, 0)$, monotonic decreasing and left-continuous on $(0, 1]$; (3) For any $x \in (-\infty, -1) \cup (1, +\infty)$, $E(x) = 0$;*

E is called a normal fuzzy structured element if the fuzzy structured element E satisfies:(1) $E(x) > 0$ for all $x \in (-1, 1)$; (2) $E(x)$ is continuous, strictly monotonic increasing on $[-1, 0)$ and also continuous, strictly monotonic decreasing on $(0, 1]$.

Theorem 2 (Local Mapping Theorem). *[8] Suppose E is a fuzzy structured element on $\mathbb{R}$ with membership function $E(x)$. $f(x)$ is monotonically bounded on $[-1, 1]$ and $\hat{f}(x)$ is extensional set-valued function of $f(x)$. Then $\hat{f}(E)$ is a bounded closed fuzzy number and membership function of $\hat{f}(E)$ is $E(\hat{f}^{-1}(x))$, where $\hat{f}^{-1}(x)$ is variable rotation symmetric function of $f(x)$ (If $f(x)$ is strictly increasing on $[-1, 1]$, then $\hat{f}^{-1}(x)$ is ordinary inverse function of $f(x)$).*

Theorem 3 (Theorem of Structured Element Expression of Fuzzy Number). *[8] For a given regular fuzzy structured element E and any bounded fuzzy number A, there exists a monotonic bounded function f on $[-1, 1]$ such that $A = \hat{f}^{-1}(E)$ (strictly, exists extensional set-valued function $\hat{f}$ such that $A = \hat{f}(E)$). We called it fuzzy number A generated by the fuzzy structured element.*

When no confusion can arise, we will use $f(x)$ to indicate extended function $\hat{f}(x)$ and use $f(E)$ to indicate $\hat{f}(E)$, respectively.

4   The Same Order Standard Monotonic Bounded Function Classes $B[-1, 1]$

Definition 4. *Let f be monotonic bounded function on $[-1, 1]$. If for any discontinuity x in $[-1, 1]$, we have*

$$f(x) = \frac{1}{2}[f(x+) + f(x-)], \tag{2}$$

where $f(x+)(f(x-))$ is the right-limit(left-limit) of $f(x)$ at the point x, then $f(x)$ is called standard monotonic bounded function on $[-1, 1]$. All same order standard monotonic bounded function on $[-1, 1]$ is denoted by $B[-1, 1]$.

It is obvious that continuous monotonic bounded function on $D[-1, 1]$ is standard monotonic bounded function.

Definition 5. *Suppose that $f \in D[-1, 1]$. We define*

$$\check{f}(x) = \begin{cases} f(-1+), & x = -1 \\ [f(x-) + f(x+)]/2, & x \in (-1, 1) \\ f(1-), & x = 1 \end{cases} \tag{3}$$

We call $\check{f}(x)$ as standardized function of $f(x)$. Obviously, $\check{f} \in B[-1, 1]$. If f is a standard monotonic bounded function, then $\check{f} = f$.

We introduce two distance formulas:

$$d_p(f,g) = \left[\int_{-1}^{1} |f(x) - g(x)|^p \mathrm{d}x \right]^{1/p} , \text{ for all } f, g \in B[-1,1], \quad (4)$$

$$d_H(f,g) = \sup_{x \in [-1,1]} |f(x) - g(x)|, \text{ for all } f, g \in B[-1,1]. \quad (5)$$

where $1 \le p < +\infty$.

Theorem 4. *Let E be a normal fuzzy structured element, K is a bounded closed interval on $\mathbb{R}$. Denote*

$$B_f(K) = \{ f : f \in B[-1,1] \text{ and } [f(-1), f(1)] \subseteq K \},$$

Metric spaces $(B[-1,1], d_H)$ and $(B_f(K), d_p)$ both are complete.

This theorem can be proved by the properties of the complete metric space, i.e. every Cauchy sequence of points in the metric space M has a limit that is also in M. Due to the space limitations of the paper, the proof has to be omitted here.

Note that the metric space $(B[-1,1], d_p)$ is not complete. For example, define $f_n \in B[-1,1]$ by

$$f_{n+1}(x) = \begin{cases} f_n(x), & x \in [-1, 1 - 1/n^2] \\ n, & x \in (1 - 1/n^2, 1] \end{cases} , (n \ge 1),$$

where $f_1(x) = 0, x \in [-1,1]$. It is obvious that $f_n(x)(n \ge 1)$ are bounded functions. Suppose $m \le n$, we have

$$d_p(f_m, f_n) = \left[\int_{-1}^{1} |f_m(t) - f_n(t)|^p \mathrm{d}t \right]^{1/p} < \left[\frac{1}{(n+1)^2} + \frac{1}{(n+2)^2} + \cdots + \frac{1}{m^2} \right]^{1/p}$$

$$< \left[\frac{1}{n} - \frac{1}{m} \right]^{1/p} < \frac{1}{n} \to 0(m, n \to \infty)$$

Thus, $\{f_n\}$ is a Cauchy Sequence, their standard function sequence $\{\check{f}_n(x)\}$ is a Cauchy Sequence in $B[-1,1]$. It is easy to know that $\{\check{f}_n(x)\}$ converges to an no upper bounded function.

In general, $f \in B[-1,1], -f \in B[-1,1]$ unless f is a constant-valued function. Because, if f isn't constant-valued function, despite $-f$ is also monotonic function, but it is not same order with f. Hence, $B[-1,1]$ cannot form group with respect to operation of addition, just can form a semigroup.

It should be noted that each element in $B[-1,1]$ is not a closed form with respect to ordinary subtraction operator. We can take example, function obtain by two monotonic function subtracted may be non-monotonic. Therefore, $B[-1,1]$ can't form linear space with respect to addition and number multiply operation.

It is obvious that $B[-1,1]$ is a convex cone with 0 as its vertex.

5   Relationship Between $B[-1,1]$ and $\tilde{N}_c(\mathbb{R})$

5.1   Two Types of Fuzzy Number Metric Spaces Induced by the Fuzzy Structured Element

Let E be symmetrical regular fuzzy structured element on real line $\mathbb{R}$ and $\tilde{N}_c(\mathbb{R})$ be the set of all bounded closed fuzzy numbers. For given function $f \in B[-1,1]$, there exists corresponding unique fuzzy number such that $A_f = f(E)$. In other words, fuzzy structured element determine a mapping from $B[-1,1]$ to $\tilde{N}_c(\mathbb{R})$.
Denote

$$H_E : B[-1,1] \to \tilde{N}_c(\mathbb{R}); f \to H_E(f) = f(E) \in \tilde{N}_c(\mathbb{R})$$

Then H_E is called fuzzy functional induced by fuzzy structured element E.
Using metrics d_p and d_H on $B[-1,1]$, mapping H_E induces distances

$$d_{Np}(A,B) = d_p(H_E^{-1}(A), H_E^{-1}(B)), \tag{6}$$

$$d_{NH}(A,B) = d_M(H_E^{-1}(A), H_E^{-1}(B)), \tag{7}$$

on $\tilde{N}_c(\mathbb{R})$, where $H_E^{-1}(A), H_E^{-1}(B)$ are preimage of mapping H_E at A and B,respectively. Suppose $A = f(E), B = f(E)$, where $f,g \in B[-1,1]$, then Eqs. (6) and (7) can also rewrite as

$$d_p(f,g) = d_p(H_E(f), H_E(g)), \tag{8}$$

$$d_H(f,g) = d_H(H_E(f), H_E(g)), \tag{9}$$

$(\tilde{N}_c(\mathbb{R}), d_{Np})$ and $(\tilde{N}_c(\mathbb{R}), d_{NH})$ are said to be distance space induced by $(B[-1,1], d_p)$ and $(B[-1,1], d_M)$, respectively. It is easy to understand that H_E is an isometric bijection of $B[-1,1]$ onto $\tilde{N}_c(\mathbb{R})$.

Using isometric bijection H_E, we can translate metric of elements in fuzzy number space to metric between the same order standard monotonic bounded functions in range of $[-1,1]$.

Then, what is the relationship between those metrics and the traditional metrics of fuzzy numbers? According to the Theorem 1 and the way of inducing the above two proposed metrics, we can get the following conclusion.

Theorem 5. *Let E be regular structured element, $u,v \in \tilde{N}_c(\mathbb{R})$, there are $f,g \in B[-1,1]$ such that $u = f(E), v = g(E)$. Denote $u_\alpha = [\underline{u}(\alpha), \overline{u}(\alpha)], v_\alpha = [\underline{v}(\alpha), \overline{v}(\alpha)]$, then*

$$d_{Np}(u,v) = \left[\int_{-1}^{1} |f(x) - g(x)|^p \mathrm{d}x \right]^{1/p}$$

$$= \left[\int_0^1 |\underline{u}(\alpha) - \underline{v}(\alpha)|^p \, \mathrm{d}\underline{E}(\alpha) + |\overline{u}(\alpha) - \overline{v}(\alpha)|^p \, \mathrm{d}\overline{E}(\alpha) \right]^{1/p} \tag{10}$$

$$d_{NH}(u,v) = \sup_{x \in [-1,1]} |f(x) - g(x)| = \sup_{x \in [-1,1]} (|\underline{u}(\alpha) - \underline{v}(\alpha)| \vee |\overline{u}(\alpha) - \overline{v}(\alpha)|) \tag{11}$$

5.2 $\tilde{N}_c(\mathbb{R})$ Is Homeomorphic to $B[-1,1]$

Proposition 1. *Suppose that* $(X, d_X), (Y, d_Y)$ *are two metric spaces.* F *is an isometric bijection from* (X, d_X) *to* (Y, d_Y). *Then* F *is continuous and inverse mapping* F^{-1} *of* F *exists and is also continuous.*

Proof. Since F is a bijection of (X, d_X) into (Y, d_Y), there exists inverse mapping F^{-1} which is also one-to-one mapping. By definition of continuous mapping, for all $x_0 \in X$ and any positive number ε, there always exists a positive number δ such that $d_Y(F(x), F(x_0)) < \varepsilon$ as $d_X(x, x_0) < \delta$. Since $d_X(x, x_0) = d_Y(F(x), F(x_0))$, given ε, it is sufficient by taking $\delta \leq \varepsilon$ (For instance, take $\delta = \varepsilon/2$). Hence, F is continuous. Similarly, we can also prove inverse mapping F^{-1} which is also continuous.

Since there exists a bijection H_E of $B[-1,1]$ into $\tilde{N}_c(\mathbb{R})$ and H_E and inverse function H_E^{-1} are continuous, thus we have conclusions as follows:

Theorem 6. *Metric spaces* $(B[-1,1], d_p)$ *and* $(\tilde{N}_c(\mathbb{R}), d_{Np})$ *are homeomorphic. Metric spaces* $(B[-1,1], d_H)$ *and* $(\tilde{N}_c(\mathbb{R}), d_{NH})$ *are homeomorphic.*

Since space $(\tilde{N}_c(R), d_{Np})$ and $(B[-1,1], d_p)$ are homeomorphic, that is, both metric spaces are topologically equivalent. So elements in both of them have consistent properties on metrics. There are one-to-one relationship between fuzzy number sequence $\{u_n\}$ of $(\tilde{N}_c(\mathbb{R}), d_{Np})$ and function sequence $\{f_n\}$, fuzzy number sequence on $(\tilde{N}_c(\mathbb{R}), d_{Np})$ and function sequence on $(B[-1,1], d_p)$ have completely same properties. Similarly, fuzzy number sequence on $(\tilde{N}_c(\mathbb{R}), d_{NH})$ and function sequence on $(B[-1,1], d_H)$ have completely same properties. Therefore, the properties of convergence sequence of general metric spaces are also founded to the convergence fuzzy number sequence. Thus, they are trivial to the following corollaries.

Corollary 1. *Fuzzy number metric space* $(\tilde{N}_c(\mathbb{R}), d_{NH})$ *is complete and* $(\tilde{N}_c(\mathbb{R}), d_{Np})$ *is not complete.*

Corollary 2. *For any nonempty closed interval* K *on* $\mathbb{R}$, *let*

$$\tilde{N}_c(K) = \{u : u \in \tilde{N}_c(R) \text{ and } \operatorname{supp} u \subseteq K\},$$

then $(\tilde{N}_c(K), d_{Np})$ *is a complete metric space.*

6   Conclusion

By using monotonic mapping of the fuzzy structured element, we have proved that the bounded fuzzy number space is homeomorphic to the space $B[-1,1]$ of monotonic bounded function with same monotonicity on $[-1,1]$. Therefore, the problem of the fuzzy number space can be transformed to one's of space $B[-1,1]$, such as convergence of sequence of fuzzy numbers, continuous of fuzzy-valued function and so on. To some extent, our study provides a new way for the study of fuzzy analysis.

Acknowledgements. This work has been partially supported by grants from National Natural Science Foundation of China (Grant NO.71331005, NO.71110107026.)

References

1. Cong-Xin, W., Ming, M.: Embedding problem of fuzzy number space: part I. Fuzzy Sets Syst. **44**(1), 33–38 (1991)
2. Congxin, W., Ming, M.: Embedding problem of fuzzy number space: part II. Fuzzy Sets Syst. **45**(2), 189–202 (1992)
3. Diamond, P., Kloeden, P.: Characterization of compact subsets of fuzzy sets. Fuzzy Sets Syst. **29**(3), 341–348 (1989)
4. Diamond, P., Kloeden, P.: Metric spaces of fuzzy sets. Fuzzy Sets Syst. **35**(2), 241–249 (1990)
5. Diamond, P., Kloeden, P.E., Kloeden, P.E., Mathematician, A., Kloeden, P.E.: Metric Spaces of Fuzzy Sets: Theory and Applications. World Scientific, Singapore (1994)
6. Gergó, L.: Generalisation of the Goetschel-Voxman embedding. Fuzzy Sets Syst. **47**(1), 105–108 (1992)
7. Goetschel, R., Voxman, W.: Topological properties of fuzzy numbers. Fuzzy Sets Syst. **10**(1), 87–99 (1983)
8. Guo, S., Su, Z., Wang, L.: Method of structured element in fuzzy analysis and calculation. Fuzzy Syst. Math. **3**, 011 (2004)
9. Guo, S.: Method of structuring element in fuzzy analysis. J. Liaoning Tech. Univ. **21**(5), 670–673 (2002)
10. Li, A., Shi, Y., He, J., Zhang, Y.: A fuzzy linear programming-based classification method. Int. J. Inf. Tech. Decis. Making **10**(06), 1161–1174 (2011)
11. Lin, K., Pai, P., Lu, Y., Chang, P.: Revenue forecasting using a least-squares support vector regression model in a fuzzy environment. Inf. Sci. **220**, 196–209 (2013)
12. Puri, M.L., Ralescu, D.A.: Differentials of fuzzy functions. J. Math. Anal. Appl. **91**(2), 552–558 (1983)
13. Reuter, U.: A fuzzy approach for modelling non-stochastic heterogeneous data in engineering based on cluster analysis. Integr. Comput. Aided Eng. **18**(3), 281–289 (2011)
14. Wang, H., Guo, S., Yue, L.: An approach to fuzzy multiple linear regression model based on the structural element theory. Syst. Eng. Theor. Pract. **34**(10), 2628 (2014)
15. Yang, M.S., Ko, C.H.: On a class of fuzzy c-numbers clustering procedures for fuzzy data. Fuzzy Sets Syst. **84**(1), 49–60 (1996)

Regression-Based Outlier Detection of Sensor Measurements Using Independent Variable Synthesis

Chang Mok Park[1(✉)] and Jesung Jeon[2]

[1] Department of Technology & Systems Management, Induk University,
Nowon-gu, Seoul 139-749, South Korea
cmpark@induk.ac.kr
[2] Department of Construction Information Engineering, Induk University,
Nowon-gu, Seoul 139-749, South Korea
jsjeon@induk.ac.kr

Abstract. We present an improved outlier detection method using a regression model. A synthesized signal using the measurements of different sensors is applied for the estimation of the model parameters. The artificial and real dataset are used to verify the proposed method. The preliminary experiments show improvement in the regression-based outlier detection method.

1 Introduction

Sensor signals are used for the security monitoring of the structure. Outlier detection is the first step for data mining with sensor measurements [1]. Outlier detection considers two areas. The first is identifying generic characteristics of the sensor measurement itself. The characteristics could be the signal distribution or temporal correlations in sensor measurements. Abrupt changes in the statistic distribution of sensor measurements can be used to detect the sensor fault [2]. Outlier detection using time-series analysis and signal prediction technique has been studied [3]. The second is identifying spatial correlation in different sensors [4].

In the conventional method, the parameter estimation of the regression model was performed using measurements among neighbor sensors. In this study, we present an improved regression-based outlier method. A new signal is synthesized using the weighted sum of sensor measurements. The regression model between a target sensor measurement and the new signal is estimated. Finally, accurate outlier detection can be performed using the residual analysis of the regression model.

2 Proposed Method

2.1 Summation of Sensor Measurements for Reducing Noise Effect

Assuming the sensor output (y) has a linear relationship with particular physical independent variable (x), the relationship can be expressed by the following equation.

© Springer International Publishing Switzerland 2015
C. Zhang et al. (Eds.): ICDS 2015, LNCS 9208, pp. 78–86, 2015.
DOI: 10.1007/978-3-319-24474-7_12

$$y = ax + b + e \qquad (1)$$

In this case, e represents the noise with the characteristics of normal distribution, N $(0, \sigma^2)$. The observations measured from the N sensors with the same linear model and the same independent variable can be expressed by the following equation.

$$
\begin{aligned}
y_1 &= ax + b + e_1 \\
y_2 &= ax + b + e_2 \\
y_3 &= ax + b + e_3 \\
&\cdots \\
y_n &= ax + b + e
\end{aligned}
\qquad (2)
$$

When summing n observations, it can be expressed by the following equation.

$$n(ax + b) + \sum_{i=1}^{n} e_i \qquad (3)$$

Because noise e has a normal distribution with 0 mean, as n increases, the noise term in Eq. (3) will converge to zero. As a result, the sum of sensor observations will be close to the following equation

$$n(ax + b) \qquad (4)$$

The sum of the observations divided by the number of sensors is approximated as the following

$$ax + b \qquad (5)$$

Therefore, in order to reduce the effect of noise of a sensor observation, the summing observations of many sensors can be used to create an observation with minimal noise effects.

2.2 Estimation of Normal Sensor Behavior for Detecting Outliers

The observations for n sensors with different linear model parameters and the same independent variable may be expressed by the following equation.

$$
\begin{aligned}
y_1 &= a_1 x + b_1 + e_1 \\
y_2 &= a_2 x + b_2 + e_2 \\
y_3 &= a_3 x + b_3 + e_3 \\
&\cdots \\
y_n &= a_n x + b_n + e_n
\end{aligned}
\qquad (6)
$$

In order to estimate the normal signal of the particular sensor observations, the observations for neighbor sensors can be used. For example, in order to estimate the normal value of the third sensor, it is possible to use the value of the second sensor. The linear equation of the second sensor can be rewritten as follows.

$$x = \frac{1}{a_2}y_2 - \frac{b_2}{a_2} - \frac{e_2}{a_2} \tag{7}$$

The linear relationship between the signal y_3, y_2 can be expressed as follows.

$$y_3 = \frac{a_3}{a_2}y_2 - \frac{a_3 b_2}{a_2} - \frac{a_3 e_2}{a_2} + e_3 \tag{8}$$

As a result, by using the data collected during a period of time in sensors 2 and 3, one can estimate the linear model, but the estimation could not be correct due to the influence of the noise e_2 and e_3. To overcome this problem, we can use the signal summation method. For example, in order to estimate the normal measurement of sensor n, it is possible to calculate the following values by adding the sensor value of the n−1 neighbors.

$$\tilde{x} = \left(\sum_{i=1}^{n-1} a_i \right) x + \sum_{i=1}^{n-1} b_i + \sum_{i=1}^{n-1} e_i \tag{9}$$

The error term is to be converged to 0, and each sum of a and b is expressed as $\tilde{a}$ and $\tilde{b}$; the above equation is expressed as follows.

$$\tilde{x} = \tilde{a}x + \tilde{b} \tag{10}$$

To rearrange the above equation relative to x, it can be expressed as follows.

$$x = \frac{1}{\tilde{a}}\tilde{x} - \frac{\tilde{b}}{\tilde{a}} \tag{11}$$

The linear relationship between y_n and combined signals $\tilde{x}$ can be expressed as follows

$$y_n = \frac{a_n}{\tilde{a}}\tilde{x} - \frac{a_n \tilde{b}}{\tilde{a}} + b_n + e_n \tag{12}$$

As a result, by using the data collected during a period of time in the n sensors, it is possible to estimate the linear model, and the normal value can be predicted by the estimated linear model. The difference between the normal value and the observed value can be verified statistically to detect outliers.

2.3   Sensor System in Which Positive and Negative Correlations Coexist

If positive, negative and zero correlations exist in the n−1 neighborhood signals, the summation of regression parameter $\tilde{a}$ in Eq. (9) is likely to converge to zero. If that occurs, the information for estimating the linear relationship between y_n and the synthesized signal $\tilde{x}$ will be lost. To overcome these problems, the correlation coefficient between y_n and the other signals can be multiplied with the observation. That is, the parameter a_i is negative in the case of the negative correlation coefficient, so the multiplication of the negative correlation coefficient with the observed signal makes the parameter a_i into a positive value.

A sample signal system is assumed as follows. All parameters are positive values (Fig. 1).

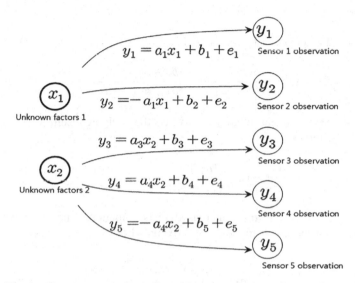

$$y_1 = a_1 x_1 + b_1 + e_1 \quad \text{Sensor 1 observation}$$

$$y_2 = -a_1 x_1 + b_2 + e_2 \quad \text{Sensor 2 observation}$$

$$y_3 = a_3 x_2 + b_3 + e_3 \quad \text{Sensor 3 observation}$$

$$y_4 = a_4 x_2 + b_4 + e_4 \quad \text{Sensor 4 observation}$$

$$y_5 = -a_4 x_2 + b_5 + e_5 \quad \text{Sensor 5 observation}$$

Fig. 1. Five sensor systems affected by two unknown physical factors.

For the outlier analysis of target sensor 5, the weighted sum $\tilde{x}$ using y_1, y_2, y_3, y_4 can be written in the following formula.

$$\tilde{x} = C_{15}(a_1 x_1 + b_1 + e_1) + C_{25}(-a_1 x_1 + b_2 + e_2) \\ + C_{35}(a_3 x_2 + b_3 + e_3) + C_{45}(a_4 x_2 + b_4 + e_4) \tag{13}$$

C_{ij} = correlation coefficient of i sensor observation and j sensor observation
The above equation can be summarized by the following.

$$\tilde{x} = (C_{15}a_1 - C_{25}a_1)x_1 + (C_{35}a_3 + C_{45}a_4)x_2 + C_{15}b_1 + C_{15}e_1 + C_{25}b_2 + C_{25}e_2 \\ + C_{35}b_3 + C_{35}e_3 + C_{45}b_4 + C_{45}e_4 \tag{14}$$

The correlation coefficient among the observations can be assumed by the following.

$$C_{15} \approx 0, \ C_{25} \approx 0, \ C_{35} \approx -1, \ C_{45} \approx -1 \tag{15}$$

The weighted sum of observations (14) can be approximated as follows using values in (15).

$$\tilde{x} = -(a_3 + a_4)x_2 - b_3 - e_3 - b_4 - e_4 \tag{16}$$

The above equation can be summarized as follows.

$$\tilde{x} = -(a_3 + a_4)x_2 - (b_3 + b_4) - (e_3 + e_4) \tag{17}$$

As a result, Eq. (17) can be rearranged relative to x_2

$$x_2 = -\frac{1}{(a_3 + a_4)}\tilde{x} - \frac{(b_3 + b_4)}{(a_3 + a_4)} - \frac{(e_3 + e_4)}{(a_3 + a_4)} \tag{18}$$

Consequently, the linear relations between the weighted sum $\tilde{x}$ and y_5 can be summarized as follows.

$$y_5 = \frac{a_4}{(a_3 + a_4)}\tilde{x} + \frac{a_4(b_3 + b_4)}{(a_3 + a_4)} + b_5 + \frac{a_4(e_3 + e_4)}{(a_3 + a_4)} + e_5 \tag{19}$$

If the number of noise terms is increased, the summation of noises converges to 0. It can be seen that the linear model is approximated by

$$y_5 = \frac{a_4}{(a_3 + a_4)}\tilde{x} + \frac{a_4(b_3 + b_4)}{(a_3 + a_4)} + b_5 \tag{20}$$

2.4   Detection of Outliers in Regression Model

A common statistic for outlier detection is the residual (observation - prediction). If very statistically large residuals are observed, they are detected as outliers. Residuals follow the normal distribution, which has the average of 0 and a standard deviation. However, the standard deviation of these residuals is different in normal situations. Therefore, standardized residuals are used. The standardized residuals are calculated by dividing the estimates of their standard errors. Standardized residuals follow the t distribution with the n-p-2 degrees of freedom. The number of independent variables is k. The number of observations is n. The independent variable is x_i. The dependent variable is y_i, and the predicted value is $\hat{y}_i$. The $Ttest_i$ is the probability that a standardized residual is larger than $Rstudent_i$.

$$Ttest_i = t(Rstudent_i, df) \tag{21}$$

$$Rstudent_i = \frac{e_i}{\sqrt{MMSE(1 - leverage_i)}}, \quad MMSE = (MSE - \frac{e_i^2}{(1 - leverage_i)df}) \frac{df}{df - 1},$$

$$df = n - k - 1, \quad MSE = \frac{SSE}{n - k - 1}, \quad leverage_i = \frac{1}{n} + \frac{(x_i - \bar{x})^2}{SSE}, \quad SSE$$

$$= \sum_{i=1}^{n} e_i^2, \quad e_i = y_i - \hat{y}_i$$

If $Ttest_i$ is smaller than the reference value, the observation is confirmed as an outlier. 0.05 is the common criteria.

3 Experiment Using Artificial Data and Real Sensor Data

3.1 Artificial Data Set

Assume unknown physical independent variables x_1, x_2. The six sensors' observations are generated using the following linear models. Noises are generated from the normal distribution $N(0.4)$. The number of observations for each sensor is 16.

$$y_1 = -1.3489 * x_1 - 1.0039 + e_1 \qquad\qquad y_4 = 1.0274 * x_2 - 0.6883 + e_4$$
$$y_2 = -0.7657 * x_1 - 1.5991 * x_2 + 0.0873 + e_2 \quad y_5 = 1.0842 * x_2 + 1.0343 + e_5$$
$$y_3 = -1.3983 * x_2 - 0.9203 + e_3 \qquad\qquad y_6 = 1.3966 * x_2 + 1.1118 + e_6$$

As shown in the Fig. 2, the coefficient determination measured at each signal shows a low value because of the influence of noise. The synthesized signal using simple summation brings more drop-effect coefficient determination. On the other hand, the higher degree of correlation is shown in the case where the synthesized signal is coming from the summation using a correlation coefficient weight (Fig. 3).

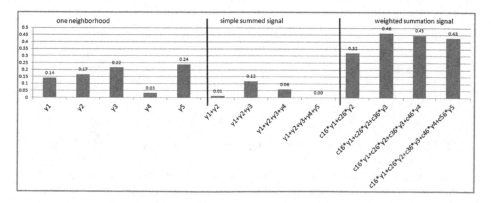

Fig. 2. Coefficient determinations of artificial data set

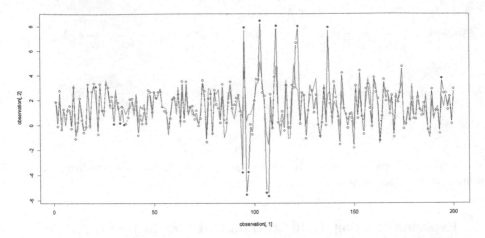

Fig. 3. Outlier detection of artificial data set

We produced six pieces of virtual data. We synthesized the independent variable from the observed values of the five sensors. The regression analysis of the synthesized signal and the sixth signal was performed. Some outliers were randomly inserted into the period of 80 to 140. The results of the detection of outliers are shown in the following figure. The line with circles represents the observations. The line without circles shows the prediction. The solid circle denotes the detected outliers. Most of the outliers were detected. The reference value for the outliers was 0.005.

3.2   Real Data Set

Six pore water pressures of a dam were measured in 3 years. The moving window size was selected as 16. A temporal variation of the coefficient of determination between the first sensor and second sensors is shown as follows (Fig. 4).

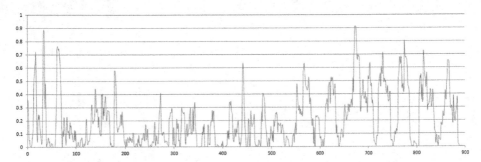

Fig. 4. Temporal variations of coefficient of determination between 1st and 2nd sensors

The correlation between the synthesized signal (correlation weighted summation) and the target signal shows the improved appearance degree of correlation, as shown in the Fig. 5.

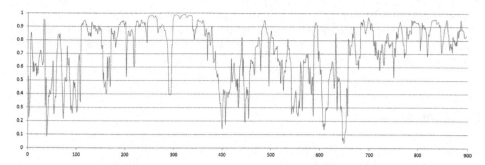

Fig. 5. Temporal variations of coefficient of determination between synthesized signal and 2nd sensor

We synthesized the independent variable from the observed values of the five sensors. The regression analysis of the synthesized signal and the sixth signal was performed. The results of the detection of outliers are shown in Fig. 6. The line with circles represents the observations. The line without circles shows the prediction. The solid circle denotes detected outliers. The reference value for the outliers was 0.005.

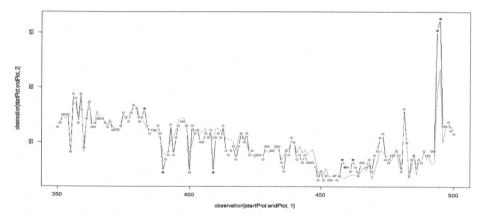

Fig. 6. Outlier detection of real data set

4 Conclusion

An efficient regression-based outlier detection method has been described in this paper. Estimating a correct regression model is an important part of estimation-based outlier detection. This research proposes a weighted summation approach for making a synthesized independent variable from the observed values. A reliable regression model can be estimated from the synthesized signal. The proposed method was successfully applied in an artificial data set and to real sensor measurements in a dam. Future research will focus on using the proposed method to achieve precise model estimation in various sensor environments.

Acknowledgments. This research was supported by a grant (14SCIP-B065985-02) from the Smart Civil Infrastructure Research Program funded by the Ministry of Land, Infrastructure and Transport (MOLIT) of the Korean government and the Korea Agency for Infrastructure Technology Advancement (KAIA).

References

1. Zhang, Y., Meratnia, N., Havinga, P.: Outlier detection techniques for wireless sensor networks: a survey. IEEE Commun. Surv. Tutorials **12–2**, 159–170 (2010)
2. Sharma, A.B., Golubchik, L., Govindan, R.: Sensor faults: Detection methods and prevalence in real-world datasets. ACM Trans. Sensor Netw. **6**(3), 1–39 (2010)
3. Ni, K., Ramanathan, N., Chehade, M.N.H., Balzano, L., Nair, S., Zahedi, S., Pottie, G., Hansen, M., Srivastava, M., Kohle, E.: Sensor network data fault types. ACM Trans. Sensor Netw. **5**(3), 1–29 (2009)
4. Mínguez, R., Reguero, B.G., Luceño, A., Méndez, F.J.: Regression models for outlier identification (Hurricanes and Typhooons) in wave hindcast databases. J. Atmospheric Ocean. Technol. **29**(2), 267–285 (2012)

Supervised Object Boundary Detection Based on Structured Forests

Fan Meng[1,2,3], Zhiquan Qi[1,2(✉)], Limeng Cui[1,2,4],
Zhensong Chen[1,2,3], and Yong Shi[1,2,3(✉)]

[1] Key Laboratory of Big Data Mining and Knowledge Management,
CAS, Beijing 100190, China
{qizhiquan,yshi}@ucas.ac.cn
[2] Research Center on Fictitious Economy and Data Science,
CAS, Beijing 100190, China
[3] School of Management, University of Chinese Academy Sciences,
Beijing 100190, China
[4] School of Computer and Control Engineering,
University of Chinese Academy Sciences, Beijing 100190, China

Abstract. Object boundary detection is an interesting and challenging topic in computer vision. Learning and combining the local, mid-level and high-level information play an important role in most of the recent approaches. However, few characteristics of a certain type of object are exploited. In this paper, we propose a novel supervised machine learning framework for object boundary detection, which makes use of the specific object features, such as boundary shape, directions and intensity. In the learning process, structured forest models are employed to tackle the high dimensional multi-class problem. Various experiment results show that our framework outperforms the competing models in the proposed data set, indicating that our framework is highly effective in modeling boundary for specific type of objects.

1 Introduction

Object boundary detection is an interesting and challenging topic in computer vision. The detected object boundaries provide much information about the shape, location and size of certain objects, which can be widely used in object detection [1–3] and image segmentation [4, 5].

As the most object boundaries are edges, edge detection is usually considered as the starting point of object boundary detection. Among the classical edge detectors, Canny [6] is the most popular one that make use of local features. However, local edge information is not sufficient for object detection if the background is complex or textured. To address this problem, some other cues, such as mid-level information and high level-information, are introduced to edge detection. From this way, several advances are made recently, in which a learning step to combine the multi-level cues are usually required to obtain a precise description of object boundaries and the learning process are often complicated and time-consuming [7–9].

C. Zhang et al. (Eds.): ICDS 2015, LNCS 9208, pp. 87–94, 2015.
DOI: 10.1007/978-3-319-24474-7_13

Most of the existing approaches make efforts to build global models, which can be used to detect boundaries of many types of objects. As a result, the specific information, such as shape and size, for a certain type of objects is usually dropped carelessly. In a great amount of cases, the purpose of object boundary detection is to identify a specific type of objects. For example, in pedestrian detection, the pedestrians are the interesting object, in vehicle tracking only vehicles detection are desired and in crack detection, the interesting object are cracks [11, 12]. From this view, inspired by [10], we deal with the object boundary detection problem in a novel perspective, which can make use of the specific characteristics of the focused objects.

In this paper, we build a task-oriented framework to train a model in a supervised way to detect a certain type of objects. Different from other methods that try to build a model to detection all kinds of objects, we aim at finding the boundaries of only some specific types of objects. Our framework is demonstrated in Fig. 1. Suppose the interesting object we want to detect is the toy sheep and there is a cup as noisy. To build our model, we first construct dataset with annotations of edges of toys. Then a structured forest is trained on the training set to detect the specific edges of the toy, which can capture more information of the toy edges than former method. To detect the boundaries of the toys in a new image, we run the structured forest, and the detection results are shown in the third column from left. The right column shows the object boundary detection results using the pre-trained model on BSDS500 [10]. It is obvious that our task-oriented model performs much better.

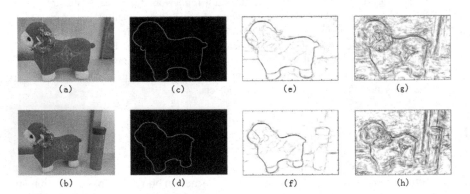

Fig. 1. Demonstration of the framework (a) and (b) two examples of original images with sheep as the interesting object, and a cup as noisy in (b); (c) and (d) the ground truths of the original images, note that cup in (b) has not annotation; (e) and (f) boundary detection results using the task-oriented data set, note that cup boundaries in (f) are much more weaker than the boundaries of the sheep; (g) and (h) boundary detection results using the pre-trained edge detection model on BSDS500. Note that, the task-oriented model outperforms the pre-trained model, although the pre-trained one obtains the state-of-the-art edge detection result on BSDS500 [10].

The rest of this paper is organized as follow: Sect. 2 presents the related work in object boundary detection. In Sect. 3, we provide a detailed description of proposed approaches. The experiments of the method are in Sect. 4. At last, we conclude our paper in Sect. 5.

2 Related Work

As object boundaries carry much information of the object, object boundary detection is a very developed topic in computer vision. It can be applied in many image processing tasks. In this section, we briefly review the recent advances in object boundary detection.

The early trials for objection boundary detection are conducted following classical edge detection [13]. The most used edge detector is Canny [6], which exploits the local information of pixels. The Canny detector doesn't take advantage of the mid-level information and high-level information, which may lead some misdetections when the background are cluttered or the textures are strong.

To improve detect accuracy, methods combining low-, mid-, and high-level information are proposed. In [14], the authors present a method that combines top-down and bottom-up processes to make efficient segmentation to handle the complex background. In [15], a Bayesian framework is introduced to integrate both low-level and high-level information, the results are promising but the computational complexity is the bottleneck.

Several learning strategies to learn and combine cues in different level are also proposed. Literature [16] presents probabilistic boosting tree to combine the cues. Some researchers propose a three-stage strategies to combine the low-, mid-, and high-level information for horse boundaries detection [17]. Literature [18] develops a Boundary-Fragment-Model that extract discriminative boundary fragments for further boundary detection.

The first machine learning based edge detection method is Boosted Edge Learning (BEL) [19], which conduct pixel wise prediction of edge in an effective way, utilizing the aperture information of the certain pixel. As it follows a boosting framework, other discriminate models such as MCLP [20, 21] and SVMs [22–26] can be used in it. The work in [10] presents a novel structured forest model for fast edge detection, achieving the state-of-the-art performance and speed. This paper is motivated by [10, 19]. We utilize the structured forest to model the presence of edge, and design our framework in a task-oriented manner.

3 Proposed Framework

In this section, we elaborate the proposed object boundary detection framework.

3.1 Problem Description

Note that in most cases, the purpose of object detection is to find out the specific objects and the objects remain unchanged in the whole problem. So we can divide the all kinds of detection objects into small problems, each of which aims at identifying a certain type of objects. The purpose of this paper is to deal with such small problems. Based on these settings, the problem can be described as following: there is one or more types of objects in a set of image with the type of interest object fixed, the purpose is to identify the boundaries of the objects of interest and the boundaries of other objects can be considered as noisy.

3.2   Structured Forest

We regard this problem as a machine learning problem, in which we have to predict the probability to be a boundary point for every pixel in the image with a great amount of features. This problem is a high-dimensional multi-class problem, and an efficient and effective classifier is desired. In the experiments, structured forest [10] is used due to its speed and accuracy outperforming the other models.

Structured forest origins from random forest. Instead of predicting a value of an input as random forest, structured forest provides a structured output for a given input. In this way, the model can model the local structure of the image and the results are more robust.

In this model, the feature of every point is a structure centered on it. The channel features used are constructed based on the [27], furthermore similarity features are design with an intermediate mapping.

3.3   Proposed Framework

Different from the former method, we don't have to design an approach to combine the cues of different level, in our framework, a supervised machine learning strategy is employed, which can automatically capture the differences between the given object type and the others in graphics. We use a labeled training set to train our model that can discriminate the boundaries of the given type of object from others. Figure 2 shows the proposed framework. There are three steps in this framework.

The first step is image annotation. In this step, only the given type of objects are given annotations and the training set is conducted.

The second step is model training. In this step, integral channel features and self-similarity features are used to train the structured forests.

The third step is boundary detection. Given a testing image, the trained model is utilized identify the boundaries of trained objectives.

4   Experiments

In this section, we present the performance of our framework. We build a new data set to evaluate the performance.

4.1   Data Set

The built data set named Supervised Sheep and Dog, or SSD for short. It contains 12 images with fixed size of 320*480, each of which has a sheep or dog in it. There are noises in every image, some of which are weak and the others strong. The main noises are cup and books.

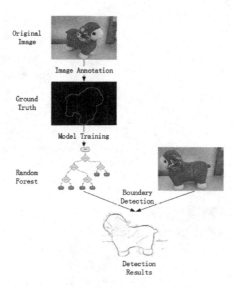

Fig. 2. The proposed framework

4.2 Experiments

To evaluate the performance we conduct several experiments, in which training images and testing images change from one to another. Specifically, our experiments design as below:

- Noise Free Sheep Model for Boundary Detection;
- Noised Sheep Model for Boundary Detection;
- Noise Free Dog Model for Boundary Detection;
- Noised Dog Model for Boundary Detection;
- Noise Free Dog & Sheep Model for Boundary Detection;
- Noised Dog & Sheep Model for Boundary Detection;

The experimental results are shown in Fig. 3. The original images lie in the left column, the boundary detection results using BSDS500 model are in the right column. The 6 columns in the middle are corresponding to the 6 experiments. In each of the column, original images represent training data, boundary maps are the testing results.

As we can see from Fig. 3, our models significantly outperform the BSDS model, indicating the supervised learning strategy can capture the object specific features.

Comparing column 2 and 3, we can conclude that training from hard situation can improve the detection accuracy. The columns 4&5 and 6&7 go the same way. When we train the model with sheep and test that on dogs, the results are still promising, presenting that the object type doesn't mean a very small class, one model trained in the framework can used for the detecting of several type of objects which sharing some similarities.

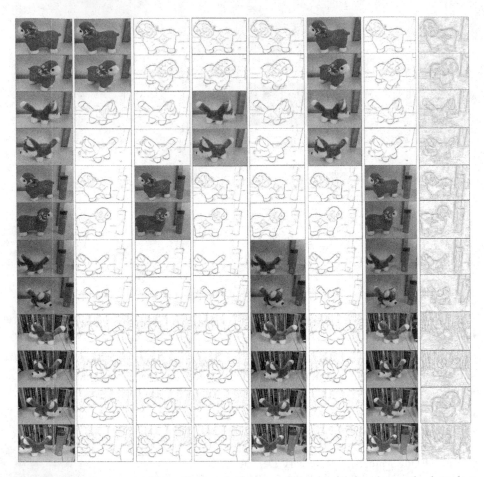

Fig. 3. The experiment results. The original images lie in the left column, the boundary detection results using BSDS500 model are in the right column. The 6 columns in the middle are corresponding to the 6 experiments. In each of the column, original images represent training data, boundary maps are the testing results.

5 Conclusion

In this paper, we propose a novel supervised object boundary detection framework, which can take advantage of the object specific information. The extensive experiments prove the significant improve than the general state-of-the-art edge detection algorithms. To support the conclusion in this paper, more experiments are supposed to be conducted and that will be the further research focus.

Acknowledgments. This work is partly supported by National Natural Science Foundation of China under Grants (Grant No. 71331005, 71110107026, 61402429). I would like to express my gratitude to my supervisor Prof. Shi and Dr. Qi who helped me a lot in studying and everyday life. I also would like to thank Jason and Limeng for the inspiring discussions and suggestions. Last my thanks would go to my girlfriend Jing, who makes my life more colorful.

References

1. Viola, P., Jones, M.: Robust real-time object detection. Int. J. Comput. Vis. **4**, 51–52 (2001)
2. Viola, P., Jones, M.: Rapid object detection using a boosted cascade of simple features. In: Proceedings of the 2001 IEEE Computer Society Conference on Computer Vision and Pattern Recognition, CVPR 2001, vol. 1. IEEE (2001)
3. Lim, J.J., Zitnick, C.L., Dollár, P.: Sketch tokens: a learned mid-level representation for contour and object detection. In: 2013 IEEE Conference on Computer Vision and Pattern Recognition (CVPR). IEEE (2013)
4. Arbelaez, P., et al.: Contour detection and hierarchical image segmentation. IEEE Trans. Pattern Anal. Mach. Intell. **33**(5), 898–916 (2011)
5. Fan, J., et al.: Automatic image segmentation by integrating color-edge extraction and seeded region growing. IEEE Trans. Image Process. **10**(10), 1454–1466 (2001)
6. Canny, J.: A computational approach to edge detection. IEEE Trans. Pattern Anal. Mach. Intell. **6**, 679–698 (1986)
7. He, X., Zemel, R.S., Carreira-Perpinan, M.A.: Multiscale conditional random fields for image labelling. In: Proceedings of IEEE Conference on Computer Vision and Pattern Recognition (2004)
8. Kumar, M.P., Torr, P.H.S., Zisserman, A.: OBJCUT. In: Proceedings of IEEE Conference on Computer Vision and Pattern Recognition (2005)
9. Wang, Y., Ji, Q.: A dynamic conditional random field model for object segmentation in image sequences. In: Proceedings of IEEE Conference on Computer Vision and Pattern Recognition, San Diego, CA, June 2005
10. Dollár, P., Zitnick, C.: Fast edge detection using structured forests. Pattern Anal. Mach. Intell. **PP**(99), 1 (2014)
11. Oliveira, H., Correia, P.L.: Automatic road crack detection and characterization. IEEE Trans. Intell. Transp. Syst. **14**(1), 155–168 (2013)
12. Zou, Q., et al.: CrackTree: automatic crack detection from pavement images. Pattern Recogn. Lett. **33**(3), 227–238 (2012)
13. Konishi, S., et al.: Statistical edge detection: learning and evaluating edge cues. IEEE Trans. Pattern Anal. Mach. Intell. **25**(1), 57–74 (2003)
14. Borenstein, E., Ullman, S.: Combined top-down/bottom-up segmentation. IEEE Trans. Pattern Anal. Mach. Intell. **30**(12), 2109–2125 (2008)
15. Tu, Z., et al.: Image parsing: unifying segmentation, detection, and recognition. Int. J. Comput. Vis. **63**(2), 113–140 (2005)
16. Tu, Z.: Probabilistic boosting-tree: learning discriminative models for classification, recognition, and clustering. In: Tenth IEEE International Conference on Computer Vision, ICCV 2005, vol. 2. IEEE (2005)
17. Zheng, S., Yuille, A., Zhuowen, T.: Detecting object boundaries using low-, mid-, and high-level information. Comput. Vis. Image Underst. **114**(10), 1055–1067 (2010)
18. Opelt, A., Pinz, A., Zisserman, A.: A boundary-fragment-model for object detection. In: Leonardis, A., Bischof, H., Pinz, A. (eds.) ECCV 2006. LNCS, vol. 3952, pp. 575–588. Springer, Heidelberg (2006)

19. Dollár, P., Tu, Z., Belongie, S.: Supervised learning of edges and object boundaries. In: 2006 IEEE Computer Society Conference on Computer Vision and Pattern Recognition, vol. 2. IEEE (2006)
20. Shi, Y., Peng, Y.: Multiple Criteria and Multiple Constraint Levels Linear Programming: Concepts, Techniques and Applications. World Scientific, New Jersey (2001)
21. Shi, Y.: Multiple criteria optimization-based data mining methods and applications: a systematic survey. Knowl. Inf. Syst. **24**(3), 369–391 (2010)
22. Vapnik, V.N., Vapnik, V.: Statistical Learning Theory, vol. 1. Wiley, New York (1998)
23. Viola, P., Jones, M.: Robust real-time object detection. Int. J. Comput. Vis. **4**, 34–47 (2001)
24. Tian, Y.J., Qi, Z.Q., Ju, X.C., Shi, Y., Liu, X.H.: Nonparallel support vector machines for pattern classification. IEEE Trans. Cybernetics **44**(7), 1067–1079 (2013)
25. Qi, Z., Tian, Y., Shi, Y.: Successive overrelaxation for laplacian support vector machine. IEEE Trans. Neural Netw. Learn. Syst. (2014). doi:10.1109/TNNLS.2014.2320738
26. Qi, Z., Tian, Y., Shi, Y.: Robust twin support vector machine for pattern classification. Pattern Recogn. **46**(1), 305–316 (2013)
27. Dollár, P., et al.: Integral channel features. In: BMVC, vol. 2(3) (2009)

Pavement Distress Detection Using Random Decision Forests

Limeng Cui[1,2,3], Zhiquan Qi[1,2(✉)], Zhensong Chen[1,2,4], Fan Meng[1,2,4],
and Yong Shi[1,24(✉)]

[1] Key Laboratory of Big Data Mining and Knowledge Management,
CAS, Beijing 100190, China
[2] Research Center on Fictious Economy and Data Science,
CAS, Beijing 100190, China
[3] School of Computer and Control Engineering, UCAS, Beijing 100190, China
[4] School of Management, UCAS, Beijing 100190, China
{qizhiquan,yshi}@ucas.ac.cn

Abstract. Pavement distress detection is a key technology to evaluate
pavement surface and crack severity. However, there are many challenging problems when using pavement distress detection technology to do
road maintenance, such as the inference of textured surroundings with
similar intensity to the distresses, the existence of intensity inhomogene-
ity along the distresses and the requirement of real-time detection in
practice. To address these problems, we propose a novel method for pavement distress detection based on random decision forests. By introducing
the color gradient features at multiple scales commonly used in contour detection, we extend the feature set of traditional distress detection
methods and get the represented crack with richer information. During
the process of training, we apply a subsampling strategy at each node to
maintain the diversity of trees. With this work, we finally solve all the
three problems mentioned above. In addition, according to the characteristics of random decision forests, our method is easy to parallel and
able to conduct real-time detection. Experimental results show that our
approach is faster and more accurate than existing methods.

1 Introduction

Pavement distresses, usually in the form of cracks, reduces the road performance and constrains passing vehicles [17]. Under this circumstance, road maintenance equipment are required, which relying on effective pavement distress
detection system. The traditional manual methods are time-consuming, dangerous and labor-intensive [6], on the contrary, automatic pavement distress detection becomes an active area. Remarkable achievements [4,5,31] have been made
in this field. However, the real-time distress detection still remains challenges.
Some methods have very low processing speed or low accuracy. Others only deal
with certain types of distress.

With the development of machine learning, methods based on neural
network [11], Markov random field [7] and wavelet [26] are introduced in this

© Springer International Publishing Switzerland 2015
C. Zhang et al. (Eds.): ICDS 2015, LNCS 9208, pp. 95–102, 2015.
DOI: 10.1007/978-3-319-24474-7_14

area successively. Machine learning shows promising performance in distress detection. It captures the distinguishing features of distress, and it is adaptive to tasks. In these methods, images are divided into small blocks. Common used features such as mean and standard values are computed on these blocks. But these methods may generate a set of disjoint fragments instead of complete crack curves, due to noises such as textured surrounding or oil spot.

In this paper, we propose a novel pavement distress detection method based on random decision forests. Due to its flexibility, efficiency and good generalization ability, random decision forests have been using broadly in the image processing area [2,25]. The training of each tree is independent, so the algorithm is easy to paralleled and very fast. Here we use two kinds of features: the common used features such as mean and standard deviation value and color gradient feature over multiples scales. These features can characterize distress region much better.

A series of experiments are conducted to test the performance of our proposed method. We test our method under different scales of training data, and compare our method with state-of-the-art pavement distress detection methods. The results show that our method is promising.

2   Related Work

There have been many methods proposed for pavement distress detection. In this section, a brief review of pavement distress detection is given. A recent research of evaluating multiple pavement distress detection can be found in [29].

Some researchers [12,15] apply the intuitive idea that the defect region is darker than its surroundings. These methods are straight-forward, but noises such as the water stain or the shadow may negatively affect the general precision. Method [1] tries to improve the performance of Sobel using bidimensional empirical mode decomposition (BEMD). But this method may not handle well the cracks with poor continuity.

In recent years, machine learning methods also show great robustness in distress detection. In literature [11], artificial neural network models are used in automatic thresholding of the images and in the classification stage. In literature [7], a crack image is projected onto a regular lattice, which allows the definition of a Markovian crack model. Wavelet-based method [30] uses wavelet transform to separate distresses from noises. However, this method can not detect cracks with high curvature or potholes with complex topology.

In addition, some block-based methods extract small patches from the original images and calculate features on these patches. For example, literature [27] uses a morphology method to describe a succession of cracks. Literature [10] uses longitudinal, transverse and diagonal crack seed to connect the detected regions. However, these methods may generate a set of unconnected regions instead of a complete distress. In order to overcome the above shortages, CrackTree [31] conducts recursive edge pruning in the minimum spanning tree (MST) to improve the continuity of the detected cracks. Features used in these methods are quite intuitive, such as mean, standard deviation, width of boundary rectangle, difference of mean and standard deviation of two cells on each side of the connected region [14]. We assume these features can not capture the overall information of distresses. Since the distress detection method can be considered as a specific contour detection problem, the features commonly used in contour detection are introduced in our method.

In general, the existing methods do not perform well in detecting complete crack curves. And the noise background also brings challenges to the distress detection. We apply a large pool of features which can capture the distress from various aspects to bridge this gap. In addition, since multiple decision trees can be trained and applied simultaneously, our method shows promising processing speed. Besides, as a boosting framework, other methods such as MCLP [23,24] and SVMs [20–22] can be used in it.

3 Automatic Pavement Distress Detection

In this section we begin with a brief review of random decision forests [9,13], and then introduce our method in details.

3.1 Feature Extraction

Suppose we have a set of image I with a corresponding set of manually labeled sketches G which indicates the edge of distress regions. 16×16 image patches $x \in \mathcal{X}$ are extracted from the original images using a sliding window. Features are computed on these patches.

Many existing methods [14,16,18] use mean and standard deviation value as features. Two matrices are computed for each original image: the mean matrix M_m with each block's average intensity and standard deviation matrix STD_m with the corresponding standard deviation value std. These feature are computed on gray level image. And they can't characterize the distress comprehensively. Inspired by Dollá et al. [9], we also apply a large set features at multiple scales, orientations and so on. These features tend to be much more general. As a result, applying the method to another domain is straightforward. Which kind of crack can be detected by this method mainly depends on the training set.

3.2 Training Random Decision Forests

Random decision forests have successfully applied in many fields such as image labeling [13], object categorization [28] and image segmentation [25]. The method is extremely fast for the training and tend not to overfit.

Training Stage: We extract image patches by using a sliding window and compute its features. Next, a weak classifier is trained at each node to decide whether a pixel is in a defect region or not according to a certain probability. Given a trained tree, a pixel is routed recursively left or right until a leaf is reached. Individual tree tends to overfit, random decision forests bridge this gap by merging multiple decision trees together.

A subsampling strategy is applied to maintain the diversity of trees. Each tree $T \in \mathcal{F}$ is trained independently on a random subset of the training set $\mathcal{D} \subseteq \mathcal{X} \times \mathcal{Y}$. A decision tree can predict the class of a sample $x_i \in \mathcal{X}$ by branching it left or right until a leaf is reached. Each sample is passed to the left or right subtree, weighted by $q(-1|x_i)$ and $q(+1|x_i)$ respectively, where $q(+1|x_i)$ denotes the probability that x_i is a positive sample.

The node of tree is characterized by two functions: $q(-1|x_i)$ and $q(+1|x)$. The sample x is routed to the left decision sub-tree t_l if $q(-1|x_i) - \frac{1}{2} > \varepsilon$, or to the right decision sub-tree t_l if $q(+1|x_i) - \frac{1}{2} > \varepsilon$, where ε is a threshold. Besides, if the sample is near the decision boundary, it is passed to both sub-trees.

Computing Probability: Given a trained tree, the probability $p(y|x)$ that sample x belongs to class y is defined recursively:

$$p(y|x) = q(+1|x) \cdot p_r(y|x) + q(-1|x) \cdot p_l(y|x) \tag{1}$$

where $p_l(y|x)$ and $p_r(y|x)$ are posteriors of the left and right trees.

The final prediction of a sample $x \in \mathcal{X}$ given a forest $\mathcal{F}$ can be obtained from the individual tree predictions:

$$\overline{p(y|x)} = \frac{1}{N} \sum_{t \in \mathcal{F}} p_t(y|x) \tag{2}$$

where N indicates the total tree number in the forest.

3.3   Binarization

The output of the above stage yields the probability of each pixel being in a distress region. The pixels in distress regions tend to have the high probability, others tend to have the low probability. A threshold θ_1 is introduced to remove the distress free regions. The noises such as shadows or texture surrounding can be eliminated effectively after the above section. But water stain and oil spot may not be removed throughly. We use another threshold θ_2 to small connected fragments (less than θ_2 pixels).

4   Experimental Results

In this section we compare the performance of our proposed method with Canny [3], BEL [9] and CrackIT [18]. Part of the Matlab code is supported on Piotr's Computer Vision Toolbox [8] and CrackIT [19]. The experiments are conducted on a pavement surface image database proposed by Oliveira et al. [18]. These images are captured during a visual survey along a Portuguese road. To obtain the ground truth, we outline the distress in each image using a image annotated program. All experiments are conducted on a desktop with AMD FX(tm)-4300 Quad-Core Processor and 4G RAM.

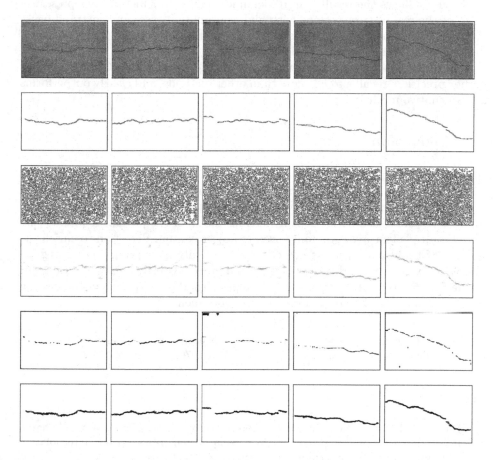

Fig. 1. Pavement distress detection results on four algorithms. (From top to down: Canny, BEL, CrackIT and our method.)

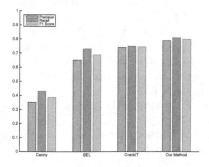

Fig. 2. Precision, Recall and F1 Score of various methods.

Figure 1 shows the results on five sample images. Our method has preserved most of the real distress regions with high continuity. Noises and textured background are suppressed. Other methods are suffered from the interferences of discontinuous fragments and various noises.

Figure 2 shows the average performance of different methods. Our method has higher precision, recall and F1 score than other methods, and clearly outperforms all alternative methods.

5   Conclusion

In this paper, we propose an automatic pavement distress detection method. Our innovation is as following shown: Firstly, the introducing of random decision forests makes it possible to compute the probability of each pixel being in a distress region. Secondly, to capture various facets of the pavement distress, we apply multiple features commonly used in object contour detection to enrich the feature of traditional distress detection set. Thirdly, a subsampling strategy is applied to maintain the diversity of trees and prevent overfitting. In addition, our framework has powerful learning ability. Our method shows promising processing speed and state-of-the-art accuracy in all experiments.

Acknowledgments. This work is supported by National Natural Science Foundation of China under Grants (Grant No. 71331005, 71110107026, 61402429).

References

1. Bhuiyan, S.M., Attoh-Okine, N.O., Barner, K.E., Ayenu-Prah, A.Y., Adhami, R.R.: Bidimensional empirical mode decomposition using various interpolation techniques. Adv. Adapt. Data Anal. **1**(02), 309–338 (2009)
2. Bulo, S.R., Kontschieder, P.: Neural decision forests for semantic image labelling. In: 2014 IEEE Conference on Computer Vision and Pattern Recognition (CVPR), pp. 81–88. IEEE (2014)
3. Canny, J.: A computational approach to edge detection. IEEE Trans. Pattern Anal. Mach. Intell. **8**(6), 679–698 (1986)
4. Cheng, H., Chen, J.R., Glazier, C., Hu, Y.: Novel approach to pavement cracking detection based on fuzzy set theory. J. Comput. Civ. Eng. **13**(4), 270–280 (1999)
5. Cheng, H., Wang, J., Hu, Y., Glazier, C., Shi, X., Chen, X.: Novel approach to pavement cracking detection based on neural network. Transp. Res. Rec.: J. Transp. Res. Board **1764**(1), 119–127 (2001)
6. Cheng, H.D., Miyojim, M.: Automatic pavement distress detection system. Inf. Sci. **108**(1), 219–240 (1998)
7. Delagnes, P., Barba, D.: A Markov random field for rectilinear structure extraction in pavement distress image analysis. In: Proceedings of the International Conference on Image Processing 1995, vol. 1, pp. 446–449. IEEE (1995)
8. Dollár, P.: Piotr's Computer Vision Matlab Toolbox (PMT). http://vision.ucsd.edu/~pdollar/toolbox/doc/index.html

9. Dollar, P., Tu, Z., Belongie, S.: Supervised learning of edges and object boundaries. In: 2006 IEEE Computer Society Conference on Computer Vision and Pattern Recognition, vol. 2, pp. 1964–1971. IEEE (2006)

10. Huang, Y., Xu, B.: Automatic inspection of pavement cracking distress. J. Electron. Imaging 15(1), 013017 (2006)

11. Kaseko, M.S., Ritchie, S.G.: A neural network-based methodology for pavement crack detection and classification. Transp. Res. Part C: Emerg. Technol. 1(4), 275–291 (1993)

12. Kirschke, K., Velinsky, S.: Histogram-based approach for automated pavement-crack sensing. J. Transp. Eng. 118(5), 700–710 (1992)

13. Kontschieder, P., Bulo, S.R., Bischof, H., Pelillo, M.: Structured class-labels in random forests for semantic image labelling. In: 2011 IEEE International Conference on Computer Vision (ICCV), pp. 2190–2197. IEEE (2011)

14. Nguyen, T.S., Avila, M., Begot, S.: Automatic detection and classification of defect on road pavement using anisotropy measure. In: European Signal Processing Conference, pp. 617–621 (2009)

15. Oh, H., Garrick, N.W., Achenie, L.E.: Segmentation algorithm using iterative clipping for processing noisy pavement images. In: Second International Conference on Imaging Technologies: Techniques and Applications in Civil Engineering (1998)

16. Oliveira, H., Correia, P.L.: Supervised strategies for crack detection in images of road pavement flexible surfaces. In: Proceedings of the European Signal Processing Conference (EUSIPCO 2008), pp. 25–29 (2008)

17. Oliveira, H., Correia, P.L.: Automatic road crack segmentation using entropy and image dynamic thresholding. In: European Signal Processing Conference (EUSIPCO), vol. 17, 622–626 (2009)

18. Oliveira, H., Correia, P.L.: Automatic road crack detection and characterization. IEEE Trans. Intell. Transp. Syst. 14(1), 155–168 (2013)

19. Oliveira, H., Correia, P.L.: Crackit–an image processing toolbox for crack detection and characterization. In: 2014 IEEE International Conference on Image Processing (ICIP), pp. 798–802. IEEE (2014)

20. Qi, Z., Tian, Y., Shi, Y.: Twin support vector machine with universum data. Neural Netw. 36, 112–119 (2012)

21. Qi, Z., Tian, Y., Shi, Y.: Robust twin support vector machine for pattern classification. Pattern Recogn. 46(1), 305–316 (2013)

22. Qi, Z., Tian, Y., Shi, Y.: Structural twin support vector machine for classification. Knowl.-Based Syst. 43, 74–81 (2013)

23. Shi, Y.: Multiple criteria optimization-based data mining methods and applications: a systematic survey. Knowl. Inf. Syst. 24(3), 369–391 (2010)

24. Shi, Y., Peng, Y.: Multiple Criteria and Multiple Constraint Levels Linear Programming: Concepts, Techniques and Applications. World Scientific, New Jersey (2001)

25. Shotton, J., Johnson, M., Cipolla, R.: Semantic texton forests for image categorization and segmentation. In: IEEE Conference on Computer Vision and Pattern Recognition, CVPR 2008, pp. 1–8. IEEE (2008)

26. Subirats, P., Dumoulin, J., Legeay, V., Barba, D.: Automation of pavement surface crack detection using the continuous wavelet transform. In: 2006 IEEE International Conference on Image Processing, pp. 3037–3040. IEEE (2006)

27. Tanaka, N., Uematsu, K.: A crack detection method in road surface images using morphology. In: MVA, vol. 98, pp. 17–19 (1998)

28. Tu, Z.: Probabilistic boosting-tree: learning discriminative models for classification, recognition, and clustering. In: Tenth IEEE International Conference on Computer Vision, ICCV 2005, vol. 2, pp. 1589–1596. IEEE (2005)
29. Xu, W., Tang, Z., Zhou, J., Ding, J.: Pavement crack detection based on saliency and statistical features. In: ICIP, pp. 4093–4097 (2013)
30. Zhou, J., Huang, P.S., Chiang, F.P.: Wavelet-based pavement distress detection and evaluation. Opt. Eng. **45**(2), 027007 (2006)
31. Zou, Q., Cao, Y., Li, Q., Mao, Q., Wang, S.: Cracktree: automatic crack detection from pavement images. Pattern Recogn. Lett. **33**(3), 227–238 (2012)

STMM: Semantic and Temporal-Aware Markov Chain Model for Mobility Prediction

Hamidu Abdel-Fatao[✉], Jiuyong Li, and Jixue Liu

School of Information Technology & Mathematical Sciences,
University of South Australia, Adelaide, Australia
hamidu.abdel-fatao@mymail.unisa.edu.au

Abstract. Information theoretic measures and probabilistic techniques have been applied successfully to human mobility datasets to show that human mobility is highly predictable up to an upper bound of 95 % prediction accuracy. Motivated by this finding, we propose a novel *Semantic and Temporal-aware Mobility Markov chain (STMM)* model to predict anticipated mobility of a target individual. Despite being an extensively studied topic in recent years, human mobility prediction by the vast majority of existing studies have mostly focused on predicting the geospatial context, and in rare cases, the temporal context of human mobility. We argue that an explicit and comprehensive analysis of semantic and temporal context of users' mobility is necessary for realistic understanding and prediction of mobility. In line with this, our proposed model simultaneously utilizes semantic and temporal features of a target individual's historical mobility data to predict their mobility, given his/her current location context (time and semantic tag of the location). We evaluate our approach on a real world GPS trajectory dataset.

1 Introduction

Advances in mobile computing in recent years have led to the deployment of many important contextually intelligent applications. One such application that has drawn immense attention from business and research communities is *location prediction*. Location prediction, typically built on some probabilistic/statistical models aims at utilizing historical mobility behaviours to forecast anticipated movement of an individual. This problem has become a hot topic lately because prediction of human mobility is fundamental to a plethora of applications such as traffic engineering, targeted advertisement, counter terrorism etc.

Recently, many studies on the predictability of human mobility [1–5] have emerged, the most of which have claimed high prediction accuracies using their algorithms, in some cases up to 95 % [2,4]. The high prediction accuracies of these algorithms can be ascribed to the high regularity hence high predictability intrinsic in human mobility [3,5,6].

Despite being quite successful in predicting human mobility, existing works share some major drawbacks. Firstly, the vast majority of the existing works [6,7] have only focused on prediction in geo-spatial space without considering the

© Springer International Publishing Switzerland 2015
C. Zhang et al. (Eds.): ICDS 2015, LNCS 9208, pp. 103–111, 2015.
DOI: 10.1007/978-3-319-24474-7_15

semantic dimension of users' mobility. We argue that semantic tags of locations reflect the types of activities likely to be undertaken in these locations (e.g. dining in restaurants), hence useful and necessary for predicting mobility. Also, these geo-spatial prediction based works suffer from over-fitting problems [5] besides the fact that they often are computationally expensive [6]. This drawback can be attributed to the fact that these approaches deal directly with massive volumes of raw mobility data which consist of long sequences of geographically points.

Secondly, except for a few works [6,7], the majority of the existing works are time-unaware in the sense that, they neglect the temporal dimension of users' mobility (such as time of the day) in their models. Consequently, they can only tell *where* but not *when* a user is likely to visit a location. Neglecting the temporal dimension can have severe implications on some applications that heavily rely on temporal information for effective function. For example, in homeland security, temporal information is vital in predicting the anticipated movement of a suspect if a potential crime is to be averted.

Motivated by these gaps, we propose a *Semantic and Temporal-aware Mobility Markov chain (STMM)* model for mobility prediction. More precisely, given the current location context (timestamp and semantic tag of location) and historical GPS trajectories of a target user, we exploit semantic and temporal features of his/her historical mobility behaviour to forecast his/her next move using a two stage strategy. Firstly, using Bayes rule, we find the stationary distribution of posterior probabilities of visiting locations having specific semantic tags during specified timeslots. We then build a second order mobility transition matrix and develop a second order Markov chain model for predicting most likely next location that the user will visit in the next timeslot, using the transition matrix and the stationary posterior probability distributions.

To the best of our knowledge, the most closely related work is Gambs et al. [4] in which an n-order Mobility Markov Chain (n-MMC) model is develop to predict Points of Interest (PoIs) - similar to our semantic tags that users are likely to visit. However, in n-MMC (see Fig. 1a) the probability of each destination PoI is computed only based on the present and immediate past PoIs that a user visited without using temporal information. In contrast, in STMM (see Fig. 1b and c) we firstly decompose each day into 4-hourly, 6 non-overlapping timeslots. For example 00.00–03:59 am and 00.04–07:59 am etc. are the first and second timeslots respectively. We then estimate a probability for semantic tag of each destination location during a specified timeslot as a random function of semantic tags of

(a) n-MMC

	Destination		
Origin	Home	Work	Shop
Home,Work	0.64	0.00	0.36
Home,Shop	0.84	0.16	0.16
Work,Home	0.00	0.83	0.17
Work,Shop	0.92	0.08	0.00
Shop,Home	0.00	1.00	0.00
Shop,Work	0.78	0.00	0.22

(b) 2-STMM

	Destination t_4		
Origin $t_2 \to t_3$	Home	Work	Shop
Home,Work	0.42	0.00	0.58
Home,Shop	0.33	0.67	0.16
Work,Home	0.00	0.49	0.51
Work,Shop	1.00	0.08	0.00
Shop,Home	0.00	0.00	0.00
Shop,Work	0.00	0.00	0.00

(c) 2-STMM

	Destination t_5		
Origin $t_3 \to t_4$	Home	Work	Shop
Home,Work	0.63	0.00	0.37
Home,Shop	0.69	0.31	0.16
Work,Home	0.00	0.54	0.46
Work,Shop	0.92	0.08	0.00
Shop,Home	0.00	1.00	0.00
Shop,Work	0.86	0.00	0.14

Fig. 1. User mobility model

the current timeslot and immediate past timeslot. Our approach is significantly different and more precise than to n-MMC [4] because the probability of visiting any particular location based on our model naturally varies depending on the timeslot under consideration, whereas in n-MMC the probability always stays the same regardless of temporal information.

The main contributions of this study are summarized as follows.

- We propose a Bayes rule based approach to estimate probability of an individual visiting a location with a specific semantic tag at a specified timeslot.
- We develop a second order STMM for predicting the anticipated next locations having specific of an individual during a specified timeslot.

We use experiments to validate our work. The rest of this paper is organized as follows. We describe data preprocessing and explain relevant concepts in Sect. 2, detail our proposed model in Sect. 3, and present our experiments in Sect. 4. We then conclude the paper in Sect. 5.

2   Preliminaries

2.1   Data Pre-processing

Trajectory Point denoted by $p = (x, y, t)$ is a geospatial point associated with a timestamp t, where x and y are *latitude* and *longitude* respectively of p at t. Trajec-

Table 1. A sample trajectory dataset

UserID	Date	Time	Latitude	Longitude
1509	2008-02-06	16:29:31	123.5322	42.30713
1509	2008-02-06	16:29:36	123.53218	42.30713
1509	2008-02-06	16:29:41	123.53217	42.30713
1509	2008-02-06	16:29:46	123.53217	42.30714
1509	2008-02-06	16:29:51	123.53217	42.30713

tory points organized sequentially in ascending of timestamps represent mobility traces, known simply as *trajectory*.

Definition 1. *A trajectorydenoted by* $\mathcal{P} = \langle p_1, p_2, ..., p_z \rangle$ *is a sequence of trajectory points organised in ascending order of timestamps, where* $\{p_i \in \mathbb{P} : p_i = (x_i, y_i, t_i)\}$ *is a trajectory point and* $t_i < t_{i+1}, \forall i \in [1, z]$.

Typically, raw trajectory points (see Table 1) are sampled at a high frequency and results in very large volumes of data. Analysing such datas directly involves significant computational overheads. We therefore transform users' historical trajectory datasets using a series of steps described briefly as follows.

Firstly, we identify significant geo-spatial places visited by users for various activities in each day called *stay points* from their historical trajectory datasets.

Definition 2. *Stay Point denoted by* $s = [(x, y), t_a, t_s]$ *is a geographical area characterized by a maximum distance threshold* δ_d *where a user stayed for at least a minimum threshold period of time* δ_t, *and* x, y, t_a *and* $(t_s \geq \delta_t)$ *are respectively latitude, longitude, arrival time and stay time of* s.

For stay point extraction, we use a well known stay point extraction algorithm by Li et al. [8] whose principle is consistent with our Definition 2.

Secondly, we perform a density-based clustering algorithm *OPTICS* to group stay points possibly representing the same location but having slightly different coordinates into non-overlapping clusters. We represent each discovered cluster with a single point called *Reference Point* defined below.

Definition 3. *A Reference Point denoted by $r = [(x_r, y_r), t_a, t_s]$, is a representative of a cluster of stay points $S_c = \{s'_1, s'_2, ..., s'_q\}$, where (x_r, y_r) is the average coordinate of the stay points $s'_i \in S_c$, t_a and t_s are respectively the earliest arrival time and mean stay time of the stay points in S_c.*

Finally, we assign a semantic tag e.g. park, shop etc. to each reference point using Foursquare[1] category database. We rely on proximity of PoIs to reference points to assign appropriate semantic tags and name each a *semantic location*

3   Methodology

In this section we formulate *visit probability* and present our STMM model. We commence with the following preamble.

Let $T_s(u) = \{L_1, L_2, ..., L_m\}$ denote a finite set of historical semantic locations visited by a user u and let $\tau(u) = \{l_1, l_2, ..., l_m\}$ be a set of semantic tags where $l_i \in \tau(u)$ is the semantic tag associated with $L_i \in T_s(u)$ $(1 \leq i \leq m)$. Also, let $T = \{t_1, t_2, ..., t_k\}$ be a set of predefined timeslots in a day.

Assuming Table 2 (our running example) represents statistics of historical visit behaviours of a user u. Table 2a corresponds to u's historical visits to locations having specific semantic tags without considering temporal information, and Table 2b is u's historical visits to locations having specific semantic tags during specified timeslots.

Location	Frequency
Work	38
Restaurant	32
Shopping	14
Cinema	6

(a) General Visit

Location	Frequency		
	t_3	t_4	t_5
Work	19	17	2
Restaurant	5	19	8
Shopping	2	5	7
Cinema	0	2	4

(b) Temporal Visit

Table 2. User historical mobility

3.1   Formulation of Visit Probability

Definition 4. *Given a finite set of semantic locations T visited by a user u having a corresponding set of semantic tags $\tau(u)$, and a set of timeslots T, visit probability denoted by $\lambda_{l_i}^{t_j}(u)$ of a semantic location $L_i \in T_s(u)$ is a numerical estimate of the likelihood that u will visit a semantic tag l_i of L_i during $t_j \in T$.*

---

[1] www.foursquare.com.

We express a visit probability of a semantic location L_i in terms of two component probabilities coined as (i) *Semantic feature-correlated (SFC)* visit probability (ii) *Temporal feature-correlated (TFC)* visit probability.

Location	$P(l_i)$
Work	0.42
Restaurant	0.36
Shopping	0.15
Cinema	0.07

(a) SFC Probabilities

Location	$P(t_j|l_i)$		
	t_3	t_4	t_5
Work	0.50	0.45	0.05
Restaurant	0.16	0.59	0.25
Shopping	0.14	0.36	0.50
Cinema	0.00	0.33	0.67

(b) TIC Probabilities

Table 3. SFC and TIC probabilities

SFC visit probability of a location having semantic tag l_i denoted by $P(l_i)$, is a *prior probability* of visit to l_i expressed as a ratio of number of times u visited l_i to the total number of visits to all semantic tags in u's location history. Table 3a exemplifies SFC probabilities computed from Table 2a. TFC visit probability of $l_i \in \tau(u)$ during $t_j \in T$ ($1 \le j \le k$) denoted by $P(t_j|l_i)$ is a *conditional probability* that a visit occurred during t_j given that l_i is been visited by u. Table 3b shows TFC probabilities obtained from Table 2b.

In line with Definition 4, we compute visit probability of a semantic location by applying the Bayes' rule to SFC and TIC probabilities. Accordingly, visit probability of a location having semantic tag l_i during timeslot t_j is given by

$$\lambda_{l_i}^{t_j}(u) = \frac{P(l_i)P(t_j|l_i)}{[P(l_i)P(t_j|l_i))] + \sum_{w=1, i\neq w} [P(l_w)P(t_j|l_w)]} \tag{1}$$

where $\{0 \le \lambda_{l_i}^{t_j}(u) \le 1\}$ and $(l_i, l_w \in \tau(u))$.

Applying Eq. 1 to Table 3 yields visit probabilities for semantic tags visited during each timeslots in Table 4. Each column in Table 4 is a probability vector showing distribution of $\lambda_{l_i}^{t_j}(u)$ for each $l_i \in L_u$ during t_j, where $\sum_{t_j \in T} \lambda_{l_i}^{t_j}(u) = 1$.

Table 4. Visit probabilities

Location	$\lambda_{l_i}^{t_j}(u)$		
	t_3	t_4	t_5
Work	0.73	0.40	0.09
Restaurant	0.20	0.44	0.39
Shopping	0.07	0.11	0.32
Cinema	0.00	0.05	0.20

3.2 Location Prediction

In this section, we highlight basic principles of Markov chain-based predictors and show how we apply the principles to STMM for mobility prediction.

Markov chain (MC) is a "memoryless" stochastic process in which the probability of occurrence of the next state of a system depends only on the present state and independent of preceding states. This intuitively simple yet mathematically tractable concept is widely used for the prediction of sequential events in a myriad of applications such as mobility prediction, gene sequencing etc.

Markov chains have been adapted by a number of works on predicting human mobility [2,4,9] to incorporate some amount of memory. Specifically, these works model users' mobility as a Markov process in which the probability of visiting a location depends on n-previous locations already visited. Accordingly, we define below an *n-order STMM* that takes into account semantic and temporal information to model users' mobility as a Markov process.

Definition 5. *An n-order STMM is a discrete stochastic process with limited memory in which the probability of visiting a location having a specific semantic* *tag l_w during timeslot t_{j+1} only depends semantic tags of n locations visited during timeslots $\{t_j, t_{j-1}, ..., t_{j-n+1}\}$.*

In line with Definition 5, the probability that a user u's next location will be a location with semantic tag l_w during timeslot t_{j+1} can be expressed as $P[(l_w, t_{j+1})|(l_i, t_j), (l_{i-1}, t_{j-1}), ..., (l_{i-n+1}, t_{j-n+1})]$.

A number of studies [1, 2, 4] have established that second order MCs have the best accuracies up to 95 % for predicting human mobility, and that higher order MCs (>2) are not necessarily more accurate but often less precise. Backed by these findings, we develop a second order STMM (2-*STMM*) in which the probability of visiting a location having specific semantic tag during timeslot t_{j+1} depends of semantic tags of locations visited during the current and immediate past timeslots t_j and t_{j-1}. A crucial challenge for successful mobility prediction based on 2-STMM is how to estimate transition probabilities defined below.

Definition 6. *A transition probability (p_{hiw}^j) with respect to 2-STMM is the probability that a user will move to a destination location having semantic tag l_w during timeslot t_{j+1} given that the user has successively visited locations having semantic tags l_h and l_i during timeslots t_{j-1} and t_j respectively.*

We denote a transition from locations with semantic tags l_h and l_i during timeslots t_{j-1} and t_j respectively to a destination location with semantic tag l_w during timeslot t_{j+1} by $[l_h^{t_{j-1}}, l_i^{t_j} \rightarrow l_w^{t_{j+1}}]$. The transition probability is computed as

$$p_{hiw}^j = \frac{count[l_h^{t_{j-1}}, l_i^{t_j} \rightarrow l_w^{t_{j+1}}]}{\sum count[l_h^{t_{j-1}}, l_i^{t_j} \rightarrow l_*^{t_{j+1}}]} \tag{2}$$

where l_* is semantic tag of any location at t_{j+1}. We predict semantic tag l_{pre} of most likely next location and its probability by computing r.h.s. of Eq. 3.

$$P[(l_{pre}, t_{j+1})|(l_i, t_j), (l_{i-1}, t_{j-1})] = \arg\max_w\{P[(l_w, t_{j+1})|(l_i, t_j), (l_{i-1}, t_{j-1})]\} \tag{3}$$

Let probability vectors λ_j and λ_{j-1} represent distributions of visit probabilities of semantic tags of locations during timeslots t_j and t_{j-1} respectively. We represent the initial probability distribution of 2-STMM by the joint distribution of λ_j and λ_{j-1} given by $\lambda_{2j} = \lambda_j\lambda_{j-1}$ where $\lambda_{2j} = \{\lambda_{l_1}^{2j}, \lambda_{l_2}^{2j}, ..., \lambda_{l_n}^{2j}\}$. Given initial probability distribution and a matrix of transition probabilities for a target user u, the r.h.s. of Eq. 3 is calculated using

$$P[(l_{pre}, t_{j+1})|(l_i, t_j), (l_{i-1}, t_{j-1})] = \arg\max_w\{\sum_{l_i \in \tau(u)} \lambda_{l_i}^{2j} p_{hiw}^j\} \tag{4}$$

4 Experiments

4.1 Dataset, Evaluation Metrics and Baselines

In this work, we utilized *GeoLife* dataset[2], a real-world GPS trajectory dataset collected from 182 individuals mostly in Shanghai over 5 years (April 2007– August 2012) using GPS devices. We chose users with sufficiently large number of trajectories (i.e. having trajectories spanning a period of at least one week) in order to increase our chances of finding trajectories which exhibit routine mobility behaviours. We found that trajectories of 149 users satisfied this requirement and processed their datasets as per our description in Sect. 2.

We evaluate the performance of our model using the metric *prediction accuracy* (γ) [2], given by $\gamma = \dfrac{\text{number of correct prediction}}{\text{total number of predictions}}$. In our experiments, we split our pre-processed dataset into 60 %, 70 % and 80 % training sets and hold off 40 %, 30 % and 20 % respectively for testing. Note that, due to the source of our dataset, we only rely on this approach for evaluation. We compare prediction accuracy of 2-STMM with two approaches namely (*i*) *Most Frequent Location Model (MF)* coined from [10], and (*ii*) Next Place Prediction using Mobility Markov Chains (*n*-MMC) [4]. MF assigns probability to the semantic tag of each location visited during a specified timeslot as a proportion of visits to semantic tags of all locations visited during that timeslot. This model, which relies heavily on frequency of historical visits, is simple and yet intuitive for prediction of human mobility. For example, if one is asked to guess the most likely location of a friend at 11 am, one will probable suggest the place of work based on historic observations.

In *n*-MMC the authors develop a second order Markov chain model to predict the next PoI a user is likely to visit (see Fig 1a). At first glance, their approach looks similar to our 2-STMM model. However, our model makes explicit use of temporal information to predict semantic tags (similar to PoIs) of locations that a user is likely to visit during a specified timeslot. For comparison, we utilise semantic tags of locations visited daily by users without regards to temporal dimension to build the *n*-MMC model for prediction of semantic tags.

Results and Discussions

Comparison with Baselines. The overall prediction accuracies of MF, *n*-MMC and 2-STMM for User 153 in the dataset are compared in Fig. 2. We chose user 153 because, after pre-processing our dataset, this user's history contained the largest number of semantic locations. We observed that, across all the three approaches,

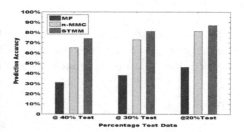

Fig. 2. Prediction accuracy of user 153

---

[2] http://research.microsoft.com/en-us/downloads/b16d359d-d164-469e-9fd4-daa38f2b2e13/.

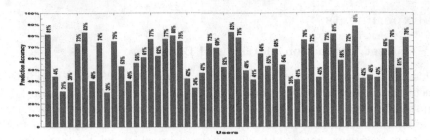

Fig. 3. Prediction accuracy across users

prediction accuracy increases as the percentage of training dataset increases. However, for all percentages of training datasets the accuracy of MF is the worst among the three methods. This is understandable and expected since MF only relies on the frequencies of visit to semantic tags of locations during a specified timeslot for prediction. The prediction accuracy of n-MMC is better compared with MF model and still considered good despite the fact that this results is slightly lower than that our 2-STMM model. The 2-STMM model achieves the highest accuracy ranging of 88 % significantly outperforming both baseline approaches. The improvement over n-MMC is attributable to the additional temporal dimension of user mobility we took into account in our approach.

Prediction Accuracy Across Users. To investigate how prediction accuracy varies with varying amounts of users' location histories, we randomly selected 50 users and trained our 2-STMM model on their preprocessed datasets according to the description given in Sect. 2. For each user, we used 80 % of preprocessed dataset for training the model and 20 % for testing. Figure 3 shows the results obtained. The highest and lowest prediction accuracy stood at 88 % and 31 % respectively. We observed that low accuracies were associated with users with short location histories, while users with long histories exhibited high prediction accuracies. Overall we achieved average accuracy of 59.82 % across all users.

5   Conclusion

In this work we present STMM model that incorporates semantic and temporal information to predict users' mobility. We compare our model with existing models to show that our approach has significantly higher of prediction accuracy.

References

1. Asahara, A., Maruyama, K., Sato, A., Seto, K.: Pedestrian-movement prediction based on mixed Markov-chain model. In: GIS 2011, New York, NY, USA (2011)
2. Lu, X., Wetter, E., Bharti, N., Tatem, A.J., Bengtsson, L.: Approaching the limit of predictability in human mobility. Sci. Rep. **3**, 2923 (2013)

3. Song, C., Qu, Z., Blumm, N., Barabási, A.-L.: Limits of predictability in human mobility. Science **327**(5968), 1018–1021 (2010)
4. Gambs, S., Killijian, M.-O., del Prado Cortez, M.N.: Next place prediction using mobility Markov chains. In: MPM 2012, New York, NY, USA, pp. 3:1–3:6 (2012)
5. Baumann, P., Kleiminger, W., Santini, S.: The influence of temporal and spatial features on the performance of next-place prediction algorithms. In: UbiComp 2013, New York, NY, USA, pp. 449–458 (2013)
6. Gidófalvi, G., Dong, F.: When and where next: individual mobility prediction. In: Proceedings of the First ACM SIGSPATIAL International Workshop on Mobile Geographic Information Systems - MobiGIS 2012, p. 57 (2012)
7. Yang, N., Kong, X., Wang, F., Yu, P.S.: When and where: predicting human movements based on social spatial-temporal events. In: Proceedings of 2014 SIAM International Conference on Data Mining abs/1407.1 (2014)
8. Li, Q., Zheng, Y., Xie, X., Chen, Y., Liu, W., Ma, W.-Y.: Mining user similarity based on location history. In: Proceedings of the 16th ACM SIGSPATIAL International Conference on Advances in GIS, New York, NY, USA (2008)
9. Smith, G., Wieser, R., Goulding, J., Barrack, D.: A refined limit on the predictability of human mobility. In: IEEE International Conference on Pervasive Computing and Communications (PerCom), pp. 88–94 (2014)
10. Cho, E., Myers, S.A., Leskovec, J.: Friendship and mobility: user movement in location-based social networks. In: Proceedings of the 17th ACM SIGKDD International Conference on Knowledge Discovery and Data Mining, KDD 2011, pp. 1082–1090. ACM, New York (2011)

3D Model-Based Food Traceability Information Extraction Framework

Bo Mao[1(✉)], Jing He[1,2], Jie Cao[1], Stephen Bigger[2],
and Todor Vasiljevic[2]

[1] College of Information Engineering,
Nanjing University of Finance and Economic, Nanjing 210003, China
{bo.mao,jie.cao}@njue.edu.cn, jing.he@vu.edu.au
[2] Victoria University, Melbourne, Australia
{Stephen.Bigger,Todor.Vasiljevic}@vu.edu.au

Abstract. In this paper, we propose a 3D model-based food traceability information extraction method for processing video surveillance data. The proposed method first builds a 3D model of the surveillance area. Then, the video cameras are mapped in the 3D model and the coordinate transform functions from the 2D camera coordinates to the 3D model coordinates are calculated. Next, the object detection method is applied to identify the target which is then mapped into the 3D coordinates so that its 3D trajectory can be generated. Finally, we merge multiple trajectories from different cameras to create the complete traceability information for the target object. According to the experimental results, the proposed method can efficiently extract useful traceability information for a video surveillance system.

1 Introduction

With the development of the economy in China, people have started to pay increasing attention to the quality of food which is essential for their health. Different methods are applied to ensure the safety of food. A traceability system is one of the key technologies to improve food quality by tracking the chain of food production. In countries such as the EU, USA and Japan, food tracking systems are a mandatory requirement for food companies. For example, the UK has a system to record the status (birth, growth and sale) of every cow by the use of an RFID ear tag.

In China, an RFID-based traceability system is also under construction by some large food producers, however a video surveillance system is more common and can be easily applied in small companies to prove the quality of their product. In this paper, we propose a framework that can automatically extract traceability information from a video surveillance system. This framework is based on the identification of the target object and makes use of the 3D model to gain the spatio-temporal trajectories of the target objects. Finally, multiple trajectories from different cameras are joined together to form the whole traceability track of the target objects. In this traceability track, every moment is recorded by the camera and have the photo evident the photos are made available for the public to check. Meanwhile, the video data are dramatically

© Springer International Publishing Switzerland 2015
C. Zhang et al. (Eds.): ICDS 2015, LNCS 9208, pp. 112–119, 2015.
DOI: 10.1007/978-3-319-24474-7_16

compressed into the key images in the track, so long-term video traceability can be preserved at a low cost for further use.

The proposed framework has two main advantages compared with the existing system: first, photogrammetry is used to generate the 3D spatiotemporal trajectory of the target object in video surveillance; second, multi-trajectories from different cameras are combined as a whole traceable track. This framework is implemented in a grain company to track its rice production. According to the experiment results, the framework can efficiently and accurately extract the traceability trajectories of the people and vehicles. The rest of paper is structured as follows: the related work is described in Sect. 2; Sect. 3 describes the proposed framework in detail; Sect. 4 overviews the case study and experimental results; Sect. 5 summarizes the whole paper and suggests future studies.

2 Related Work

2.1 Traceability System

Recently, one of the most important research trends in the food sector has been electronic traceability and condition monitoring using RFID and WSN [1]. There have been some practical implementations in companies that are now using RFID for food supply chain in Italy, France, UK, Sweden, the USA and Canada [2–7]. Some electronic chain traceability systems have been proposed, such as the one in Frederiksen et al. [8] that proposed an Internet-based traceability system for fresh fish. Seino et al. [9] proposed a similar system for fish traceability by using QR codes after discarding the use of RFID due to the cost of this technology at that moment. Grabacki et al. [10] introduced the concept of using an RFID for the seafood industry in Alaska and they predicted that this would be the key technology in the supply chains of the future. More recently, research has demonstrated the use of RFID applications in the live fish supply chain, in intercontinental fresh fish logistic chains [11] and for monitoring the temperature of fish during the cold chain using RFID loggers [12]. The benefits of using RFID in the fish supply chain were also recognized by the Scandinavian fishing industry, with the main objective of developing and evaluating a traceability system [13]. With regard to WSN systems, Lin et al. [14] proposed a WSN-based traceability system for aquaculture that can automate many monitoring tasks and improve information flow.

2.2 3D Videogrammetry

Videogrammetry is a measurement technique which is mainly based on the principles of Photogrammetry [15]. Videogrammetry refers to video images taken with a camcorder or the movie function on a digital still camera. A video movie consists of sequences of images (or frames). If the video speed is 25 fps (frames per second) and the duration is 1 min (i.e. 60 s), there are 25 frames per second or overall 1500 images. Hiroshi et al. [16] worked on the automatic modeling of a 3D city map from a real-world video. They proposed an efficient method for making a 3D map from real-world video data. Their proposed method was an automatic organization method by collating the real-world video data with the map information using DP matching. They also devised a system which was able to generate a 3D virtual map automatically in VRML format. Clip et al. [17] proposed a Mobile 3D City Reconstruction system. It is an efficient flexible capture and reconstruction system for the automatic reconstruction of large scale urban scenes. Zhang et al. [18] introduced a concept for consistent depth map recovery from a video sequence. Video image sequence frames were used and depth maps from these frames were created. In this method, they used the structure from motion (SFM) technique to recover the camera parameters, after which disparity initialization, bundle optimization, and space-time fusion techniques were used to create depth maps. These depth maps are useful for creating a virtual 3-D model of an area or object. Hengel et al. [19] developed a method and system (named the Video Trace) which interactively generates realistic 3D models of objects from video. This research shows that it is possible to retrieval the 3D trajectories of a target object from a video surveillance system, which has not been applied in a food traceability framework as far as we know. Singh et al. [20] developed a multi-camera setup and method for camera calibration from video image frames. From the video data, image frames were created for close range photogrammetric work.

3   Methodology

In the proposed framework, we first create the 3D models of the surveillance target, such as food storage or a production line. Then, the cameras of the surveillance system are mapped on to the 3D models and calculate the transform function for each camera. The transform function $F(a, b) = (x, y, z)$ takes the image coordinate (a, b) of a camera as the input parameter and returns its corresponding coordinate in 3D model (x, y, z). In this case, we assume that objects are located on the horizontal surface of the 3D models such as the ground plan, tabletop and so on, therefore the transform function F is an injective mapping. Next, we analyze the video surveillance data and extract the interesting objects, such as people or products and obtain their trajectories based on transform function F. Finally, the multiple trajectories of a target object from different cameras are connected as a complete traceability track, according to their spatial distributions. In this section, we discuss the framework in detail.

3.1   3D Model Generation

There are many methods by which to generate 3D models of the production environment, but it is usually difficult and costly to generate accurate 3D models. In this paper, we create models with the CAD and satellite images. These models are mainly used for videogrammetry, so the geometry is more considered than the visual effects.

3.2   Transform Function

The extracted frames with a target object are difficult to process because there is a lack of spatial-temporal information. From the frame image, it is difficult to identify the real location of the target object in the world coordinate system. Therefore, we propose a transform function to convert the object coordinates in the 2D frame into the 3D real world. The inner orientation defines the geometric parameters of the imaging process. The exterior orientation of a camera defines its location in space and its view direction. This information is difficult to gather for the video surveillance system in which some cameras are installed overhead.

In this paper, we propose a simple transform function to map the image coordinates into the real world coordinates. We assume that the target object is located in a plane. For the on-plane surface, we can use the triangulation method to simulate the on-plane surface with smaller planes.

Suppose that three vertexes of a triangular area in the real world are (C1, C2, C3) and the corresponding coordinates in the camera/frame image are (c1, c2, c3). We define the transform matrix M. Therefore, we have the following equation:

$$
\begin{bmatrix} c1.x & c1.y & 1 \\ c2.x & c2.y & 1 \\ c3.x & c3.y & 1 \end{bmatrix} M = \begin{bmatrix} C1.x & C1.y & C1.z \\ C2.x & C2.y & C2.z \\ C3.x & C3.y & C3.z \end{bmatrix} \tag{1}
$$

Since c1, c2 and c3 are not in a line, we can calculate M based on Eq. (1) as follows:

$$
M = \begin{bmatrix} c1.x & c1.y & 1 \\ c2.x & c2.y & 1 \\ c3.x & c3.y & 1 \end{bmatrix}^{-1} \begin{bmatrix} C1.x & C1.y & C1.z \\ C2.x & C2.y & C2.z \\ C3.x & C3.y & C3.z \end{bmatrix} \tag{2}
$$

In our implementation, we label several ground references and measure their relative location with the Electronic Total Station, as shown. Then, we manually record the corresponding coordinates of these references in the camera to generate the transform matrix M. If it is difficult to measure the ground truth, we can simply set the reference points in the 3D models and map them into the camera. For example, we first find the coordinate in the 3D models of some corner on the ground, then its corresponding coordinate in the camera can be calculated based on locating the corner in the monitoring frame.

For a complex area, we need to define a multi-triangular mesh to represent the no-plane surface. Therefore, multiple transform functions are required for these complex area.

3.3   Multiple Camera Integration

By converting the 2D image coordinate into a 3D real world, we not only obtain more semantic information but also gain the ability to combine multiple cameras into a unified system that can continuously monitor a target object from start to end. This is quite important for the traceability system.

Unlike existing target recognition-based surveillance systems, the proposed framework has better accuracy with less computation, since we identify target objects

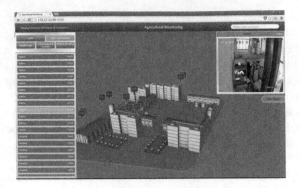

Fig. 1. 3D model based video surveillance system.

based on their spatiotemporal distribution. It is easily to connect two trajectories in a unified 3D reference coordinate system, therefore, we do not need to identify which vehicle in one camera is the same in the other as the existing methods do.

Meanwhile, we could optimize the distribution of cameras in the surveillance system based on the created 3D models with per-analysis. Currently many surveillance systems are installed based on the experience of the installer, which may not always be right. With the 3D models in the monitoring area, we can calculate the coverage and shielded area of each camera. More importantly, it is possible to find the exact relationship between the multi-cameras to build a unified monitoring system without dead angles, using the least number of cameras.

4   Results

4.1   3D Models

We partially implemented the proposed system in a rice production company. Over 200 cameras are deployed in four rice processing factories located in North Jiangsu, China. We create the 3D models of these four factories based on satellite images, as shown in Fig. 2.

Meanwhile, Cesium, a JavaScript library for creating 3D globes and 2D maps similar to Google Earth in a web browser, is employed to increase the accessibility of

Fig. 2. The 3D models of rice processing factories.

the 3D models. Cesium makes use of WebGL for hardware-accelerated graphics, so no plugins are required to view the 3D models. Figure 1 shows the browser-based 3D monitoring interface. We can check the real-time video stream or history trajectories through the browser on both the PC and mobile devices, as shown in Fig. 1.

4.2   Object Detection

In order to deal with the huge volume of data from the surveillance system, we select several key cameras from which to extract the trajectories of the target object which will reduce the network and computation load dramatically. We write a script to automatically download the video from NVRs and analyse the frames in a centralized server. In the next step, these object detection methods will be deployed in NVRs to save the network traffic.

In this framework, we detect the object using the existing algorithm background difference method. The implementation is based on OpenCV. The object detection results are listed in Fig. 3. The target is indicated with a green rectangle.

Fig. 3. Object detection results

4.3   Object Detection

Based on the proposed transformation function, all detected objects are converted into a 3D model reference coordinate system. Therefore, multiple trajectories can be easily connected, as shown in Fig. 4. The traceability information is extracted from the video surveillance system and can be used for visualization and other analysis applications.

Fig. 4. Trajectory generation

5 Conclusion

In this paper, we proposed a 3D model-based food traceability information extraction method. This method involves 3D model construction, 2D–3D transformation, object detection and trajectory integration. The system was deployed in a rice factory as a partial implementation of the proposed framework. The results indicate that the proposed method is effective and can find all the traceability information on the target of interest. However, we still need to overcome the matching error from 2D to 3D. In the future, we will focus on how to automatically adjust the transform function based on the information from multiple cameras. Also, the object detection method will be improved to suit different application areas.

Acknowledgments. This work was supported by the National Natural Science Foundation of China (Grant No. 41201486), the National Key Technologies R&D Program of China (Grant No. 2013BAH16F 2015BAD18B02 and 2015BAK36B02), and the project of the Priority Academic Program Development of Jiangsu Higher Education Institutions (PAPD) in the Collaborative Innovation Center of Modern Grain Circulation and Security, Nanjing University of Finance and Economics.

References

1. Myhre, B., Netland, T., Vevle, G.: The footprint of food-a suggested traceability solution based on EPCIS. In: Proceedings of the 5th European Workshop on RFID Systems and Technologies (RFID SysTech 2009), Bremen, Germany (2009)
2. Angeles, R.: RFID technologies: supply-chain applications and implementation issues. Inf. Syst. Manage. **22**(1), 51–65 (2005)
3. Jones, P., Clarke-Hill, C., Comfort, D., Hilliear, D., Shears, P.: Radio frequency identification and food retailing. UK Br. Food J. **107**(6), 356–360 (2005)
4. Regattieri, A., Gamberi, M., Manzini, R.: Traceability of food products: general framework and experimental evidence. J. Food Eng. **81**(2), 347–356 (2007)
5. Connolly, C.: Sensor trends in processing and packaging of foods and pharmaceuticals. Sens. Rev. **27**(2), 103–108 (2007)
6. Launois, A.: RFID tracking system stores wine bottle data. http://www.foodproductiondaily.com/news/ng.asp?id=84511. Accessed 03 June 2015
7. Kumar, P., Reinitz, H.W., Simunovic, J., Sandeep, K.P., Franzon, P.D.: Overview of RFID technology and its applications in the food industry. J. Food Sci. **74**, 101–105 (2009)
8. Frederiksen, M., Osterberg, C., Silberg, S., Larsen, E., Bremmer, A.: Info-fish. Development and validation of an Internet-based traceability system in a Danish domestic fresh fish chain. J. Aquat. Food Prod. Technol. **11**(2), 13–34 (2002)
9. Seino, K., Kuwabara, S., Mikami, S., Takahashi, Y., Yoshikawa, M., Narumi, H., Koganezaki, K., Wakabayashi, T., Nagano, A.: Development of the traceability system which secures the safety of fishery products using the QR Code and a digital signature. In: Proceedings of Marine Technology Society/IEEE Techno-Ocean, Kobe, Japan, vol. 1, pp. 476–481 (2004)

10. Grabacki, S.T., Ronchetti, M., Humphrey, T., Hedgepeth, O.: How it will transform packaging, distribution and handling of Alaska seafood. In: Anchorage, Alaska: International Smoked Seafood Conference Proceedings Alaska Sea Grant College, Program, AK-SG-08-02, pp. 101–106 (2007)
11. Abad, E., Palacio, F., Nuin, M., González de Zárate, A., Juarros, A., Gómez, J.M., Marco, S.: RFID smart tag for traceability and cold chain monitoring of foods: demonstration in an intercontinental fresh fish logistic chain. J. Food Eng. **93**, 394–399 (2009)
12. Tingman, W., Jian, Z., Xiaoshuan, Z.: Fish product quality evaluation based on temperature monitoring in cold chain. Afr. J. Biotechnol. **9**(37), 6146–6151 (2010)
13. Thakur, M., Ringsberg, H.: Impacts of using the EPCIS standard in two fish supply chain. In: Food Integrity and Traceability Conference, Belfast, pp. 21–24 (2001)
14. Lin, Q., Jian, Z., Xu, M., Zetian, F., Wei, C., Xiaoshuan, Z.: Developing WSN-based traceability system for recirculation aquaculture. Math. Comput. Model. **53**, 2162–2172 (2011)
15. Gruen, A.: Fundamentals of videogrammetry-a review. Hum. Mov. Sci. **16**, 155–187 (1997)
16. Hiroshi, K., Tomoyuki, Y., Katsushi, I., Masao, S.: Automatic Modeling of a 3D City Map from Real-World Video. Institute of Industrial Science, University of Tokyo, Japan (1999)
17. Clipp, B., Raguram, R., Frahm, J., Welch, G., Pollefeys, M.: A Mobile 3D City Reconstruction System. UNC Chapel Hill, ETH, Zurich (2008)
18. Zhang, G., Jia, J., Wong, T., Bao, H.: Consistent depth maps recovery from a video sequence. IEEE Trans. Pattern Anal. Mach. Intell. **31**(6), 974–988 (2009)
19. Hengel, A., Dick, A., Thormahlen, T., Ward, B., Philip, H, Torr, S.: VideoTrace: rapid interactive scene modelling from video. ACM Trans. Graph. **26**(3) (2007)
20. Singh, S., Mandla, V., Jain, K.: Design and calibration of multi camera setup for 3D city modeling. Int. J. Eng. Res. Technol. (IJERT) **2**(5) (2013)

A Spark-Based Big Data Platform for Massive Remote Sensing Data Processing

Zhongyi Sun[1], Fengke Chen[1], Mingmin Chi[1,2]([✉]), and Yangyong Zhu[1]

[1] School of Computer Science, Shanghai Key Laboratory of Data Science,
Key Laboratory for Information Science of Electromagnetic Waves (MoE),
Fudan University, Shanghai, China
mmchi@fudan.edu.cn
[2] State Key Laboratory of Satellite Ocean Environment Dynamics,
Second Institute of Oceanography (SOA), Hangzhou, China

Abstract. With the fast development of remote sensing techniques, the volume of acquired data grows exponentially. This brings a big challenge to process massive remote sensing data. In the paper, an in-memory computing framework is proposed to address this problem. Here, Spark is an open-source distributed computing platform with Hadoop YARN as resource scheduler and HDFS as cloud storage system. On the Spark-based platform, data loaded into memory in the first iteration can be reused in the subsequent iterations. This mechanism makes Spark much suitable for running multi-iteration algorithms compared to MapReduce which has to load data in each iteration. The experiments are carried out on massive remote sensing data using multi-iteration singular value decomposition (SVD) algorithm. The results show that Spark-based SVD can obtain significantly faster computation timethan that by MapReduce, usually by one order of magnitude.

Keywords: Big data · Remote sensing · Spark · Hadoop

1   Introduction

With the fast development of remote sensing techniques, massive amounts of high spacial and spectral resolution images can be acquired for various applications, such as hazard monitoring and urban planning. This brings big opportunities for various applications based on the massive remote sensing data but also big challenges for big data storage and computation.

Usually, parallel and distributed computations are utilized to deal with the computational challenges of big remote sensing data. The parallel computing platform is often based on Compute Unified Device Architecture (CUDA) created by NVIDIA and implemented by the graphics processing units (GPUs) [4]. Thanks to efficiency and programmability of the CUDA GPUs, the technique has been successfully used in remote sensing applications, e.g., Cloud tracking and Reconstruction [9], remote sensing image fusion [17], and color balancing [15]. Similarly, the heterogeneous system OpenCL by combining multi-core

© Springer International Publishing Switzerland 2015
C. Zhang et al. (Eds.): ICDS 2015, LNCS 9208, pp. 120–126, 2015.
DOI: 10.1007/978-3-319-24474-7_17

GPU and CPU with operation system has been used to remote sensing data processing [1,3].

Although GPUs are capable of speeding up remote sensing data processing, it is still hard for a single computer, even a extremely expensive minicomputer or a PC server to analyze the big remote sensing data. Hadoop [2,6] based distributed storage and computing cluster provides a new resolution to the computation problem of big data. The work in [8,14] demonstrated that the performance in speed of MapReduce [6] based algorithm has an advantage over the single-thread process algorithm. However, in the MapReduce-based platform, the entire data set has to be loaded from hard disks to memory at each iteration, which takes a lot of time when processing massive data by multi-iteration data analysis algorithms.

To attack this problem, usually an open-source in-memory distributed computing framework, namely, Spark [16] is exploited for distributed computation. In the Spark-based platform, the data loaded into memory in the first iteration can be reused in the subsequent iterations. This mechanism makes Spark much suitable for running multi-iteration algorithms compared to MapReduce which has to load data in each iteration. In [16], multi-iterations programs using Spark based algorithm is up to 100x faster than Hadoop MapReduce in memory, or 10x faster on disk. The Spark-based platform has been used to graph data applications [10], large scale security monitoring [13], log analysis [12] and so on.

As we know, Spark has not been used for processing remote sensing big data. In the paper, Spark-based platform is proposed to fulfil a multi-iteration algorithm for remote sensing application. In particular, the Hadoop Distributed File System (shorted as HDFS) is adopted and Hadoop YARN as resource scheduler. Here, the feature extraction algorithm, i.e., singular value decomposition(shorted as SVD) is implemented to evaluate the effectiveness of the proposed distributed platform. The experiments are carried out on two real-world massive remote sensing data. The results show that Spark-based SVD can obtain significantly faster computation time than that by MapReduce, usually by one order of magnitude.

The rest of the paper is organized as follows. The next section describes the preliminary knowledge of the proposed big data Architecture. The applied remote sensing datasets and machine learning algorithms are briefly described in Sect. 3. Section 3.2 reports and discusses the results provided by the SVD algorithm and different data sets. Finally, Sect. 4 draws the conclusions of this paper.

2   The Big Remote Sensing Data Architecture

In the paper, massive remote sensing data are dealt with in the big data processing architecture. In the following, the proposed architecture is first described. Then, the distributed computing models, i.e., MapReduce and Spark, and the related storage system are briefly introduced as follows.

2.1   Big Remote Sensing Data Architecture

The big remote sensing data are acquired from different sources, such as remote sensing data and data from the Internet and then input to the system. In the data processing stage, HDFS is chosen as the distributed file system. Then, big data in remote sensing are loaded to the HDFS at the beginning. In-memory based Spark, is chosen as the main principal distributed computing framework. Meanwhile, Hadoop MapReduce is also been integrated into the platform. Apache YARN is chosen as the scheduler responsible for allocating resources to various running applications between the HDFS and the distributed computing programming models, i.e., MapReduce and Spark. This means that the proposed platform supports the algorithm implemented by both Spark and MapReduce to process remote sensing data. Meanwhile, the set of data analysis algorithms, i.e., a machine learning library (MLlib) can be implemented in the Spark programming model. Similarly, MapReduce builds Apache Mahout, a scalable machine learning and data mining library. On top of the big data processing stage, different remote sensing processing tasks can be fulfilled, e.g., feature extraction and image classification.

2.2   Hadoop

Hadoop is a series of technology for distributed storage and processing of big data. It is an open source framework developed by the Apache Software Foundation. Hadoop is fault tolerant, scalable, and extremely simple to expand. Hadoop is capable of processing massive amounts of data sets which are unable to be dealt with or originally need expensive super-computers. Nowadays, Hadoop can manage thousands of computers, storage and process massive data in a PeraByte level. The core of Hadoop consists of two parts, a storage part Hadoop Distributed File System (shorted as HDFS) and a processing part MapReduce, which are introduced as follows.

HDFS. HDFS [2] is a Java-based file system designed for large data storage which was inspired from Google File System (shorted as GFS) [7]. The purpose of HDFS is to enhance the I/O performance of data storage and to ensure that the distributed storage system is scalable, fault tolerant. HDFS break data down into smaller pieces which called blocks and distribute them throughout the cluster. Each block of data is independently replicated at multiple servers. When a duplicate of a block is lost due to a hardware failure, HDFS can automatically provide the nearest duplicate instead and creates another duplicate of the block. HDFS supports redundant data storage which not only offers the tolerance to hardware failure, but also allows that Hadoop can divide a large task into small pieces and runs them on separate servers.

MapReduce. MapReduce [6] is the core of Hadoop. It is a programming model and an associated implementation for processing and generating large data sets.

Before the invention of the MapReduce, open multi-processing (shorted as OpenMP [5]) and many other models were popular in the field of distributed computing. Most of these models require a very long learning curve to master. However, MapReduce is a simplified data processing model. Users only need to modify the Map and Reduce functions according to the requirements of the task. A Map function processes a key/value pair to generate a set of intermediate key/value pair, and a Reduce function merges all intermediate values associated with the same intermediate key. This model can realize many real-world applications.

2.3 Spark

The Apache Spark [16] is a fast and general engine for large-scale data processing implemented in Scala [11]. Even though the MapReduce model has achieved an unprecedented success in implementing many real-world distributed tasks, it is not suitable for the applications built around a cyclic data flow model. The Spark is proposed to handle these applications while retaining the similar excellent properties of MapReduce, i.e., scalability and fault tolerance. Spark has an advanced DAG execution engine that supports cyclic data flow and in-memory computing. In some specific applications, Spark may work 100 times faster than Hadoop [16].

The resilient distributed dataset (shorted as RDD) is used for the fundamental programming abstraction in Spark. The RDD is a logical collection of data partitioned across machines and can be rebuilt if a partition is lost. An RDD can be explicitly cached in memory across machines and reused for later MapReduce-like parallel operations. For the algorithms whose main body is a loop calculation, the intermediate RDD data sets do not need to read and to write from the hard disk at each iterative manner. This is one of the major reasons why Spark works faster. RDDs can be created in two ways, i.e., parallelizing an existing RDD and referencing a dataset in an external storage system. RDDs support many useful parallel operations in the latest release.

3 Experimental Results

To evaluate the effectiveness of the proposed big data platform for processing massive remote sensing data, a multi-iteration singular value decomposition (SVD) is implemented in both Spark and MapReduce platforms in terms of hyperspectral remote sensing data in different magnitudes of spatial resolutions.

In the followings, the datasets utilized are firstly introduced and then the corresponding experimental results are reported.

3.1 Datasets

The experiment is evaluated on two public remote sensing images briefly described as follows:

Paiva: It is a hyperspectral and high-resolution (1.3 m) image taken over the urban area of Pavia by the airborne ROSIS-03 optical sensor. The image consists of 1096*715 pixels with 103 bands ranging from 0.43 to 0.86 μm in the center of Pavia (denoted as (denoted as PaviaCenter), Pavia, Italy.

IndianPine: It is a hyperspectral image over the Indian_Pine test site on June 1992 by the AVIRIS instrument. The image size is 145*145 pixels with 220 bands from 0.37-2.5 μm.

Table 1. The details for the datasets used in the experiments.

Dataset	Indian_Pines	Pavia
Number of pixels	34947	468666
Number of bands	200	102

The details of the datasets are summarized in Table 1.

3.2   Experiment Results

In order to evaluate the effectiveness of the proposed platform, the computation times are compared in terms of the SVD algorithm based on both the Spark and MapReduce platform. SVD is an effective algorithm for feature extraction (reduction) but time-consuming. The implementation of SVD in the distributed platform can greatly accelerate the algorithm. In the real environment of the experiments, the computation time cost is significantly influenced by the status of the experimental cluster. Accordingly, the results in a single trial could be unreliable. To ensure the robustness of the experiment results, all time costs are referred to the average ones over ten trials.

The time costs of implementing the SVD algorithms are shown in Fig. 1(a) and (b) using the Mahout (MapReduce) and MLlib (Spark) for the datasets Indian_Pine and Paiva, Respectively. From the experiments, one can see that the time cost of the SVD implemented by MapReduce is slightly faster than that by Spark on the same datasets when the singular value is taken as 1 due to

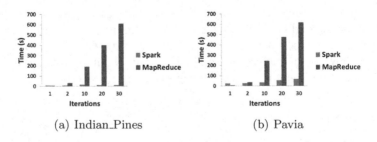

(a) Indian_Pines   (b) Pavia

Fig. 1. Time costs for the SVD algorithm with Spark and MapReduce, respectively.

the higher hardware resource requirements of Spark. In the following iterations, the time costs of SVD implemented by MapReduce significantly increases due to the I/O operations. However, the time costs for Spark only slightly increase to run the decomposition computation in the distributed environment.

4   Conclusion

In the paper, a big data platform has been proposed to process massive remote sensing data processing, where Spark is utilized for distributed computation to avoid the expensive I/O operations compared to the MapReduce model as the principle distributed computing framework. In particular, the proposed framework is comporised of YRAN as distributed resource scheduler and HDFS as distributed file system. To evaluate the effectiveness for massive remote sensing processing, the multi-iteration Singular Value Decomposition (SVD) has been implemented in the proposed platform by both Spark and MapReduce models. The experiments show that the time cost on the Spark-based platform is far less than that on the MapReduce platform.

Acknowledgement. This work was supported in part by Natural Science Foundation of China under contract 71331005, in part by Shanghai Science and Technology Development Funds (13dz2260200, 13511504300), and in part by the Open Foundation of Second Institute of Oceanography (SOA).

References

1. Bilotta, G., Sánchez, R.Z., Ganci, G.: Optimizing satellite monitoring of volcanic areas through gpus and multi-core cpus image processing: An opencl case study. Selected Topics in Applied Earth Observations and Remote Sensing, IEEE Journal of **6**(6), 2445–2452 (2013)
2. Borthakur, D.: The hadoop distributed file system: architecture and design. Hadoop Project Website **11**, 21 (2007)
3. Callico, G., Lopez, S., Aguilar, B., Lopez, J., Sarmiento, R.: Parallel implementation of the modified vertex component analysis algorithm for hyperspectral unmixing using opencl (2014)
4. CUDA: http://www.nvidia.com/object/cuda_home_new.html/
5. Dagum, L., Menon, R.: Openmp: an industry standard api for shared-memory programming. IEEE Comput. Sci. Eng. **5**(1), 46–55 (1998)
6. Dean, J., Ghemawat, S.: Mapreduce: simplified data processing on large clusters. Commun. ACM **51**(1), 107–113 (2008)
7. Ghemawat, S., Gobioff, H., Leung, S.T.: The google file system. In: ACM SIGOPS Operating Systems Review, vol. 37, pp. 29–43. ACM (2003)
8. Golpayegani, N., Halem, M.: Cloud computing for satellite data processing on high end compute clusters. In: IEEE International Conference on Cloud Computing, 2009. CLOUD 2009, pp. 88–92. IEEE (2009)
9. Grauer-Gray, S., Kambhamettu, C., Palaniappan, K.: Gpu implementation of belief propagation using cuda for cloud tracking and reconstruction. In: IAPR Workshop on Pattern Recognition in Remote Sensing (PRRS 2008), vol. 4, p. 2 (2008)

10. Johnpaul, C., Thampi, N.S.: Distributed in-memory cluster computing approach in scala for solving graph data applications. In: 2014 International Conference on Advances in Electronics, Computers and Communications (ICAECC), pp. 1–6. IEEE (2014)
11. Programming Language, S.: http://www.scala-lang.org
12. Lin, X., Wang, P., Wu, B.: Log analysis in cloud computing environment with hadoop and spark. In: 2013 5th IEEE International Conference on Broadband Network & Multimedia Technology (IC-BNMT), pp. 273–276. IEEE (2013)
13. Marchal, S., Jiang, X., State, R., Engel, T.: A big data architecture for large scale security monitoring. In: 2014 IEEE International Congress on Big Data (BigData Congress), pp. 56–63. IEEE (2014)
14. Pan, X., Zhang, S.: A remote sensing image cloud processing system based on hadoop. In: 2012 IEEE 2nd International Conference on Cloud Computing and Intelligent Systems (CCIS), vol. 1, pp. 492–494. IEEE (2012)
15. Tan, Y.K.A., Tan, W.J., Kwoh, L.K.: Fast colour balance adjustment of ikonos imagery using cuda. In: IEEE International Geoscience and Remote Sensing Symposium, 2008. IGARSS 2008, vol. 2, pp. II-1052. IEEE (2008)
16. Zaharia, M., Chowdhury, M., Franklin, M.J., Shenker, S., Stoica, I.: Spark: cluster computing with working sets. In: Proceedings of the 2nd USENIX Conference on Hot Topics in Cloud Computing, pp. 10–10 (2010)
17. Zhao, J., Zhou, H.: Design and optimization of remote sensing image fusion parallel algorithms based on cpu-gpu heterogeneous platforms. In: 2011 4th International Congress on Image and Signal Processing (CISP), vol. 3, pp. 1623–1627. IEEE (2011)

A Vehicle Routing Problem with Time Windows for Attended Home Distribution

Yi Qu, Feng Wu[⊠], and Wei Zong

Department of Industrial Engineering, School of Management, Xi'an Jiaotong University, 28 Xianning West Road, Xi'an 710049, People's Republic of China
fengwu@mail.xjtu.edu.cn

Abstract. The reliable and efficient last three mile of delivery results in enormous challenges for city logistics. In recent years, the combination of telematics based big data collection and O2O e-commerce has built the ground for time-dependent vehicle routing, which becomes extremely important in the home delivery applications. This paper proposes a logistics platform to solve the order fulfillment problem of on-demand delivery service with large quantities of orders. The problem can be considered as a special vehicle routing problem with considering the link time and cost between the store and the delivery destinations designated by customers, who are associated with time windows and vehicles with capacity. We then propose a Genetic Algorithm (GA) method. Experimental results show that the proposed approach is highly feasible and very potential in dealing with the present order fulfillment problem.

1 Introduction

According to the current figures, 65 % consumption of goods is to take place in around three kilometers, except staple commodities such as houses and cars. In this category of O2O services, most of the demands take place within three kilometers, of which the most typical pattern is restaurant takeout, laundry washing send, and the planned purchase of supermarkets in some areas. These all belong to the convenience and urgent demand of the people. The three mile delivery is currently regarded as one of the most expensive, least efficient and most polluting sections of the entire supply chain by Gevaers et al. 2010 [1]. Increasing customer requirements exacerbate flexibility of delivery. In urban areas, traffic infrastructure is often used to capacity, resulting in traffic jams. City logistics service providers compete against other road user for the scarce traffic space, which cannot be extended unlimitedly. Defiance of varying infrastructure utilization may lead to lower service quality, higher pollution and higher realization costs of delivery by Eglese et al. 2006 [2] and Maden et al. 2010 [3].

In a living delivery circle of three kilometers, instead of delivering from house to house by motor vehicle, the express of a short radius of three kilometers is a much more common logistics forms. Within the scope of a given distribution, such as in the district of three kilometers radius, users and logistics delivery staff are both disperse in this district, stores include restaurants, department stores, supermarkets, laundries, etc. Different from traditional logistics, in a three-kilometer business circle, a courier pickup and delivery cross the whole district, which constitute a discrete distribution network.

C. Zhang et al. (Eds.): ICDS 2015, LNCS 9208, pp. 127–134, 2015.
DOI: 10.1007/978-3-319-24474-7_18

In every business circle, generally with a point of service as its logistical support, information systems within the Terminal, a small amount of chilled, frozen, space. As every order is usually small but serves rather large number of customers with dispersed locations, it is crucial to carefully design the routes of the vehicles in order to reduce its operating cost while improving the service quality to customers.

This paper proposed adopted the logistics optimization platform based on intelligent scheduling and debris management mode, on which the dynamic information of a marching courier will be updated to the information system in real time, based on which the systems get the feedback of dynamic scheduling at work, when the delivery proceed, it will inevitably lead to some pieces of time, such as delivery waiting time, empty turn-back fragments, or fragments between two deliveries, which can share the cost to every single delivery active to reduce the whole costs through the intelligent scheduling to improve the efficiency of logistics operation, reduce logistics costs, improve service levels.

The paper is organized as follows. Section 2 reviews the literature on pickup and delivery problems with time window constraints, related problems and the methodologies. Section 3 describes the model assumptions. Section 4 reports on the computational experiments, followed by the managerial implications in Sect. 5. Finally, the conclusion and future research are discussed in Sect. 6.

2 Literature Review

As stated before, two main bodies of are relevant to our problem. The first is the vehicle routing problem with time windows, in which goods are transported by a fleet of vehicles between the depot and customers within their time windows. The second one is the vehicle scheduling problem (VSP) which is a major research field of logistics scheduling problems. We survey the literature in two parts.

Vehicle routing problem (VRP from now on) is the classic problem initially described Dantzig and Ramser in 1959 [4] and it derives from the traveling salesman problem or arc routing problem. This is basically a reflection of real life distribution problems like delivering and picking up passengers, mail, packages and different kind of goods. Since its proposition by Dantzig, it has received much attention in the scientific community and a lot of exact and also heuristic methods have been proposed to solve it. The VRP is a classic problem that represents the real life situations from distribution field. The VRP is a classic problem that represents the real life situations from distribution field. In theory it derives from two basic optimization problems: the traveling salesman problem (TSP) talked by Shmoys et al. 1985 [5], and arc routing problem. Numbers of methods have been developed to solve it, some are exact methods and others tried to solve it with heuristics. These methods have largely been used to solve VRP, some with more success than others as Hà et al. 2014 [6] and C. Liong, 2008 [7]. The VRP expands on the TSP with the addition of the bases.

VRP with time windows (VRPTW) is the standard extension by Toth and Vigo [8]. In this variation the customers have given time window when they are available for pickup of the goods. Variation of this kind of problem implements the soft time windows, where customer still operates outside of the time windows but visiting them in that time involves some form of penalty. This kind of the problem usually has a complex way of calculating the cost of the trips, where the creator has to decide what is more important to service all of the customers within the given time windows or to find the shortest route despite breaking some of the time constraints.

As mentioned before, there is an extensive amount of publications relating to container assignment for distribution problems. Most studies focus on the utilization of vehicular fleets and the corresponding resource assignment such as containers, 1993 [9] and vehicles, 1999 [10]. Sheu, 2006 [11] has proposed a dynamic customer resource model for city logistics distribution operations to reduce the aggregate operational costs and average lead time. Logistic activities scheduling is to make the optimized scheme for logistic activities including the start time, finishing time and the sequences of activities. The vehicle scheduling problem (VSP) is a major research field of logistics scheduling problems.

3   Model Assumptions

This paper addresses the daily scheduling problem of vehicles of home delivery. This section provides a formal description of the problem.

3.1   Assumptions

The problem consists in determining a set of routes of minimal overall cost in order to serve all delivery demands of all customers under the obvious time window and vehicle cost constraints and the following assumptions.

- There is more than one logistic vehicle. Each vehicle can undertake several distribution activities. The number of activities is not less than one.
- There is more than one store, and each store has several orders to distribution. And only one order can be process at a time for each store.
- Each vehicle can process only one activity at a time and each activity.
- The starting time of the first distribution activity is set at zero-time.
- Activities of each store are processed in sequence.
- The original location and destination of each activity are fixed and known.

  Each activity can be processed without interruption on one vehicle.

3.2   Parameters

The parameters and decision variables are defined in the following

- $V = \{V_1, V_2, \cdots, V_m\}$ indexed k, be a set of m logistic vehicle. Each vehicle V_k consists of a sequence of distribution activities. Let $V_{kl}, l \in \{1, 2, \cdots m_k\}$, m_k be activity l in sequence V_k. m_k denotes the number of activities in sequence V_k.
- Let $D = \{D_1, D_2, \cdots, D_n\}$ indexed i, be a set of store. Each store consists of a sequence of orders. Let $D_{ih}, h \in \{1, 2, \cdots n_i\}$, n_i be order h in sequence D_n.

- SD_i denotes the earliest available time of store i to process an activity and ED_i denotes the latest available time. Therefore the time window for store i is (SD_i, ED_i).in which the store i is available to process activities. The available time period is $TD_i = ED_i - SD_i$.
- $tV_{kl}D_{ih}$ is the operation time of the vehicle V_k process the order of the store D_n.
- $SV_{kl}D_{ih}$ and $EV_{kl}D_{ih}$ denote the starting time and the finishing time of order D_{ih} on distribution activities V_{kl} respectively. Therefore, $TV_{kl}D_{ih} = EV_{kl}D_{ih} - SV_{kl}D_{ih}$ is the processing time of order D_{ih}.
- Let $LV_{kl}D_{ih}D_{jg}$ be the joint time to connect two distribution activities between finishing time of store D_i which is processed on vehicle V_{kl} and the starting time of its immediate predecessors distribution activity $V_{k(l-1)}$ and store $D_j i, j \in \{1, 2, \cdots n\}, i, j \in \{1, 2, \cdots m\}$.

In this passage the objective is to minimize the total finishing time of all activities. And The total time cost C : $C = C_1 + C_2$, where C_1 denotes the total direct time of vehicles to finish their activities assigned, C_2 denotes the joint time associated to connect two sequential activities of store D_n which is processed on vehicle V_{kl} and its immediate predecessors activity $V_{k(l-1)}$.

Let $XV_{kl}D_{ih}$ is a variable. If the store order D_{ih} is processed $C_1 = \sum_{k=1}^{m} \sum_{i=1}^{n} \sum_{l=1}^{m_k} \sum_{h=1}^{n_i} XV_{kl}D_{ih}tV_{kl}D_{ih}$ on vehicle V_{kl}, then $XV_{kl}D_{ih} = 1$, otherwise, $XV_{kl}D_{ih} = 0$. So the total direct time of vehicles is:

$$C_1 = \sum_{k=1}^{m} \sum_{i=1}^{n} \sum_{l=1}^{m_k} \sum_{h=1}^{n_i} XV_{kl}D_{ih}tV_{kl}D_{ih} \tag{1}$$

In order to analysis the joint time, let $XV_{k(l-1)}D_{jg}$ is a variable. If the immediate predecessor activity $XV_{k(l-1)}D_{jg}$ of order D_{jg} is processed on vehicle V_{kl}, then $XV_{k(l-1)}D_{jg} = 1$, otherwise, $XV_{k(l-1)}D_{jg} = 0$. Only if $XV_{kl}D_{ih} = 1$ and $XV_{k(l-1)}D_{jg} = 1$ which mean that vehicle V_{kl} and its immediate predecessors activity $V_{k(l-1)}$ are order D_{ih} and D_{jg} respectively, $LV_{kl}D_{ih}D_{jg}$ can be included in C_2. So the joint time associated to connect two sequential activities of store is:

$$C_2 = \sum_{k=1}^{m} \sum_{i=1}^{n} \sum_{l=1}^{m_k} \sum_{j=1}^{n} \sum_{h=1}^{n_k} \sum_{g=1}^{n_k} XV_{kl}D_{ih}XV_{k(l-1)}D_{jg}LV_{kl}D_{ih}D_{jg} \tag{2}$$

Therefore the total time C to finish all orders is as following:

$$C = \sum_{k=1}^{m} \sum_{i=1}^{n} \sum_{l=1}^{m_k} \sum_{h=1}^{n_i} XV_{kl}D_{ih}tV_{kl}D_{ih}$$
$$+ \sum_{k=1}^{m} \sum_{i=1}^{n} \sum_{l=1}^{m_k} \sum_{j=1}^{n} \sum_{h=1}^{n_k} \sum_{g=1}^{n_k} XV_{kl}D_{ih}XV_{k(l-1)}D_{jg}LV_{kl}D_{ih}D_{jg} \tag{3}$$

For the second objective, the finishing time of all tasks is determined by the finishing time of the last activity. The starting time of activity D_{ih} of store i should be the latest time between the finishing time of its immediate predecessor activity $V_{k(l-1)}$ of store j, $V_{k(l-1)}D_{jg}$ plus the joint time between two activities, and the finishing time of the immediate predecessor activity V_{kl} of store I, $EV_{kl}D_{ih}$ plus the joint time between two activities. Therefore:

$$SV_{kl}D_{ih} = \max\{EV_{kl}D_{ih} + LV_{kl}D_{ih}D_{jg}, EV_{k(l-1)}D_{jg}\} \tag{4}$$

The finishing time of activity D_{ih} is as following:

$$EV_{kl}D_{ih} = \max\{EV_{kl}D_{ih} + LV_{kl}D_{ih}D_{jg}, EV_{k(l-1)}D_{jg}\} + tV_{kl}D_{ih} \tag{5}$$

3.3 Mathematical Model

Therefore, a scheduling model aiming at minimizing total operation time is formulated as follows:

$$C = \sum_{k=1}^{m}\sum_{i=1}^{n}\sum_{l=1}^{m_k}\sum_{h=1}^{n_i} XV_{kl}D_{ih}tV_{kl}D_{ih}$$

$$+ \sum_{k=1}^{m}\sum_{i=1}^{n}\sum_{l=1}^{m_k}\sum_{j=1}^{n}\sum_{h=1}^{n_k}\sum_{g=1}^{n_k} XV_{kl}D_{ih}XV_{k(l-1)}D_{jg}LV_{kl}D_{ih}D_{jg} \tag{6}$$

s.t.

$$SV_{kl}D_{ih} - SV_{k(l-1)}D_{jg} \geq TV_{k(l-1)}D_{jg} + LV_{kl}D_{ih}D_{jg}$$

$$SV_{kl}D_{ih} - SV_{k(l-1)}D_{i(h-1)} \geq TV_{k(l-1)}D_{i(h-1)} + LV_{kl}D_{ih}D_{jg}$$

$$S_{D_i} \leq SV_{kl}D_{ih}$$

$$EV_{kl}D_{ih} \leq E_{D_i}$$

Constraint ensures that the time difference between the starting time of activity V_{kl} on resource i and the starting time of the immediate predecessor activity $V_{k(l-1)}D_{jg}$ of store j is not less than the processing time of activity $V_{k(l-1)}$ of store i plus the joint time between the two activities. And the difference of starting time of two sequential activities in of a vehicle V_{kl} is not less than the processing time of immediate predecessor activity $TV_{k(l-1)}D_{i(h-1)}$ plus the joint time between two resources. The starting time of activity V_{kl} of store i is not earlier than the earliest available time of store I while the finishing time of activity V_{kl} of store i is not later than the latest available time of store i.

4   The Algorithm

The proposed activities scheduling model is a typical optimization problem in which cost time is objectives to be optimized. Therefore an improved GA is designed in this paper to solve the logistic scheduling problem.

It is needed not only to assign each activity a resource but also to make sequences of activities on the resources simultaneously in the logistic scheduling problem. Therefore, the genes of the chromosomes describe not only the assignment of activities to the resources, but also the sequence of the activities in the resources. A task-based representation is proposed in this paper. The chromosome consists of two strings. The first string is the activity-based representation which determines the sequence of activities. The second string is the resource-based representation which denotes the selected resources for corresponding activities of all tasks. Each chromosome represents a solution of scheduling. It has been proven that perverting the diversity of GA population can diminish the risk of premature convergence by Sevaux et al. 2006 [12]. A simple and stricter rule is imposed in this paper to keep the diversity of the population, i.e., the fitness of any two feasible chromosomes must be different.

5   Computational Tests

A logistics market is taken as an example to bench- mark the proposed model and algorithm. The scenarios of logistic tasks and resources nodes are shown in Tables 1 and 2. There are five vehicles which can be divided into several activities and eight stores available at that time. The data in Table 1 indicate the time needed for the vehicle on the first column to process the activity on the first row respectively. The dash mark in the table denotes that the vehicle on the first column could not be used to process the activity. The second row shows the time windows for stores on the top row.

Table 1. Time windows

	D_1	D_2	D_3	D_4	D_5	D_6	D_7	D_8
Time windows	8–30	5–28	0–30	4–32	0–25	8–24	0–18	0–12
V_1	6	8	/	8	/	6	/	6
V_2	4	/	14	8	/	12	2	12
V_3	8	8	4	6	9	8	5	8
V_4	/	/	/	10	/	/	8	3
V_5	12	4	/	12	/	10	/	8

The data in the Table 2 denote the time needed to link two activities processed by the vehicle on the left of the row and on the top of the column respectively.

The improved genetic Algorithm described above has been programmed in the Matlab language, the larger the population size, the better the quality of solutions and longer computing times. After many trials, we found that setting population size at 100, mutation rates among 0.01–0.02, cross over rate of GA among 0.8–0.9. The algorithm

Table 2. The link time

	D_1	D_2	D_3	D_4	D_5	D_6	D_7	D_8
D_1	1.45	0.45	0.15	0.05	2.5	1.05	0.8	1.25
D_2	1.25	2.1	1.4	2.3	1.25	/	1.65	0.7
D_3	0.8	0.55	2.75	0.3	2.05	1.65	/	0.55
D_4	0.15	0.7	1.95	0.95	0.4	0.7	0.55	/
D_5	2.5	1.35	0.05	1.65	/	1.25	2.05	0.4
D_6	/	/	0.5	1.8	1.35	2.1	0.55	0.7
D_7	0.15	0.5	/	0.2	0.05	1.4	2.7	1.95
D_8	0.05	1.8	0.2	/	1.65	2.3	0.3	0.95

was terminated after 200 generations of the genetic algorithm. The solutions are shown in Table 3. Among the three solutions with zero tardiness in Table 3, No.8 solution has the shortest finish time. Therefore, No.8 solution is selected as the best satisfied solution.

Table 3. The solutions

No	1	2	3	4	5	6	7	8
Time	24.7	30.6	26.1	29.9	30.1	28.7	27.7	25.1

6 Conclusion

In this paper, a system has been proposed to solve the vehicle problem with a large number of orders for stores. A model is utilized to distribution orders based on time of operation to the delivery vehicles. Then a genetic algorithm (GA) is used to optimize the vehicle route which has the shortest time.

Experimental results show that the system is promising in dealing with the distribution problem of store. The average time to distribution for the store is decreased, ensuring a higher service level. Further investigations are recommended to use the proposed approach to solve other similar optimization problems such as distribution according to distance.

References

1. Gevaers, R., Van de Voorde, E., Vanelslander, T.: Characteristics and typology of last-mile logistics from an innovation perspective in an urban context. In: Proceedings of WCTR 2010, Lisbon, Portugal (2010)
2. Eglese, R., Maden, W., Slater, A.: A road timetable to aid vehicle routing and scheduling. Comput. Oper. Res. **33**(12), 3508–3519 (2006)
3. Maden, W., Eglese, R., Black, D.: Vehicle routing and scheduling with time-varying data: a case study. J. Oper. Res. Soc. **61**, 515–522 (2010)

4. Dantzig, G.B., Ramser, J.H.: The truck dispatching problem. Manage. Sci. **4**, 80–91 (1959)
5. Shmoys, D.B., Lenstra, J.K., Kan, A.H.G.R., Lawler, E.L.: The Traveling Salesman Problem. Wiley, Chichester (1985)
6. Hà, M.H., Bostel, N., Langevin, A., Rousseau, L.-M.: An exact algorithm and a metaheuristic for the generalized vehicle routing problem with flexible fleet size. Comput. Oper. Res. **43**, 9–19 (2014)
7. Liong, C., Ismail, W.: Vehicle routing problem: models and solutions. J. Qual. Technol. **4** (1), 205–218 (2008)
8. Toth, P., Vigo, D.: An exact algorithm for the vehicle routing problem with backhauls. Transportation Science **31**, 372–385 (1997)
9. Crainic, T.G., Delorme, L.: Dual-ascent procedures for multi commodity location- allocation problems with balancing requirements. Transp Sci **27**, 90–101 (1993)
10. Hall, R.W.: Stochastic freight flow patterns: implications for fleet optimization. Transp. Res. A **33**(6), 449–465 (1999)
11. Jiuh-Biing, S.: A novel dynamic resource allocation model for demand- responsive city logistics distribution operations. Transp. Res. E **42**, 445–472 (2006)
12. Sensen, K., Sevaux, M.: MAjPM: memetic algorithms with population management. Comput. Oper. Res. **33**, 1214–1225 (2006)

Active Class Discovery by Querying Pairwise Label Homogeneity

Yifan Fu[1], Junbin Gao[1]([✉]), and Xingquan Zhu[2]

[1] School of Computing and Mathematics, Charles Sturt University,
Bathurst, NSW 2795, Australia
{yfu,jbgao}@csu.edu.au
[2] Department of Computer and Electrical Engineering and Computer Science,
Florida Atlantic University, Boca Raton, Fl 33431, USA
xzhu3@fau.edu

Abstract. Active learning traditionally focuses on labeling the most informative instances for some well defined learning tasks with known class labels, and a labeler is provided to label each queried instance. In an extreme case, the whole active learning task may start without any available information about the tasks, for instance, no labeled data are available at the initial stage and the labeler is incapable of providing the ground truth to each queried instance. In this paper, we propose an active class discovery method for the case where no randomly labeled instances exist to kick-off the learning circle and the labeler only has weak knowledge to answer whether a pair of instances belong to the same class or not. To roughly identify the classes in the data, a Minimum Spanning Tree based query strategy is employed to discover a number of classes from unlabeled data. Experiments and comparisons demonstrate superior performance of the proposed method for class discovery tasks.

Keywords: Active learning · Active class discovery · Pairwise constraint · Minimum spanning tree

1 Introduction

Active learning offers a solution by labeling a subset of the most informative data, with the objective of minimizing the labeling costs without significantly compromising the accuracy of the classifier trained from the labeled data. To date, most existing active learning methods assume that the total number of classes are known and that the labeler has expertise to provide a ground truth label for each queried instance. Under these circumstances, some randomly selected instances are labeled as the initial training set, so the active learning process can kick-off to gradually expand the training set.

However, in some cases, the class information in the data may be unknown beforehand. Because there is no labeled information available, the labeler may not accurately provide the ground truth to each queried instance, but can only answer simple questions like: whether a pair of instances belong to the same class

© Springer International Publishing Switzerland 2015
C. Zhang et al. (Eds.): ICDS 2015, LNCS 9208, pp. 135–140, 2015.
DOI: 10.1007/978-3-319-24474-7_19

or not? For this type of query, the labeler does not need to know the number and the type of classes in the data, but simply provides yes or no answers. In this paper, we refer to this as a "pairwise constraint" query.

For tasks with incomplete class information, Several methods exist to discover rare class samples by using likelihood [1], gradient [2] or clustering [3] criteria. However, all these methods assume that the number of classes (including rare classes) are known beforehand. Moreover, they all assume that labelers can provide ground truth labels for each queried instance, which is hardly the case in reality because the labeler may not have knowledge to label new class samples.

To this end, we propose a novel active class discovery method to roughly identify the classes in the data sets, where no randomly labeled instances exist to kick-off the learning circle and the labeler only has weak knowledge to answer whether a pair of instances belong to the same class or not. Our innovation is to explore the unknown classes efficiency with minimum query costs.

2   Active Class Discovery Based on Pairwise Constraint

2.1   Problem Formulation

Given a set of instances denoted by $\mathcal{D} = \{x_1, ..., x_n\}$, with each instance $x_i \in \mathbb{R}^{f \times 1}$ denoted by f features. The class label of x_i is denoted by y_i, which is unknown. The total class space is denoted by $\mathbb{L}$, which is also unknown and needs to be discovered and during active learning process. Our **aims** is to identify prt or all classes in D with minimum query efforts.

2.2   MST Based Class Discovery

Exhaustively querying pairwise instance relationships to determine the number of classes in D is expensive and out of question. To reduce the query costs, we propose to query the pairwise relationships on a small representative instance subset Γ, which is chosen in a random manner. After the classes on Γ are discovered, we can directly determine the number of classes in the original unlabeled data set D.

To save query costs, we built minimum spanning trees (MST) from Γ, and use MSTs to query pairwise instance relationships, through which we can discover the initial classes in D. Our method begins with a tree consisting of a single randomly picked vertex, which forms the initial forest. At each time, we select an unvisited vertex x^* in Γ, which has the minimum distance to the forest, and query its pairwise relationships with a set formed by one vertex from each tree in the current forest. According to the query results, we determine whether to extend the current forest by building a new tree, or to include x^* into one of the existing trees. We continuously increase the number of visited vertices, one vertex at a time, until all vertices in Γ are visited. Because the vertices connected in the same tree have the same pairwise constraints with x^*, we only query the pairwise relationship between x^* and one vertex in each tree, which effectively reduces the query cost. Algorithm 1 explains the general process of *Class Discovery.*

Algorithm 1. Active Class Discovery Process

Require: an unlabeled sample set D.
Ensure: discover the classes in the optimal subset Γ.
1: randomly choose k samples to generate a sample set Γ;
2: $x_{init} \leftarrow$ a random instance in Γ;
3: $T_1 \leftarrow x_{init}$;
4: $\Omega_T \leftarrow T_1$; MST forest with one tree;
5: **while** not all vertices in Γ are visited **do**
6:　$x^* \leftarrow$ instance with minimum distance to Ω_T;
7:　$\Psi \leftarrow \{x_1, \ldots, x_{|\Omega_T|}\}$, where $x_i \in T_i, (1 \le i \le |\Omega_T|)$ is one instance randomly selected from each tree;
8:　query (x^*, x_i), where $x_i \in \Psi, 1 \le i \le |\Omega_T|$;
9:　**if** exist $(x^*, x_i) \in$ **"Same Class"** **then**
10:　　$T_i \leftarrow x^*$, where $x_i \in T_i$;
11:　**else**
12:　　$T_{|\Omega_T|+1} \leftarrow x^*, \Omega_T \leftarrow T_{|\Omega_T|+1}$;
13:　**end if**
14: **end while**

---

3 Experiments

We implement our method and several baseline approaches using Java and WEKA data mining tools, and compare their performances on ten benchmark data sets, as shown in Table 1.

Table 1. A simple description of the benchmark data

ID	Dataset	Instances	Features	Classes
1	segement-challenge (sc)	1500	20	7
2	poker	25010	11	10
3	covertype	5000	10	7
4	letter recognition (lr)	20000	16	26
5	glass	214	10	6
6	vowel	990	10	11
7	MNIST	60000	50	10
8	fbis.wc	2463	2001	17
9	ERA	1000	5	19
10	yeast	1484	8	10

3.1 Query Number Comparisons Using Different Query Strategies

In Fig. 1, we report the query numbers with respect to different query strategies for class discovery. These methods are all built based on pairwise relationship queries, including a random selection in *RanPQC*, a maximum distance selection in *MaxSTC*, and a minimum distance selection in *MinSTC*. We apply these methods to help discover classes based on the representative instance subset built using the density-distance metric. In our implementation, *MaxSTC* has a similar framework with our *MinSTC*, which starts with a single vertex, and continuously increases the size of a tree, one edge at a time, until it spans all vertices. In contrast to *MinSTC*, the vertex having the longest distance to the existing tree vertices is visited each time. It also queries the pairwise constraints between the added vertex and the existing vertices in the trees to determine whether to build a new tree or include the instance into one of the existing trees. *RanPQC* randomly selects a pair of instances to query its label relationship at each time until the number of classes in the representative subset is identified.

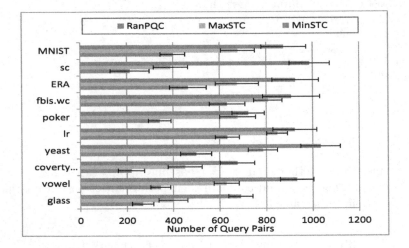

Fig. 1. Query number comparison with different query strategies.

For all benchmark data sets, *MaxSTC* and *MinSTC*, which share the same framework, are always superior to *RanPQC*. This observation suggests that using a heuristic strategy in pair query effectively reduces the query cost. Moreover, *MinSTC* performs better than *MaxSTC*. This is because the two instances near in the topology are more similar, with a high probability of belonging to the same class. When selecting the instance by using *MinSTC* strategy, a selected instance x is more likely from one of the existing groups, so only a very few queries are needed to validate whether x is from an existing class, or whether it is from a new class. On the other hand, an instance x selected by *MaxSTC* is dissimilar to the existing trees. So one has to query the pairwise relationships between x and all of the existing trees, and then starts to build a new tree (if x does not belong to any of the existing class).

3.2   Class Discovery Effectiveness Using Different Query Strategies

In Fig. 2, we report the discovered classes using different query strategies with the same number of queried pairs (i.e. 380 pairs). For all benchmark data sets, our new method *MinSTC* discovered most or even all classes in the datasets, which demonstrates that our active class discovery strategy is effective to discover classes with low query cost. Moreover, the performance of *MaxSTC* is always superior to *RanPQC*. This is mainly because the instance selected by MaxSTC is different from the existing trees and has higher possibility to find a new class than a randomly chosen instance has. Since *MinSTC* prefers the instance more similar to one of existing groups, it is capable of identifying the class of the selected instance with less queries than *MaxSTC* is. Accordingly, *MaxSTC* can find more classes than *MinSTC* as we expected.

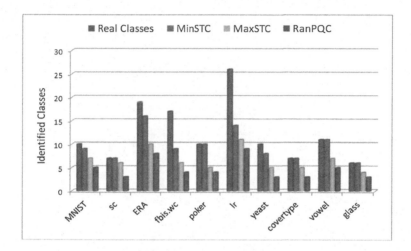

Fig. 2. Class Discovery comparison with different query strategies when querying 380 pairs.

4   Conclusions

In this paper, we propose a active class discovery paradigm where an unlabeled data set is given for active learning and the labeler does not know the number of classes in the data. To solve the problem, we introduce a MST based framework that discovers a number of candidate classes from the unlabeled data set. Experiments and comparisons demonstrate that our new active learning framework achieves superior performance compared to various baseline methods.

Acknowledgements. This work is supported by the Australian Research Council (ARC) through Discovery Project Grant DP130100364.

References

1. Pelleg, D., Moore, A.: Active learning for anomaly and rare category detection. In: Neural Information Processing System (2004)
2. He, J., Carbonell, J.: Nearest-neighbor-based active learning for rare category detection. In: Neural Information Processing System (2007)
3. Vatturi, P., Wong, W.K.: Category detection using hierarchical mean shift. In: SIGKDD, pp. 847–856 (2009)

Discovering Productive Periodic Frequent Patterns in Transactional Databases

Vincent Mwintieru Nofong[✉]

School of Information Technology and Mathematical Science,
University of South Australia, Adelaide, Australia
vincent.nofong@mymail.unisa.edu.au

Abstract. Periodic frequent pattern mining is an important data mining task for various decision making. However, it often presents a large number of periodic frequent patterns, most of which are not useful as their periodicities are due to random occurrence of uncorrelated items. Such periodic frequent patterns would most often be detrimental in decision making where correlations between the items of periodic frequent patterns are vital. To enable mine the periodic frequent patterns with correlated items, we employ a correlation test on periodic frequent patterns and introduce the productive periodic frequent patterns as the set of periodic frequent patterns with correlated items. We finally develop PPFP, an efficient Productive Periodic Frequent Pattern mining framework. PPFP is efficient and the productiveness measure removes the periodic frequent patterns with uncorrelated items.

Keywords: Frequent patterns · Periodic frequent patterns · Productiveness measure

1 Introduction

Periodicity detection in data has been widely studied in two distinct areas based on the data types: (i) time series data [2], and (ii) transactional data [3–10]. In time-series data, periodicity is detected under the names *segment* and/or *symbol periodicity* [2] while in transactional data it is detected under the names *periodic frequent patterns* (PFPs) [3–5,9,10] or *regular frequent patterns* (RFPs) [6–8]. Though transactional data can always be accumulated as time-series data, our work focuses on addressing some challenges on periodicity detection in transactional data.

PFP mining in transactional data was proposed by Tanbeer et al. in [10]. They used the maximal period among the occurrence periods of a pattern as its periodicity. Though this concept has been accepted and used in PFP mining in works such as [3–5,9], Rashid et al. [7] recently argued the proposed periodicity measure in [10] as inappropriate and susceptible to noise. To improve the definition, they define a patterns' periodicity based on the maximum variance of its periods and named the periodic patterns as *regular frequent patterns* (RFPs). Their concept has also been accepted and used in works such as [6,8].

© Springer International Publishing Switzerland 2015
C. Zhang et al. (Eds.): ICDS 2015, LNCS 9208, pp. 141–150, 2015.
DOI: 10.1007/978-3-319-24474-7_20

Though PFP mining in transactional data is useful in decision making such as predicting future customers' behaviours, disease control and website management, it is faced with two major challenges. Firstly, a large number of PFPs are often reported, of which most are not of interest to users since their periodicities are due to random occurrence of uncorrelated items. Such PFPs would most often be detrimental in decision making because they do not exhibit any inherent relationship among items. Secondly, in decision making where PFPs with similar periods are required, existing works often report PFPs with distinct periods making it difficult identifying PFPs with similar periods for decision making.

Motivated by these challenges on PFP mining in transactional data, we use a method to mine the set of productive PFPs as follows. Firstly, we restrict our periodicity measure to enable mine PFPs with similar periods. Subsequently, we employ a productiveness measure to mine the set of productive PFPs, that is, PFPs with inherent item relationships. We make the following contributions to the discovery of PFPs. We present a periodicity measure for mining the set of PFPs with similar periods and introduce the productive PFPs set. We propose and develop *PPFP*, an efficient productive PFP mining framework.

2   Preliminaries

Let $I = \langle i_1, i_2,..., i_n \rangle$ be a set of literals, called items. Then, a transaction is a nonempty set of items. A pattern S is a set of transactions satisfying some conditions of measures like frequency. A pattern is of length-k if it has k items, for example, $S = \{a, b, c\}$ is a length-3 pattern. Given a database of n transactions, $\mathbf{D} = < d_1, d_2, d_3, \ldots, d_n >$, where each d_m in $\mathbf{D}$ is identified by TID, m, which is also the time stamp. The *cover* of a pattern S in $\mathbf{D}$, $cov_{\mathbf{D}}(S)$, is the set of $TIDs$ of transactions that contain S. That is, $cov_{\mathbf{D}}(S) = \{m : d_m \in \mathbf{D} \wedge S \subseteq d_m\}$. We use the notation $e.cov_{\mathbf{D}}(S)$ to indicate the extension of $cov_{\mathbf{D}}(S)$ by the starting time 0 and the last time n. That is, $e.cov_{\mathbf{D}}(S) = \{0 \cup cov_{\mathbf{D}}(S) \cup n\}$, where $n = |\mathbf{D}|$. Because of set operation, n will not be duplicated even if it is already in $cov_{\mathbf{D}}(S)$. The *support* of a pattern S in $\mathbf{D}$, $sup_{\mathbf{D}}(S)$, is defined as, $sup_{\mathbf{D}}(S) = \frac{|cov_{\mathbf{D}}(S)|}{|\mathbf{D}|}$.

Frequent pattern mining is the process of discovering all patterns in a database, $\mathbf{D}$, whose supports are equal to or larger than a user specified minimum support (η). A pattern S in $\mathbf{D}$ is said to be productive in $\mathbf{D}$ if [11]: for all S_1, S_2 (such that, $S_1 \subset S$, $S_2 \subset S$, $S_1 \cup S_2 = S$, $S_1 \cap S_2 = \emptyset$), $sup_{\mathbf{D}}(S) > sup_{\mathbf{D}}(S_1) sup_{\mathbf{D}}(S_2)$.

Given a pattern S, let $m_j, m_{j+1} \in e.cov_{\mathbf{D}}(S)$ be two consecutive $TIDs$ of S. Then $p_j^S = m_{j+1} - m_j$ is the jth period of S. The set of all periods of S obtained from its extended cover, $e.cov_{\mathbf{D}}(S)$, is denoted as $P^S = \{p_1^S, \cdots, p_r^S\}$ where $r = |e.cov_{\mathbf{D}}(S)|$. For example, given $e.cov_{\mathbf{D}}(S) = \{0, 1, 4, 6\}$, then $p_1^S = (1 - 0) = 1$, $p_2^S = (4 - 1) = 3$, and, $P^S = \{1, 3, 2, 0\}$. To mine PFPs in transactional data, Tanbeer et al. [10] proposed a periodicity measure on patterns as follows.

Definition 1. *[10] Given a database* $\mathbf{D}$, *a pattern* S *and its set of periods* P^S *in* $\mathbf{D}$, *the periodicity of* S, $Per(S)$, *is defined as,* $Per(S) = \max\{p | p \in P^S\}$.

The periodicity of a pattern S in Definition 1, is the maximum period (time-interval) for which S does not appear in $\mathbf{D}$. For a given maximum threshold, say $maxPer$, Tanbeer et al. [10] consider a pattern S as periodic if $Per(S) \leq maxPer$. Definition 1 and the concept of periodic patterns proposed in [10] is used in PFP mining by works such as [3–5,9]. Recently, Rashid et al. [7] argued that the periodicity evaluation in [10] is inappropriate and susceptible to noise. To address this issue, they define the periodicity of a pattern under the name patterns' *regularity* as follows.

Definition 2. *[7] Given a database* $\mathbf{D}$, *a pattern* S *and its set of periods* P^S *in* $\mathbf{D}$, *the regularity of* S, $Reg(S)$, *is defined as* $Reg(S) = var(P^S)$, *where* $var(P^S)$ *is the variance of* P^S.

For a given maximum threshold, say $maxVar$, Rashid et al. [7] consider a pattern S as regular (periodic) if $Rer(S) \leq maxVar$. This has also been accepted and used in mining PFPs under the name *regular frequent patterns* in [6,8].

Table 1. Database

TID	Transaction
1	$\{a, b, c, f\}$
2	$\{d, e\}$
3	$\{a, f\}$
4	$\{c, d, e\}$
5	$\{a, b, f\}$
6	$\{b, d, e\}$
7	$\{a, c, f\}$
8	$\{c, d, e\}$
9	$\{a, b, f\}$
10	$\{a, d, e, f\}$

Though Definitions 1 and 2 have been accepted and used in mining PFPs, they often report a large number of PFPs, of which most are not useful as they are periodic due to random occurrence of uncorrelated items. Such PFPs will often be detrimental in decision making since they do not encode inherent relationships. It is also worth noting that works such as [3–10] often report a set of PFPs which have totally distinct regular periods in databases. For instance, in Table 2 (which shows the occurrence properties of the length-1 transactions from Table 1), given $maxPer = 3$, Definition 1 will report items $\{a\}$, $\{c\}$, $\{d\}$, $\{e\}$ and $\{f\}$ as periodic. Similarly, given $maxReg = 0.8$, Definition 2 will report items $\{a\}$, $\{c\}$, $\{d\}$, $\{e\}$ and $\{f\}$ as periodic (regular).

However, from Fig. 1, if we consider the support trends with time, $\{a\}$ and $\{f\}$ have similar occurrence periods which are totally distinct from those of

Table 2. Periodic intervals

Item	TID set	Period, P	$\bar{x}(P)$	$std(P)$	$var(P)$	$max(P)$
a	$\{1,3,5,7,9,10\}$	$\{1,2,2,2,2,1,0\}$	1.429	0.728	0.530	2
b	$\{1,5,6,9\}$	$\{1,4,1,3,1\}$	2.0	0.943	0.889	4
c	$\{1,4,7,8\}$	$\{1,3,3,1,2\}$	2.0	0.894	0.799	3
d	$\{2,4,6,8,10\}$	$\{2,2,2,2,2,0\}$	1.667	0.745	0.555	2
e	$\{2,4,6,8,10\}$	$\{2,2,2,2,2,0\}$	1.667	0.745	0.555	2
f	$\{1,3,5,7,9,10\}$	$\{1,2,2,2,2,1,0\}$	1.429	0.728	0.530	2

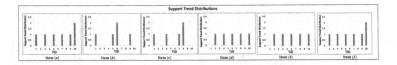

Fig. 1. Support trend distributions of length-1 items in Table 1

$\{d\}$ and $\{e\}$, and that of $\{c\}$. In decision making such as analysis of associated purchases where PFPs with similar occurrence periods are required, users will have to manually select from the reported PFPs those with similar periods.

3   Definitions and Problem Statement

With Definitions 1 and 2, sets of PFPs will be reported, however, some reported PFPs will not be useful as they might be formed by chance. In decision making such disease control where correlations (inherent relationships) among items of PFPs are vital, PFPs without inherent item relationships can be detrimental in decision making. Additionally, the reported PFPs might have totally distinct periods and average periods. In decision making where PFPs with similar periods are required, users will have to manually select from the reported PFPs those with similar periods. To avoid the above mentioned situations, we begin by defining the periodicity of a pattern as follows.

Definition 3. *Given a database* **D***, a pattern* S *and its set of periods* P^S *in* **D***, the periodicity of* S*,* $Prd(S)$*, is defined as* $Prd(S) = \bar{x}(P^S)$*, where* $\bar{x}(P^S)$ *is the mean of* P^S*.*

Though Definition 3 will report a set of PFPs, it may not present PFPs with similar periods. To enable mine the set of PFPs with similar periods in databases, we restrict our periodicity to a range and formally define a periodic frequent pattern as follows.

Definition 4. *Given a database* **D***, minimum support threshold,* η*, periodicity threshold,* p*, difference factor,* p_1*, a pattern* S *and* P^S*,* S *is a periodic frequent pattern if* $sup_D(S) \geq \eta$*,* $(p - p_1) \leq Prd(S) - std(P^S)$ *and* $Prd(S) + std(P^S) \leq (p + p_1)$*.*

In Definition 4, $std(P^S)$ is the standard deviation, while p and p_1 are user desired periodicity threshold, and difference factor respectively. We use the range $p \pm p_1$ in Definition 4 to ensure only PFPs with similar range of regular periods are reported. For example in Table 2, if $p = 1.4$ and $p_1 = 0.8$, only $\{a\}$ and $\{f\}$ which have similar regular periods will be reported as being periodic.

Though Definition 4 will report only PFPs with similar regular periods, some might not be useful as they might be periodic due to random occurrence of uncorrelated items. Such PFPs without inherent item associations will often be detrimental in decision making where inherent item associations are vital. To ensure only PFPs with inherent item associations are reported, we test for positive correlations among items of a PFP. We employ Property 1 for this test.

Property 1. For a pattern S and its period $Prd(S)$, S is productive if for all S_1, S_2 (such that, $S_1 \subset S$, $S_2 \subset S$, $S_1 \cup S_2 = S$, $S_1 \cap S_2 = \emptyset$), $\left(\frac{|D| - Prd(S)}{Prd(S) \cdot |D|} \right) > \left(\frac{|D| - Prd(S_1)}{Prd(S_1) \cdot |D|} \times \frac{|D| - Prd(S_2)}{Prd(S_2) \cdot |D|} \right)$.

Property 1 can be proven to be same as the proposed productivity test in [11].

Proof. For any pattern S_n, $\frac{|D| - Prd(S_n)}{Prd(S_n) \cdot |D|}$ in Property 1 can be re-written as $\frac{|D| - Prd(S_n)}{Prd(S_n)} \times \frac{1}{|D|}$ where $\frac{|D| - Prd(S_n)}{Prd(S_n)} = |cov_D(S_n)|$. Hence, $\frac{|D| - Prd(S_n)}{Prd(S_n) \cdot |D|}$ can thus be expressed as $\frac{|cov_D(S_n)|}{|D|} = sup_D(S_n)$. Hence Property 1 satisfies the productiveness test proposed in [11] as: $\left(\frac{|D| - Prd(S)}{Prd(S) \cdot |D|} \right) > \left(\frac{|D| - Prd(S_1)}{Prd(S_1) \cdot |D|} \times \frac{|D| - Prd(S_2)}{Prd(S_2) \cdot |D|} \right) = sup_D(S) > sup_D(S_1) \times sup_D(S_2)$. □

Base on Property 1, we define a productive PFP as follows.

Definition 5. *A PFP, S in* **D**, *is a productive PFP if, for all S_1, S_2 such that, $S_1 \subset S$, $S_2 \subset S$, $S_1 \cup S_2 = S$, and $S_1 \cap S_2 = \emptyset$, Property 1 is satisfied.*

Definition 5 requires a PFP, S in **D** is productive if and only if every subset that can be formed from it is productive (formed by items with inherent associations) in **D**. This productiveness measure for every subset is to ensure all items of a PFP are correlated and not due to random occurrences. The measure in Property 1 covers the case where a PFP has more than two subsets of items that are independent of one another [11]. Since the supersets of a non-productive pattern will always contain the non-productive pattern, we use the productiveness of patterns as one of our pruning strategies in *PPFP* to avoid reporting PFPs with non-productive subsets. In the rest of this work, we represent the set of PFPs discovered by Definition 5 in a database **D** as **Per$_D$**. Our problem can now be defined as, mining all productive PFPs in a database, **D**, with regards to a minimum support, η, periodicity threshold, p, and difference factor p_1.

4   Mining Productive Periodic Frequent Patterns

To efficiently mine the productive PFPs, we propose *PPFP*, an efficient productive PFP mining framework shown in Algorithm 1. *PPFP* employs the Apriori-like candidate generation technique in [1]. However, it stores the set of *TIDs* for each item to avoid repeated dataset scan and for quick implementation. Two major steps are employed in *PPFP*: (i) finding the set of frequent length-1 items, and, (ii) mining the set of productive PFPs from the frequent length-1 items.

Algorithm 1. PPFP(D, η, p, p_1)

Input: Database D, minimum support η, periodicity, p and difference factor, p_1
Output: Productive PFP set Per_D

1 Create set L; Create HashMap h_n
2 **for** *each transaction* $T \in D$ **do**
3   **for** *each length-1 item* $a_y \in T$ **do**
4   **if** $a_y \notin h_n$ **then**
5   Create $cov_D(a_y) = \{TID\}$
6   Add $(a_y, cov_D(a_y))$ to h_n
7   **else**
8   Let $(a_y, cov_D(a_y)) = h_n(a_y)$
9              $cov_D(a_y) = cov_D(a_y) + TID$
10   Update h_n with $(a_y, cov_D(a_y))$

11 **for** *each item* $a_y \in h_n$ **do**
12   Let $(a_y, cov_D(a_y)) = h_n(a_y)$
13   **if** $sup_D(a_y) \geq \eta$ **then**
14   Add $(a_y, cov_D(a_y))$ to L

15 Sort L in descending order of items
16 MinePFPs(L, η, p, p_1)
17 **return** Per_D

4.1   Finding Frequent Length-1 Items

This step (Line 1 to 15 of Algorithm 1) finds the set of frequent length-1 items and their coversets in **D** with regards to the minimum support (η). As shown in Line 13 of Algorithm 1, only length-1 items whose supports in **D** are greater than η are added to L. L is then sorted in item descending order in Line 15 of Algorithm 1. The set of productive PFPs are then mined from L in Line 16 of Algorithm 1 by calling MinePFPs().

4.2   Mining Productive PFPs

This step mines all productive PFPs from L by calling MinePFPs(L, η, p, p_1) (Algorithm 2) in Line 16 of Algorithm 1. Algorithm 2 mines the set of productive PFPs from L as follows. If there are no items in L, that is, $|L| = 0$, the productive PFP mining terminates. Else, while $|L| > 0$, the productive PFPs are mined from L in the nested for-loop (from Lines 3 to 20 of Algorithm 2) as follows.

Algorithm 2. MinePFPs(L, η, p, p_1)

Input: Set L, periodicity, p, difference factor, p_1, and minimum support η
Output: Productive PFP set Per_D

1 Create set TempL $= \emptyset$
2 Let $pr_{a_n}[0, b]$ be the the length-b prefix of a_n
3 **while** $|L| > 0$ **do**
4   **for** $k = 0$ *to* $|L|$-1 **do**
5   Let $(a_k, cov_D(a_k)) = L[k]$
6   **if** $|a_k| = 1$ **then**
7   Obtain P^{a_k} from $e.cov_D(a_k)$
8   Evaluate $Prd(a_k)$ and $std(P^{a_k})$ from P^{a_k}
9   **if** a_k *is periodic* **then**
10   Add a_k to Per_D /* length-1 items are productive */

11   **for** $l = (k + 1)$ *to* $|L|$-1 **do**
12   Let $(a_l, cov_D(a_l)) = L[l]$
13   **if** $pr_{a_k}[0, |a_k|$-1$] = pr_{a_l}[0, |a_l|$-1$]$ **then**
14   Create $S = (a_k \cup a_l, cov_D(a_k) \cap cov_D(a_l))$
15   **if** $supp_D(S) \geq \eta$ *and S is productive* **then**
16   Add S to TempL
17   Get P^S from $e.cov_D(S)$; Evaluate $Prd(S)$ and $std(P^S)$ from P^S
18   **if** S *is periodic* **then**
19   Add S to Per_D /* Based on Definition 5 */

20      $L =$ TempL; TempL.clear()
21 **return** Per_D

In the first for-loop within L (from index $k = 0$ to $|L|$-1), the item a_k and $cov_D(a_k)$ at the kth-index are obtained in Line 5 as $(a_k, cov_D(a_k)) = L[k]$. If a_k is a length-1 item, P^{a_k} is obtained from $e.cov_D(a_k)$ in Line 7. $Prd(a_k)$ and $std(P^{a_k})$ are then obtained from P^{a_k} in Line 8. If a_k is periodic, it is added to Per_D in Line 10. While still at the kth-index, the second for-loop within L (from index $l = (k + 1)$ to $|L|$-1) starts in Line 11 as follows. For each item, a_l in the lth-index, a_l and $cov_D(a_l)$ are obtained in Line 12 as $(a_l, cov_D(a_l)) = L[l]$. In Line 13, if a_k and a_l have common length-$(|a_k| - 1)$ prefixes (that is, $pr_{a_k}[0, |a_k|$-1$] = pr_{a_l}[0, |a_l|$-1$]$), a candidate frequent pattern, S, is created in Line 14 as $S = (a_k \cup a_l, cov_D(S) = cov_D(a_k) \cap cov_D(a_l))$.

In Line 15, if S is frequent and productive in **D**, it is added to TempL in Line 16. This ensures only frequent and productive patterns are kept as they both follow the anti-monotone property. In Line 17, the set of periods of S, P^S are then obtained from $e.cov_D(S)$ and, $Prd(S)$, $std(P^S)$ evaluated. If $Prd(S) \pm std(P^S)$ falls within the periodicity range $(p \pm p_1)$, S is added to Per_D in Line 19. For each kth-index in the first for-loop, the second for-loop repeats till all indexes in L are iterated in the second for-loop. When both nested loops are complete, L is re-created in Line 20 from TempL, after which the content of TempL cleared. The size of L is checked and the nested looping repeats on L until $|L| = 0$.

The set of productive PFPs are then returned in Line 21 and the PFP mining process terminates. For lack of space we do not illustrate our PFP mining process.

5   Experimental Analysis

The following implementations were used in our experimental analysis:

-PPFP: This is our implementation based on Definitions 4 and 5. *PPFP* detects and reports the set of productive PFPs with similar regular periods. The productiveness measure is used as a pruning strategy to ensure PFPs due to random occurrence of uncorrelated items are removed, and for fast PFP discovery.

-PPFP+: This is our implementation based on only Definition 4 without the productiveness measure. *PPFP+* detects and reports both productive and non-productive PFPs with similar regular periods.

-Existing: This is our implementation of the approach proposed in [10]. *Existing* detects and reports PFPs whose maximum periods fall below the given periodicity threshold p.

All compared approaches are implemented in Java and experiments carried on a 64-bit Windows 7 PC (Intel Core i5, CPU 2.50GHz, 4GB). For lack of space we show results on only Kosarak25K data.

-Time Performance and Scalability. Figure 2, shows the runtime of the three compared frameworks in the Kosarak25K dataset. As can be seen, *PPFP* is significantly more time efficient in PFP discovery compared to both *PPFP+* and *Existing*. We also observed that the runtime for PFP detection were not significantly affected by increasing or decreasing periodicity threshold (p).

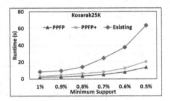

Fig. 2. Runtime at $\varepsilon = 30$

-Effect of Productiveness Measure on Reported PFPs. Table 3 shows the number of reported PFPs for the three compared approaches. We observed that the productiveness measure removes quite a number of non-productive PFPs. We also noticed that for a given minimum support, the number of detected PFPs in *Existing* increases proportionally with increasing periodicity threshold (p). In *PPFP* and *PPFP+* however, the number of detected productive PFPs and PFPs do not increase exponentially as p increases unless the difference factor

Table 3. Reported PFPs in Kosarak25K

η	PPFP			PPFP+			Existing		
	$p = 15$	$p = 150$	$p = 200$	$p = 15$	$p = 150$	$p = 200$	$p = 15$	$p = 150$	$p = 200$
	$p_1 = 14.5$	$p_1 = 135$	$p_1 = 190$	$p_1 = 14.5$	$p_1 = 135$	$p_1 = 190$			
0.8 %	13	2	13	16	4	17	1	36	62
0.7 %	13	6	45	16	9	54	1	36	62

p_1 is also incremented by the same proportion. The disadvantage of employing the maximum period in PFP mining was also observed. For instance, in the Kosarak25K dataset, though patterns such as $\{6, 11\}$, $\{1, 11\}$ and $\{6, 218\}$ have regular periods between 15 ± 14.5, they were missed by *Existing* as their noisy maximum periods, 22, 78 and 106 respectively are greater than 15.

6   Conclusions and Future Works

Productive PFPs are frequent patterns whose regular periodic occurrences in databases are not due to random occurrence of uncorrelated items. We have presented a measure to identify PFPs with similar regular periods, and a measure to identify the set of productive PFPs in databases. We subsequently develop *PPFP*, an efficient framework for mining the set of productive PFPs in transactional databases. Our future works include an extension of *PPFP* to enable predict future occurrence times of periodic frequent patterns.

References

1. Agrawal, R., Srikant, R.: Mining sequential patterns. In: 11th IEEE International Conference on Data Engineering, pp. 3–14 IEEE (1995)
2. Elfeky, M.G., Aref, W.G., Elmagarmid, A.K.: Periodicity detection in time series databases. IIEEE Trans. Knowl. Data Eng. **17**(7), 875–887 (2005)
3. Uday Kiran, R., Krishna Reddy, P.: Towards efficient mining of periodic-frequent patterns in transactional databases. In: Bringas, P.G., Hameurlain, A., Quirchmayr, G. (eds.) DEXA 2010, Part II. LNCS, vol. 6262, pp. 194–208. Springer, Heidelberg (2010)
4. Kiran, R.U., Kitsuregawa, M.: Novel techniques to reduce search space in periodic-frequent pattern mining. In: Bhowmick, S.S., Dyreson, C.E., Jensen, C.S., Lee, M.L., Muliantara, A., Thalheim, B. (eds.) DASFAA 2014, Part II. LNCS, vol. 8422, pp. 377–391. Springer, Heidelberg (2014)
5. Kiran, R.U., Reddy, P.K.: An alternative interestingness measure for mining periodic-frequent patterns. In: Yu, J.X., Kim, M.H., Unland, R. (eds.) DASFAA 2011, Part I. LNCS, vol. 6587, pp. 183–192. Springer, Heidelberg (2011)
6. Kumar, V., Valli Kumari, V.: Incremental mining for regular frequent patterns in vertical format. Int. J. Eng. Tech. **5**(2), 1506–1511 (2013)
7. Rashid, M.M., Karim, M.R., Jeong, B.-S., Choi, H.-J.: Efficient mining regularly frequent patterns in transactional databases. In: Lee, S., Peng, Z., Zhou, X., Moon, Y.-S., Unland, R., Yoo, J. (eds.) DASFAA 2012, Part I. LNCS, vol. 7238, pp. 258–271. Springer, Heidelberg (2012)
8. Rashid, M.M., Gondal, I., Kamruzzaman, J.: Regularly frequent patterns mining from sensor data stream. In: Lee, M., Hirose, A., Hou, Z.-G., Kil, R.M. (eds.) ICONIP 2013, Part II. LNCS, vol. 8227, pp. 417–424. Springer, Heidelberg (2013)
9. Surana, A., Kiran, R.U., Reddy, P.K.: An efficient approach to mine periodic-frequent patterns in transactional databases. In: Cao, L., Huang, J.Z., Bailey, J., Koh, Y.S., Luo, J. (eds.) PAKDD Workshops 2011. LNCS, vol. 7104, pp. 254–266. Springer, Heidelberg (2012)

10. Tanbeer, S.K., Ahmed, C.F., Jeong, B.-S., Lee, Y.-K.: Discovering periodic-frequent patterns in transactional databases. In: Theeramunkong, T., Kijsirikul, B., Cercone, N., Ho, T.-B. (eds.) PAKDD 2009. LNCS, vol. 5476, pp. 242–253. Springer, Heidelberg (2009)
11. Webb, G.I.: Self-sufficient itemsets: an approach to screening potentially interesting associations between items. ACM Trans. Knowl. Discov. Data 4(1), 3:1–3:20 (2010)

Building Computational Virtual Reality Environment for Anesthesia

Xinyu Cao[1], Peng Zhang[1], Jing He[1(✉)], and Guangyan Huang[2]

[1] College of Engineering and Science, Victoria University,
Melbourne, VIC, Australia
jing.he@vu.edu.au
[2] School of Information Technology, Deakin University,
Melbourne, VIC, Australia

Abstract. In this paper, a Computational Virtual Reality Environment for Anesthesia (CVREA) is proposed. Virtual reality, data mining, machine learning techniques will be explored to develop (1) an immersive and interactive training platform for anaesthetists, which can greatly improve their training and learning performance; (2) a knowledge learning environment which collects clinical data with greater richness, process data with more efficacy, and facilitate knowledge discovery in anaesthesiology.

1 Introduction

Anesthesia is crucial and indispensable for modern surgical operations. Generally speaking, anaesthetists are responsible for tranquilizing the patients during the surgery, keeping the patients' physiological status stable, and managing crisis in the operating theatre. To safely perform surgical anaesthesia, both solid theoretical knowledge and proficiency in practical skills are demanded for an anaesthetist [1]. However, the acquisition of such knowledge and practical skills takes time. The traditional training methods for anaesthesia include cadavers, video demonstration, ultrasound guidance, and most importantly an apprenticeship mode. Such apprenticeship mode employs the time-honored approach of "see one, do one, teach one", where trainees are supervised by experienced anaesthetists and hone their skills on live patients. Obviously, this apprenticeship approach is limited by the supply of real-life cases and availability of cost-intensive medical facilities. The shorter lengths of specialist training and reduction of working hours of trainees result in less exposure to the wide range of potential critical events. Consequently, trainees would become less competent to handle those critical events when they are expected to respond rapidly and correctly in independent practice [2]. Besides, critical events can evolve rapidly in practical anaesthesia, it is challenging for even the most experienced anaesthetists to correctly recognize the situation and react appropriately in a time-critical manner. Although various kinds of sophisticated monitoring equipment have been introduced into modern operating theatre to keep track of patients' physiological status, physiological data analysis techniques are so limited that anaesthetists still need to rely on their own expertise for recognition and decision-making.

C. Zhang et al. (Eds.): ICDS 2015, LNCS 9208, pp. 151–158, 2015.
DOI: 10.1007/978-3-319-24474-7_21

Therefore, this paper has two goals: (1) to propose a Computational Virtual Reality Environment for Anaesthesia (CVREA) which provides an effective and efficient training platform for anaesthetists; (2) to incorporate data mining and machine learning techniques into the proposed CVREA so that it can learn how to process physiological data via observing and analyzing the recorded training process supervised by human experts.

The rest of this paper is organized as follows: background study is conducted in Sect. 2; Sect. 3 presents the details of the project design; and finally we reach conclusion in Sect. 4.

2 Background Study

In this paper, we adopt the definition of Virtual Reality (VR) as interactive computer-generated environments that accurately simulate the realistic world and incorporate a first-person perspective. Virtual Reality has its root in the research of simulation conducted by aerospace and defense industries [2]. The first VR-based simulation system was developed by the US General Electric Company for the space program [13]. As to civilian and commercial use, flight simulator has been one of the most successful applications of VR-based simulation technology which has allegedly helped the industry reduce 50 % of human-error-related airline crashes [5]. Mortality rate of air travel is commonly used as a yardstick to benchmark the risk of anaesthesia [14–17]. Over 20 years period between 1993 and 2012, the odds of being killed on a single airline flight was 1 in 4.7 million for 78 major world airlines, 1 in 19.8 million for the best-performed airlines, and 1 in 2.0 million for the worst-performed airlines (Fig. 1). In contrast, risk of anaesthetic sole mortality in the 1990s–2000s was 34 per million for the whole world, 25 per million for the developed countries, and 141 for the developing countries (Fig. 2). Considering the anaesthetic contributory mortality, the risk of anaesthesia was even higher. The risk of anaesthesia is much higher than that of air travel.

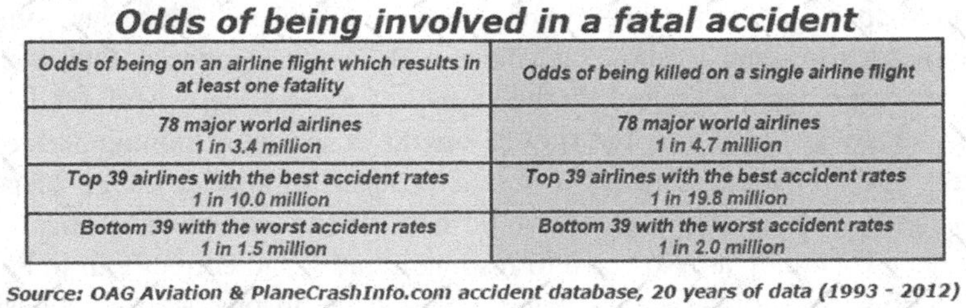

Odds of being involved in a fatal accident

Odds of being on an airline flight which results in at least one fatality	Odds of being killed on a single airline flight
78 major world airlines 1 in 3.4 million	78 major world airlines 1 in 4.7 million
Top 39 airlines with the best accident rates 1 in 10.0 million	Top 39 airlines with the best accident rates 1 in 19.8 million
Bottom 39 with the worst accident rates 1 in 1.5 million	Bottom 39 with the worst accident rates 1 in 2.0 million

Source: OAG Aviation & PlaneCrashInfo.com accident database, 20 years of data (1993 - 2012)

Fig. 1. Odds of being involved in a fatal aviation accident [18]

Comparisons between aviation and anaesthesia care are common. They are both high-technology, high-stake. And there are several significant parallels between life in the cockpit and life in the operating theatre: high-technology equipment; team work; high stress; complex and potentially unpredictable environment; time-critical data

	Events	Weighted event rate per million (95%CI)	p value for subgroup interaction	
			By HDI	By decade
Anaesthetic sole mortality				
Pre-1970s*	403/1294158	357 (324-394)	..	<0·00001
High HDI	403/1294158	357 (324-394)	NA	..
Low HDI	NR	NR	..	..
1970s-80s	86/2380920	52 (42-64)	..	..
High HDI	50/1761384	32 (24-42)	<0·00001	..
Low HDI	36/619536	101 (72-140)	..	..
1990s-2000s	186/8990012	34 (29-39)	..	..
High HDI†	151/8610720	25 (21-30)	<0·00001	..
Low HDI†	32/274692	141 (100-199)	..	..
Anaesthetic contributory mortality				
Pre-1970s*	925/1625266	650 (610-693)	..	<0·00001
High HDI	867/1447338	684 (642-729)	<0·00001	..
Low HDI	58/177928	326 (252-422)	..	..
1970s-80s	332/1176999	323 (290-360)	..	..
High HDI†	150/649744	234 (200-275)	<0·00001	..
Low HDI†	180/475127	432 (373-500)	..	..
1990s-2000s	395/5950293	143 (129-157)	..	..
High HDI	275/5641048	85 (75-96)	<0·00001	..
Low HDI	120/309245	467 (391-559)	..	..

Fig. 2. Anaesthetic mortality rate [19]

processing and reaction, to name a few. Safety is the key issue and concern shared by these two professions. After more than a century of evolvement, aviation safety has achieved remarkable result. Anaesthetists have been applying those lessons learned by aviation to make anaesthesia safer: pre-operation assessment and planning; checklist and backup plan; standardized procedure and safety protocols; systematic review of processes; and training using simulators. Both the cockpit and operating theatre are high-technology equipped (Figs. 3 and 4). Pilots and anaesthetists both have to be able to use those technologies with a great deal of proficiency and accuracy. During the operation, there are many variables to be monitored and interpreted. And there is a wide range of potential critical events to be handled. Therefore, both professions require intensive training and education. In aviation industry, sophisticated simulators have been developed using advanced hardware and software. Specific designed computer-generated flight simulation program together with the full-size cockpit replica provide an immersive and interactive environment for the trainee pilots (Fig. 3). In contrast, medical simulation is less mature and less effective. Most commonly, a medical mannequin is connected to the real monitors and anaesthetic machines via computer console (Fig. 4). This kind of simulation is less sophisticated, less flexible, and most of the time task-specific. An alternative approach is to utilized Virtual Reality technology to recreate a virtual anaesthetic scenario. Some VR-based surgical simulators have been developed for training (Fig. 4). Although these simulators have gained some success [25], they are exclusively designed for particular surgeries and hence cannot be used for anaesthesia purpose.

Modern aircrafts are equipped with various kinds of advanced sensors which capture and monitor critical parameters for the flight. These data are collected, monitored, processed, and displayed by a highly integrated system. Pilots are technically well-supported, hence can focus more on decision-making more rapidly and correctly. During a flight, the flight data recorder automatically and continuously preserves logs information about control and sensors while the cockpit voice recorder records the

Fig. 3. Left: real aircraft cockpit [20]; Middle: simulation cockpit [21]; Right: fixed base flight simulator [22]

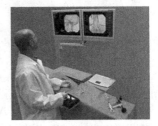

Fig. 4. Left: real operating theatre [23]; Middle: medical simulation using mannequin [24]; Right: endovascular simulator [25]

sounds in the cockpit. These recordings can be reviewed and investigated after aviation accidents and incidents. Therefore, problems can be identified and recognized. Accordingly, improvement can be achieved afterwards to make air travel safer. Advanced sensor technologies have also been introduced into operation theatres for decades. Nevertheless, the physiological data processing techniques are so limited that the anaesthetists still need to rely on their own knowledge for interpretation. Despite the complexity of physiological signals, what hinders the progress of research is often the lack of quality data. Ideally, the data should consist of as much information as possible to reproduce what happened during the operation. But in reality, the existing recordings are only partial in the sense that some valuable information is not included (surgeon's action, patient's complexion, flow of gas, vocalization of patients, etc.). Moreover, the recordings are not well-annotated since they are meant to be read by anaesthetists rather than data analyst, which makes it even harder to translate the clinical knowledge into engineering terms.

3 Project Design

The principal objective of this project is to build a Computational Virtual Reality Environment for Anaesthesia (CVREA) using virtual reality, data mining, and machine learning techniques. The proposed CVREA will serve as: (1) a training platform which simulates real anaesthesia operation and enables the trainees to effectively and efficiently practice anaesthetic skills; (2) a knowledge learning environment which can analyze physiological data, recognize patients' situation, identify critical events, predict potential crisis, and propose possible treatments.

3.1 Training Platform

The past 40 years has witnessed simulation as a powerful tool in many nonmedical fields, including aviation, nuclear power, and the military, in which sophisticated technical skills are necessary [3, 4]. One outstanding example is aviation simulator which has allegedly helped the industry reduce 50 % of human-error-related airline crashes [5]. Previous studies also have supported the efficacy of simulation in enhancing technical, behavioural, and social skills in medicine [6–10]. Among all modern simulation approaches [11], Virtual Reality is the most powerful one in that it can provide trainees and educators a realistic representation of complex clinical environments and allow trainees to develop their skills while protecting patients from unnecessary risk. Nevertheless, the application of VR-based training environment for anaesthetists so far has lagged behind other high-technology and high-risk professions mainly due to (1) limit to accurate modelling of complex human pathophysiology; (2) lack of rigorous scientific evidence of efficacy [12].

Our proposed CVREA will help trainees and anaesthetists to improve their teaching and learning performance more efficiently and more effectively. We propose to achieve this goal in three stages. Firstly, we design and implement our proposed CVREA which comprises three components: immersion, interactivity, and feedback. CVREA's software components will be implemented using OpenGL, VC++, 3DMAX modeling, and collision detection algorithm while cutting-edge VR devices will be utilized to facilitate human-computer interaction. Experienced anaesthetists will be highly involved to provide domain knowledge and be interviewed to elicit project-specific requirements with regard to anaesthetists training. Physiological data recordings of real cases will be obtained from collaborating local hospitals and employed as part of the knowledge base. Secondly, we develop and validate a scoring scheme, which leads to unbiased and structured assessment of learning performance of prospective users (trainees, anaesthetists). The proposed scoring scheme should be able to faithfully reflect users' level of competency and proficiency. Otherwise, we will not be able to keep track of users' progress and determine whether they can proceed to the next stage. Thirdly, we will establish training effect of our proposed CVREA by conducting observation and evaluation on real-life anaesthesia operations. Trainee anaesthetists have to achieve expert performance level defined in the second stage before they can proceed to this stage. Here, we essentially go back to the traditional apprenticeship mode of anaesthetist training. And we use this stage to validate CVREA's efficacy, and use the outcome as scientific evidence to build confidence of the anaesthetist society in our research.

3.2   Knowledge Learning Environment

Modern operating theatres are equipped with sophisticated sensors which are used to keep track of vital physiological parameters of the patients. Anaesthetists interpret these physiological data using their domain knowledge, make judgment, and react correspondingly. The problem is that physiological signals are very complex, and there is a wide range of possibilities. A crisis event may develop so fast that exceeds human brain's processing speed. Besides, there are still some crisis events that have not been fully understood. Even the most experienced anaesthetists cannot recognize them.

It becomes a natural idea to utilize the computational power of computers to analyze these data on behalf of anaesthetists. But there is a gap between the two disciplines. On one side, anaesthetists possess the clinical knowledge but don't know how to process the data in an engineering way. On the other side, data scientists cannot produce clinically interpretable data processing result without domain knowledge. It would be ideal if the researchers have solid knowledge from both sides. But it is hardly the case. A feasible alternative is to provide the data scientists with data well-annotated by the anaesthetists. Currently the available data recorded by the hospitals are meant for the anaesthetists rather than the data scientists. Therefore, the annotations are very simple. It is understandable since the anaesthetists had no time to give details during the operation. And they would not have time to go over thousands of historical data records and annotate them piece by piece given their busy schedules. Besides, the historical data records from the hospitals only include the sensory data and dosage of drugs. But information about other factors could also be helpful in data analysis and knowledge learning. For example, the surgeon's actions might explain sudden changes of some physiological parameters; vocalization of patients might indicate their anaesthetic is becoming "too light" [2]. It is hard to update the existing settings of operation theatres and whole data recording system to include these factors.

In our proposed CVREA, we simulate the anaesthesia scenario using real-life historical data and provide an interactive environment for the trainees and supervisors. Since the training sessions are carried out in the program-generated virtual world, data collection becomes much easier and complete. The trainees are essentially interacting with data objects. The system can record the whole process of the training session: the patient's physiological status, the trainee's actions, and the supervisor's feedbacks, etc. The anaesthetists become contributors of data. They can halt simulation for discussion, experience rare events, make errors and explore the consequences, and undertake any specific training session repetitively. The supervisors can review the training sessions, provide valuable comments and feedbacks, and evaluate trainees' performance. All these information will be recorded and then feed to the embedded data mining and machine learning algorithms. Since the training sessions are created based on real cases, the participants are actually reviewing and rehearsing the past cases, and our learning algorithms are observing the whole process and learning from the experts. To fully take advantage of the richness of data, we propose to develop a learning algorithm using data mining and machine learning techniques. The outcome will be a data processing algorithm which will not only deliver accurate alarms of immediate crisis events but also provide early warning of imminent adverse events. These alarms and warning will be fully interpretable, which means the anaesthetists can be better supported in decision making and focus on remedy. Moreover, our proposed learning algorithm can be used to facilitate discovery of new knowledge of anaesthesiology.

4 Conclusion

In this paper, we propose a Computational Virtual Reality Environment for Anaesthesia. Virtual Reality technologies are employed to simulate the real-life anaesthesia environment where anaesthetists can undertake training sessions. As a training platform, CVREA allows anaesthetists to hone their skills more efficiently, more effectively, and without posing any risk to patients. The proposed CVREA is also a knowledge learning environment. When trainees take training sessions in the virtual environment, more informative data regarding the anaesthesia operations can be collected. Knowledge learning algorithm will be developed to explore the richness of the collected data, facilitate data processing and knowledge discovery.

References

1. Grottke, O., et al.: Virtual reality-based simulator for training in regional anaesthesia. Br. J. Anaesth. **103**, 594–600 (2009). aep224
2. Burt, D.E.: Virtual reality in anaesthesia. Br. J. Anaesth. **75**(4), 472–480 (1995)
3. Wiener, E.L., Nagel, D.C. (eds.): Human Factors in Aviation. Gulf Professional Publishing, Houston (1988)
4. Wiener, E.L., Kanki, B.G., Helmreich, R.L. (eds.): Cockpit Resource Management. Gulf Professional Publishing, Houston (1993)
5. Levin, A.: Fewer crashes caused by pilots. USA Today, p. 2, March 2, 2004
6. Issenberg, S.B., et al.: Effectiveness of a computer-based system to teach bedside cardiology. Acad. Med. **74**(10), S93–S95 (1999)
7. Schwid, H.A., et al.: Use of a computerized advanced cardiac life support simulator improves retention of advanced cardiac life support guidelines better than a textbook review. Crit. Care Med. **27**(4), 821–824 (1999)
8. Logan, I.P., et al.: Virtual environment knee arthroscopic training system. Simul. Ser. **28**, 11–16 (1996)
9. Tuggy, M.L.: Virtual reality flexible sigmoidoscopy simulator training: impact on resident performance. J. Am. Board Fam. Pract. **11**(6), 426–433 (1998)
10. Small, S.D., et al.: Demonstration of high-fidelity simulation team training for emergency medicine. Acad. Emerg. Med. **6**(4), 312–323 (1999)
11. Ziv, A., Small, S.D., Wolpe, P.R.: Patient safety and simulation-based medical education. Med. Teach. **22**(5), 489–495 (2000)
12. Ziv, A., et al.: Simulation-based medical education: an ethical imperative. Acad. Med. **78**(8), 783–788 (2003)
13. Rolfe, J.M., Staples, K.J. (eds.): Flight Simulation, vol. 1. Cambridge University Press, Cambridge (1988)
14. Gaba, D.M.: Anaesthesiology as a model for patient safety in health care. BMJ. Br. Med. J. **320**(7237), 785 (2000)

158   X. Cao et al.

15. Cooper, J.B.: No myth: anesthesia is a model for addressing patient safety. Anesthesiology **97**(6), 1335–1337 (2002)
16. Lagasse, R.S.: Anesthesia safety: Model or myth. Anesthesiology **97**(6), 1609–1617 (2002)
17. Merry, A.F., et al.: International standards for a safe practice of anesthesia 2010. Can. J. Anesth./J. Can. d'anesthésie **57**(11), 1027–1034 (2010)
18. http://www.planecrashinfo.com
19. Bainbridge, D., et al.: Perioperative and anaesthetic-related mortality in developed and developing countries: a systematic review and meta-analysis. Lancet **380**(9847), 1075–1081 (2012)
20. en.wikipedia.org
21. www.simjet.com.au
22. www.virtualaviation.co.uk
23. www.pixshark.com
24. www.healthcaredesignmagazine.com
25. Kunkler, K.: The role of medical simulation: an overview. Int. J. Med. Robot. Comput. Assist. Surg. **2**(3), 203–210 (2006)

Study of the Noise Level in the Colour Fundus Images

Toufique Ahmed Soomro and Junbin Gao[✉]

School of Computing and Mathematics,
Charles Sturt University, Bathurst, NSW 2795, Australia
etoufique@yahoo.com, jbgao@csu.edu.au

Abstract. Diabetic Retinopathy (DR) causes vision loss insufficiency due to impediment rising from high sugar level conditions disturbing the retina. The Progression of DR occurs in the Foveal avascular zone (FAZ) due to loss of tiny blood vessels of capillary network. Due to image acquisition process of fundus camera, the colour retinal fundus image suffers from varying contrast and noise problems. To overcome varying contrast and noise problem in fundus image, the technique has been implemented. The technique is contained on the Retinex algorithm along with stationary wavelet transform. The technique has been applied on 36 high resolution fundus (HRF) image database contain the 18 bad quality images and 18 good quality images. The RETSWT (RETinex and Stationary Wavelet Transform) developed with introduces denoising techniques. Stationary wavelet transform is used as denoised technique. RETSWT achieved the average PSNR improvement of 2.39 db good quality images else it achieved the average PSNR improvement of 2.20 db in the bad quality images. The RETSWT image enhancement method potentially reduces the need of the invasive fluorescein angiogram in DR assessment.

1 Introduction

Eye screening using fundus imaging is essential and significant for detecting and monitoring of diabetic retinopathy (DR). The main purpose of the screening is to recognise patients with effect of DR on his vision so that crucial cure would be given for avoidance of vision loss [1]. These DR progress are characterized by the presence of pathologies such as haemorrhages, exudates and changes in the veins [2]. It has been observed that retinal vasculature features analysed in DR are the loss of tiny capillaries retinal network due to the increase in the size of the Foveal avascular zone (FAZ) [3]. Research on the investigation of colour fundus images originate that the size of the fovea avascular zone increased with the disease progress level of DR [4]. The macula region known as FAZ can be observed in colour fundus images and the perifoveal capillary network can only be seen in fundus fluorescein angiograms (FFA) [5].

The goal of the this research work is to address the issues of removal of noise from the image, when retinal imaging is performed by colour fundus camera but without contrasting agents injected into subjects. Moreover, the present procedure of assessing DR is based on the FFA images [6]. A different image enhancement method was developed to extract the retinal vasculature from digital colour fundus images [7].

© Springer International Publishing Switzerland 2015
C. Zhang et al. (Eds.): ICDS 2015, LNCS 9208, pp. 159–168, 2015.
DOI: 10.1007/978-3-319-24474-7_22

In this work, the PSNR improvement of the digital colour fundus images have been further examined using RETSWT (RETinex and Stationary Wavelet Transform) on the High-Resolution Fundus (HRF) image database [8].

The RETSWT is developed to handle the problem of varying contrast and noise level of colour fundus images. The technique contained two stages. First stage contains overcoming the problem of varying contrast in colour fundus images by using Retinex algorithm. In second stage, Stationary wavelet transform is used to handle the noise level of colour fundus images. It is the fact that medical imaging methods produce noise. Stationary wavelet transform improves the strength of signal by removing noise. The Green band image of colour fundus image possess the best contrast as compared to red and blue channel image, so it is considered as haemoglobin image because according to biological structure of retinal images, it contained the three retinal pigment macular, melanin and haemoglobin, the haemoglobin contained blood vessels so the green band image of colour fundus image gave more visualisation of blood vessels so it is considered as haemoglobin image [7].

The main theme of this work is to study the presence of noise level in the retinal fundus images. The fundus fluorescein angiograms (FFA) image contains high contrast but it is not preferred due contrast injection in to the subjects. In order to achieve the high contrast image similarly to FFA image without contrast injecting agent but noise in the colour fundus image effect the contrast. It is necessary to handle noise level of colour fundus. The novelty of this paper is presented the proposed technique named RETSWT for handling the noise level in the colour fundus images.

2 Proposed Approach

The proposed digital image enhancement technique is the combination of the two techniques Retinex and stationary wavelet technique (SWT), also known as RETSWT. The first stage of the proposed technique involves contrast normalization through the Retinex algorithm [9] and the second stage performs denoising of object of interest using stationary wavelet transform (SWT) method as depicted in Fig. 1. The three channels green, blue and red of the colour fundus image are processed by the Retinex algorithm to normalise the varied contrast. Next, SWT is performed to obtain denoised green band image. But after analysis the Results of RETSWT, the PSNR is used as evaluation parameter of its performance. The main theme of developed non-invasive image enhancement technique for colour retinal image is to get better contrast image in order to reduce the use of invasive method due to its side effects. The Retinex image contained the noise and it effects the visualisation of tiny blood vessels. The Wavelet transforms denoised technique named as stationary wavelet transform is used after Retinex algorithm to denoise Retinex image in order to get the best visualization of tiny capillaries. The proposed RETSWT technique is shown in Fig. 1. Details of the operation of proposed technique is explained in the following subsections.

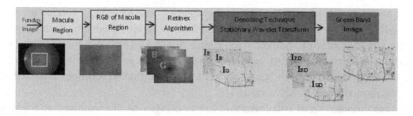

Fig. 1. Proposed image enhancement technique for colour retinal fundus image

2.1 Retinex Algorithm

As shown in Fig. 1, the RGB of colour fundus channel is processed through the Retinex algorithm to get the normalised images of it. The foveal avascular zone is considered as smallest region of the digital colour fundus image is known the macula of fundus image and it is considered as the region of interest. The McCann algorithm [9] is used for contrast normalisation and operation is based on the transformation of each colour channel from linear to logarithm form to streamline the process of multiplication to addition and division to subtraction [10]. The iterative Retinex algorithm is grounded on arithmetic operation ratio-product-reset and average. Comparing resulting in the revision of a newer product or initial estimated product in each process of pixel comparison has been performed by using ratio and product operation. The average operation is used to update the estimate reflectance of image [9]. In general, we can say that the arithmetic based operation is performed by calculating the ratio between I (in specific channel) and its spatially shifted input version and offset by some distances formulated as Eq. 1.

$$\log S^*_{x,y} = \frac{\text{Reset}\left[\left(\log M_{x,y} - \log N'_{xs,ys}\right) + \log S_{xs,ys}\right] + \log S_{x,y}}{2} \qquad (1)$$

where $\left(\log M_{x,y} - \log N'_{xs,ys}\right)$ show the ratio and $\left[\left(\log M_{x,y} - \log N'_{xs,ys}\right) + \log S_{xs,ys}\right]$ represents the product in log domain. Reset operation is achieved to update the maximum intensity giving to number iteration. The $\log S(x,y)^*$ is a result of averaging with $\log S'(x,y)$ and $\log S(x,y)^*$ itself is an updated output produced in each iteration that will be used as an input for next iteration till the final reflectance is obtained at given last iteration.

2.2 Wavelet Transform for Denoising

Image acquisition process produces the noise and which gives poor quality image. There are many techniques used for denoising the image. Wavelet transform is most used to denoise image because it removes the noise and preserve the details of image [11]. The wavelet transform is based on the suitable threshold values. There are many methods being used for setting the threshold limits of the wavelet transform [12]. The translation invariable wavelet transformation technique are widely used for images denoised and it is also known the stationary wavelet transform [13]. Stationary wavelet transform (SWT) is in category of non-orthogonal wavelet transform. Redundancy and translation invariability are main characteristics of SWT. The SWT may obtain through revision of the classical discrete wavelet transformation and give output factor to the low pass filter rather than high pass filter and gives original resolution denoised signal with application of threshold value [14].

The hard threshold and soft threshold are two types of thresholding and which are also named as shrinkage. The approximation of the noise level, which is generally premeditated from the variance of signals and achieved value is used as threshold [15, 16]. The wavelet coefficient are obtained through applying threshold values and the method to include Mallat et al.'s [17] projected Mold maximum value processing algorithm. Xu et al. [18] suggested denoising algorithm based on threshold value, Donoho et al. [16] also proposed threshold value denoising algorithm. Thresholding is not an easy task and finding the optimum threshold value (λ) is very important in wavelet based denoised technique. The resultant coefficients may contain noises due to a small threshold value thus they produce noised output signal as well. The suitable threshold is required to remove the noise as well as maintain the details of images. The method is proposed and the threshold value t proposed as Eq. 2.

$$t = C(\sigma - (AM - GM)) \tag{2}$$

The σ is the standard deviation of noisy image. We use the proposed concept by Donoho et al. [16] based on the variance of noise as shown Eq. 3.

$$t = \sigma\sqrt{2\log n} \tag{3}$$

The n is the size of the processed signal along with standard deviation and threshold value t. In this case; the standard deviation σ after wavelet sub bands the first high frequency parameters estimates gets as Eq. 4.

$$\sigma = \frac{\text{Median}(X)}{0.6745} \tag{4}$$

Generally in wavelet transform sub bands, as the level raises the coefficients of sub band come to be smoother and lost details. The term C is comprised for this purpose to make the threshold value which is given as Eq. 5,

$$C = 2(L - K) \tag{5}$$

Where L is decomposition level of wavelet transform, k is the sub bands level. The term |AM - GM| gave absolute value of difference between arithmetic mean and geometric mean of specific sub band. These proposed methods are used to get good quality denoised image with preserve image details [19]. The AM and GM mathematical shown as Eqs. 6 and 7.

$$AM = \frac{1}{M \times N} \sum_{i=1}^{M} \sum_{j=1}^{N} X(i,j) \tag{6}$$

$$GM = \left[\prod_{i=1}^{M} \prod_{j=1}^{N} X(i,j) \right]^{\frac{1}{M \times N}} \tag{7}$$

The algorithm of proposed stationary wavelet transformation is enlightened in the following steps.

1. Apply the wavelet transform on the image.
2. Calculate the threshold values according above explained methods
   a. Measure Standard deviation according to Eq. 4.
   b. Find the decomposition level of each sub band by using Eq. 5.
   c. Calculate threshold value by using Eq. 1.

2.3   Signal to Noise Ratio of the Fundus Images

Peak Signal to Noise Ratio (PSNR) is a ratio between value of signal level or image and the value of the noisy signal or image [20]. Scientifically is shown in Eq. 8.

$$PSNR = 20 \log_{10} \left(\frac{R}{\sigma} \right) \tag{8}$$

In the Eq. 8, the σ is the variance of the image intensities and R is the maximum value of the image, it may be range from 0 to 255 because it is considered as peak intensity of a digital image.

3   Result Analysis and Discussion

Consider Tables 1 and 2 in which results of 36 images of High resolution fundus (HRF) images database [21] are elaborated as example, which shows the PSNR improvement between Retinex image (PSNRRet) and Retinex denoised image of each applied denoised technique named Stationary wavelet transform are shown in Fig. 1. PSNR improvement (IMSWT) between PSNR Retinex image (PSNRRet) and PSNR of stationary wavelet transform (SWT) of denoised Retinex image (PSNRSWT) is 2.39 db in the good quality images else 2.20 db in the bad quality images. It is observed that SWT gave PSNR improvement between denoised Retinex image and Retinex image up to 2 db in the mages High resolution fundus (HRF) images database.

For further analysis, it is observed that average PSNR of Retinex images on good quality and bad quality images are 39.23 dB and 39.72 dB respectively after applying stationary wavelet transform, the average PSNR of SWT denoised images on good quality and bad quality images are 41.63 dB and 41.92 dB respectively as shown in Fig. 2.

Table 1. Good quality images of HRF images database

S.No	PSNRRet	STDRERT	PSNRSWT	STDSWT	PSNRIMP	STDIM
PSNR of good quality image						
Image 1	37.44	1.08	39.99	0.87	2.55	0.21
Image 2	38.08	0.92	40.78	0.64	2.70	0.28
Image 3	39.91	1.22	41.98	1.05	2.07	0.17
Image 4	39.95	1.24	42.12	1.03	2.17	0.21
Image 5	38.73	0.96	41.35	0.68	2.62	0.28
Image 6	38.58	1.01	41.08	0.89	2.50	0.12
Image 7	38.88	1.06	41.10	0.61	2.22	0.45
Image 8	39.08	1.25	41.58	0.99	2.50	0.26
Image 9	39.48	1.31	41.51	1.01	2.03	0.30
Image 10	39.18	1.25	41.63	1.02	2.45	0.23
Image 11	38.93	1.02	41.31	0.69	2.38	0.33
Image 12	40.64	1.74	43.98	1.39	3.34	0.35
Image 13	40.84	1.67	42.70	1.41	1.86	0.26
Image 14	39.71	1.24	43.01	0.62	3.30	0.62
Image 15	39.04	1.29	41.84	0.73	2.80	0.56
Image 16	39.09	1.21	41.02	0.59	1.93	0.62
Image 17	40.19	1.56	41.29	1.15	1.10	0.41
Image 18	38.47	1.03	41.03	0.79	2.56	0.24
Average PSNR	**39.23**	**1.23**	**41.63**	**0.90**	**2.39**	**0.33**

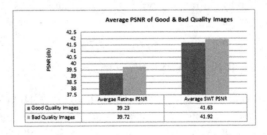

Fig. 2. Average PSNR of good & bad quality images of HRF image database

It observed that proposed technique RETSWT is working much better on bad quality images and gave almost similarly PSNR improvement of 2.2 dB as compared to 2.39 dB in the good quality images as shown in Fig. 3.

It is observed that average Standard deviation of Retinex images on good quality and bad quality images are 1.23 and 1.26 respectively, this shows that more noise is presented in the bad quality image, after applying stationary wavelet transform, the average Standard deviation of SWT denoised images on good quality and bad quality images are 0.9 and 1.02 respectively a shown in Fig. 4. This indicates that SWT algorithm reduce the noise level in the retinal fundus images and gave more details of images.

Table 2. Bad quality images of HRF image database

PSNR of bad quality image						
S.No	PSNRRet	STDRERT	PSNRSWT	STDSWT	PSNRIMP	STDIM
Image 1	39.74	1.24	41.58	1.02	1.84	0.22
Image 2	40.68	1.52	42.38	1.26	1.70	0.26
Image 3	41.52	1.62	44.35	1.41	2.83	0.21
Image 4	39.98	1.23	42.31	1.03	2.33	0.20
Image 5	42.51	1.65	43.92	1.38	1.41	0.27
Image 6	42.65	1.71	44.85	1.41	2.20	0.30
Image 7	39.77	1.19	43.63	0.95	3.86	0.24
Image 8	39.92	1.17	41.05	0.99	1.13	0.18
Image 9	38.45	1.04	41.25	0.77	2.80	0.27
Image 10	38.41	1.01	41.20	0.75	2.79	0.26
Image 11	39.19	1.21	39.68	1.01	0.49	0.20
Image 12	36.61	0.87	41.21	0.64	4.60	0.23
Image 13	37.45	0.94	38.25	0.61	0.80	0.33
Image 14	39.74	1.27	42.01	1.06	2.27	0.21
Image 15	39.47	1.18	41.70	1.03	2.23	0.15
Image 16	39.57	1.23	41.23	0.98	1.66	0.25
Image 17	39.39	1.28	41.58	1.04	2.19	0.24
Image 18	39.97	1.24	42.36	1.01	2.39	0.23
Average PSNR	**39.72**	**1.26**	**41.92**	**1.02**	**2.20**	**0.24**

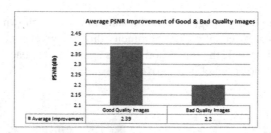

Fig. 3. Average PSNR improvement of good and bad quality images of HRF image database

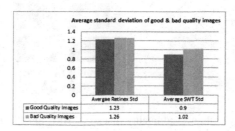

Fig. 4. Average standard deviation of good and bad quality images of HRF image database

It observed that proposed technique RETSWT is working much better on bad quality images and gave almost similarly Standard improvement of 0.24 as compared to 0.33 in the good quality images as shown in Fig. 5.

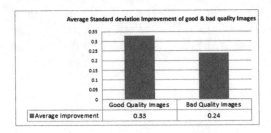

Fig. 5. Average standard deviation improvement of good and bad quality images of HRF image database

The average PSNR and Standard deviation improvement on HRF image database is 2.29 dB and 0.28 as shown in Table 3.

Table 3. PSNR and standard deviation improvement of HRF image database

Average improvement	HRF image database
PSNR (dB)	2.29
STD	0.28

The some good quality images and bad quality images are shown in the Fig. 6. It is observed that colour macular region of fundus did not give good details of blood vessels else after RETSWT, the tiny blood vessels against in the background are clearly observed as well as noise level is improved.

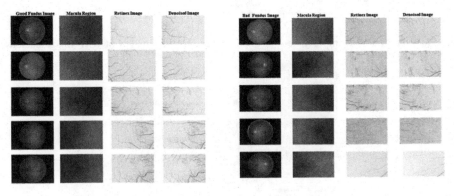

Fig. 6. Good and bad quality images of HRF image database

4   Conclusion

Due to varied and low contrast in the digital colour fundus image and presence of noise make it is difficult to analyse the tiny blood vessels in the macula region. The noises effect the contrast enhancement technique and make it difficult to analyse the capillary network of fundus image for diagnose of DR progress. Fundus Fluorescein angiography gave better contrast images; it is not considerable because it required contrast injecting agent. In this work, the RETSWT was developed by combining the Retinex technique and stationary wavelet transform. The Retinex technique is used for normalised the contrast of image and stationary wavelet transform is used to reduce noise level of image. The technique is applied on the High Resolution Fundus (HRF) image database and technique worked successfully and more tiny blood vessels are observed as well as noise level improved. For future work as it is believed that PSNR effect the contrast of image and through this techniques higher contrast image is obtained as compared to FFA image. The aim theme of this research work is to validate the effect of noise on the blood vessels and develop full image enhancement technique to get good visualisation of blood vessels in order to reduce the invasive method FFA.

Acknowledgement. The research project is supported by the Australian Research Council (ARC) through the grant DP140102270.

References

1. Zhitao, W.J.X., Qian, Z., Jiangtao, X.: Diabetic retinopathy fundus image processing based on phase information. In: International Conference on Control, Automation and Systems Engineering (CASE 2011), pp. 1–3 (2011)
2. Niemeijer, M., van Ginneken, B., Cree, M.J., Mizutani, A., Quellec, G., Sanchez, C.I., et al.: Retinopathy online challenge: automatic detection of microaneurysms in digital color fundus photographs. IEEE Trans. Med. Imaging **29**, 185–195 (2010)
3. Goh, P.: Status of diabetic retinopathy among diabetics registered to the diabetic eye registry, national eye database. Med J. Malaysia **63**, 24–28 (2007)
4. Hani, A.F.M., Nugroho, H.A., Nugroho, H.: Gaussian Bayes classifier for medical diagnosis and grading: application to diabetic retinopathy. In: 2010 IEEE EMBS Conference on Biomedical Engineering and Sciences (IECBES), pp. 52–56 (2010)
5. Nugroho, H.A.: Non-Invasive image enhancement of colour retinal fundus image for computerised diabetic retinopathy monitoring and grading system. Ph.D. Thesis Electrical and Electronics Engineering Programme, Universiti Teknologi PETRONAS (2012)
6. Malaysia, P.D.: Clinical Practice Guidelines (CPG) Management of Type 2 Diabetes Mellitus. Ministry of Health Malaysia, Malaysian Endocrine and Metabolic Society, Academy of Medicine Malaysia (2009)
7. Hani, A.F.M., Ahmed Soomro, T., Nugroho, H., Nugroho, H.A.: Enhancement of colour fundus image and FFA image using RETICA. In: 2012 IEEE EMBS Conference on Biomedical Engineering and Sciences (IECBES), pp. 831–836 (2012)
8. Budai, A., Hornegger, J., Michelson, G.: Multiscale approach for blood vessel segmentation on retinal fundus images. Invest. Ophthalmol. Vis. Sci. **50**, 325–326 (2009)

9. Funt, B., Ciurea, F., McCann, J.: Retinex in MATLAB™. J. Electron. Imaging **13**, 48–57 (2004)
10. Ying, L., Renjie, H., Guizhi, X., Changzhi, H., Yunyan, S., Lei, G., et al.: Retinex enhancement of infrared images. In: 30th Annual International Conference of the IEEE Engineering in Medicine and Biology Society (EMBS 2008), pp. 2189–2192 (2008)
11. Zhengmao, Y., Mohamadian, H., Yongmao, Y.: Quantitative effects of discrete wavelet transforms and wavelet packets on aerial digital image denoising. In: 2009 6th International Conference on Electrical Engineering, Computing Science and Automatic Control, CCE, pp. 1–5 (2009)
12. Tongzhou, Z., Yanli, W., Ying, R., Yalan, L.: Approach of image denoising based on discrete multi-wavelet transform. In: International Workshop on Intelligent Systems and Applications (ISA 2009), pp. 1–4 (2009)
13. Mitiche, L., Adamou-Mitiche, A.B.H., Naimi, H.: Medical image denoising using dual tree complex thresholding wavelet transform. In: 2013 IEEE Jordan Conference on Applied Electrical Engineering and Computing Technologies (AEECT), pp. 1–5 (2013)
14. Raj, V.N.P., Venkateswarlu, T.: Denoising of medical images using undecimated wavelet transform. In: Recent Advances in Intelligent Computational Systems (RAICS), pp. 483–488. IEEE (2011)
15. Jun-Hai, Z., Su-Fang, Z.: Image denoising via wavelet threshold: single wavelet and multiple wavelets transform. In: Proceedings of 2005 International Conference on Machine Learning and Cybernetics, vol. 5, pp. 3232–3236 (2005)
16. Donoho, D.L.: De-noising by soft-thresholding. IEEE Trans. Inf. Theory **41**, 613–627 (1995)
17. Shensa, M.: The discrete wavelet transform: wedding the a trous and Mallat algorithms. IEEE Trans. Sig. Process. **40**, 2464–2482 (1992)
18. Xu, W., Yin, X.: An Signal denoising method based on modified wavelet threshold filtering for ocean depth. In: Jin, D., Lin, S. (eds.) Advances in Computer Science, Intelligent System and Environment. AISC, vol. 105, pp. 153–158. Springer, Heidelberg (2011)
19. Li, H., Wang, S.: A new image denoising method using wavelet transform. In: International Forum on Information Technology and Applications (IFITA 2009), pp. 111–114 (2009)
20. Jong-Sen, L.: Digital image enhancement and noise filtering by use of local statistics. IEEE Trans. Pattern Anal. Mach. Intell. **2**, 165–168 (1980)
21. Odstrcilik, J., Kolar, R., Budai, A., Hornegger, J., Jan, J., Gazarek, J., et al.: Retinal vessel segmentation by improved matched filtering: evaluation on a new high-resolution fundus image database. IET Image Process. **7**(4), 373–383 (2013). http://digital-library.theiet.org/content/journals/10.1049/iet-ipr.2012.0455

Optimal Search Plan Model for Lost Aircraft

Luyao Zhu[1(✉)], Wenxi Hao[1(✉)], and Zhiwei Zhu[2(✉)]

[1] China University of Political Science and Law,
No. 27, Fuxue Street, Changping District, Beijing, China
luyao.z@hotmail.com, haowenxi108@163.com
[2] Tianjin Polytechnic University, No. 399, Binshuixi Road, Tianjin, China
812070350@qq.com

Abstract. In this passage, we intend to determinate the specific searching plan for lost aircraft on the basis of big data application. First, it uses the Neural Network Model to solve the problem about area classification by means of SOM. Then, we cope with Maximum Flow Problem by BFS, in order to the determination of cruise route.

1 Introduction

With development of computer science and statistics, *Big Data* is no longer a new word to us all. In this passage, we are focusing on figuring out the optimal searching plan for lost plane on the basis of big data application. It is not a difficulty to determine the best searching region, but how to find out the optimal searching route and allocate the searching power in the searching region is very troublesome since we have so much information to deal with during the searching period. Now we are going to make search and rescue plans, which may be related to our courses of Operational Research, Computer Science, Topology, Computer Simulation and so on. First, we will try to divide our search team into 3 groups and to allocate tasks to each one. Then, we'll attempt to find a best searching route which allows us to find the lost aircraft in the least time at the lowest cost. The searching stage can be divided into 2 sections according to spatial location, which are searching above and on the sea and searching under water. Here we are focusing on the searching above and on the sea.

1.1 Notations

Notations in Model 1

(1) s is the current iteration.
(2) α is the iteration limit.
(3) p is a target input data vector in the input data set D.
(4) $D(p)$ is a target input data vector.
(5) a is the index of the node in the map.
(6) W_a is the current weight vector of node a.
(7) b is the index of the best matching unit (BMU) in the map.
(8) $\theta(b, a, s)$ is a restraint due to distance from BMU, usually called the neighborhood function.

© Springer International Publishing Switzerland 2015
C. Zhang et al. (Eds.): ICDS 2015, LNCS 9208, pp. 169–177, 2015.
DOI: 10.1007/978-3-319-24474-7_23

(9) $\beta(s)$ is a learning restraint due to iteration progress.

Notations in Model 2

(1) nd is the number of nodes.
(2) i or j is the node, $0 < i,j < nd$.
(3) $e(i,j)$ is the path from i to j.
(4) $le(i,j)$ is the value of the path $e(i,j)$.

2   Model 1: Neural Network Model in Classification Problems

2.1   Introduction of SOM

A self-organizing map (SOM) or self-organizing feature map (SOFM) is a type of artificial neural network (ANN) that is trained using unsupervised learning to produce a low-dimensional (typically two-dimensional), discretized representation of the input space of the training samples, called a map. Self-organizing maps are different from other artificial neural networks in the sense that they use a neighborhood function to preserve the topological properties of the input space.[1]

2.2   A Variant Algorithm

(1) Randomize the map's nodes' weight vectors.
(2) Traverse each input vector in the input data set.
    (2.1) Traverse each node in the map.
        (2.1.1) Use the Euclidean distance formula to find the similarity between the input vector and the map's node's weight vector.
        (2.1.2) Track the node that produces the smallest distance (this node is the best matching unit, BMU).
    (2.2) Update the nodes in the neighborhood of the BMU (including the BMU itself) by pulling them closer to the input vector.
        (2.2.1) $W_a(s+1) = W_a(s) + \theta(b,a,s) * \beta(s) * (D(p) - W_a(s))$
(3) Increase s and repeat from step 2 while $s < \alpha$ [1].

2.3   Application of SOM

Next, we are dividing the search planes whose models are acquired from the Internet, into 3 groups according to their endurance, radar range, satellite, etc. The concrete details of their model are as follows (Table 1).
Design network structure.

(1) Input layer: 10 nodes (neuron);
(2) Output layer: $3*1 = 3$ nodes (neuron).

---

[1] http://en.wikipedia.org/wiki/Self-organizing_map.

Table 1. Model of the search plane

Type	Length (m)	Diameter (m)	Range (km)	Cruising speed(km/h)	Maximum speed(km/h)	Maximum flying height(m)	Endurance (h)	Radar	Radar range(km)	Satellite
EC-135	12.16	1.86	735	253	278	3000	3.5	2	20	0
EC-145	13.03	1.96	680	246	268	5240	4.5	1	200	1
EC-155	14.4	2.16	830	280	315	4572	3	2	20	1
EC-225	16.79	2.4	857	260.5	275.5	5900	4.5	1	200	1
AW101	22.81	3.36	1389	285	309	4575	4	1	400	1
AW609	13.3	1.12	1390	465	510	7620	3.7	1	345	0
AW139	16.65	2.36	568	290	310	3200	3.9	1	300	0
AS365	13.68	1.1	897	260	296	4300	4	1	500	0
NH90	19.4	3.2	1100	285	310	6000	4.8	1	300	1
MH-60G	19.76	2.36	600	331	361	5790	4.87	3	600	1

Train the experimental data and verify the extensive ability of the model via Matlab 2012b.

Carry out the comparison between the prediction and experimental data Matlab 2012b. The result of SOM model is as follows (Fig. 1).

```
>> sjwl
ans ='EC-225'   'AW609'   'NH90'   'MH-60G Pave Hawk'
ans ='EC-145'   'EC-155'   'AW101'
ans = 'EC-135'   'AW139'   'AS365'
```

In accordance with the result above, the first group concluding 'EC-225', 'AW609', 'NH90' and 'MH-60G Pave Hawk' is assigned to cruise at a higher altitude, since they share the similar features which shows their excellent searching capabilities. The second group consisting of 'EC-145', 'EC-155' and 'AW101' is appointed to search for useful information and cruise as far as possible because of the advantages in endurance as well as perfect radar and satellite system. The last group made up of 'EC-135', 'AW139' and 'AS365' is designated to cruise at a lower altitude, for they are more suitable to carry out low altitude tasks.

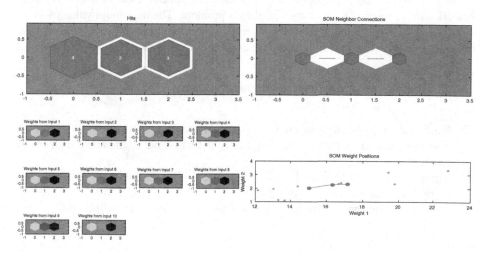

Fig. 1. SOM model analysis

When it comes to the division of the groups and the allocation of tasks, the same is true of warships and submarines. The following is the solution.

```
>> sjwll
ans = 'i'   'j'   'k'   'l'   'm'   'n'   'o'
ans =   'f'   'g'   'h'
ans =   'a'   'b'   'c'   'd'   'e'
```

3   Model 2: Maximum Flow Problem in Determination of Cruise Route

In this section, we have to figure out some dispersive objective searched-areas in searching region and make out the optimal cruise route. This is related to Maximum Flow Problem. Here, we have to make some assumptions.

Assumptions

- Assume that the number of the objective searched-areas is limited and we have made sure location and features of them in advance.
- Assume that the size scattered islands in the searching regions is small enough so that we mustn't consider how to bypass them in our searching process.
- Assume that the nodes represent the objective searched-areas.

3.1   Maximum Flow Problem

In order to improve the universality of our whole model, we will relax the assumption, which induce us to find a better solution to the problem. In fact, the new problem based on the new situation is just the Maximum Flow Problem. In optimization theory, maximum flow problems involve finding a feasible flow through a single-source, single-sink flow network that is maximal.

The maximum flow problem can be seen as a special case of more complex network flow problems, such as the circulation problem. The maximum value of an s-t flow (i.e., flow from source s to sink t) is equal to the minimum capacity of an s-t cut (i.e., cut severing s from t) in the network, as stated in the max-flow min-cut theorem.[2]

3.2   Basic Concept of the Maximum Flow Problem

(1) State space is typically modeled as a directed graph.
(2) The flow is a maximum flow, if and only if there's no augmenting path in the residual network.
(3) Minimum cut is the minimal cut in all the ones. The minimum cut is not unique, while the value of it is the only one.
(4) The flux of the maximum flow equals the capacity of the minimum cut.

---

[2] http://en.wikipedia.org/wiki/Maximum_flow_problem#cite_note-9.

In effect, the principle of the algorithm established in our paper is Ford–Fulkerson algorithm, which means as long as there is an open path through the residual graph, send the minimum of the residual capacities on the path. The Ford-Fulkerson algorithm works only if all weights are integers. Otherwise it is possible that the Ford–Fulkerson algorithm will not converge to the maximum value.

3.3 Detailed Process of the Solution

(1) Find a path from source node to sink nodes via BFS(Breadth- First Search), which is called augmenting path.
(2) If we cannot find such a path stated in step (1), the network solved in the last iteration is the maximum flow. Else, do as follows.
(3) Find the minimum from the augmenting path values.
(4) Construct a new network by subtracting the minimum value in step (3) from all the augmenting paths.
(5) Construct the maximum flow network with the minimum value obtained from step (3), which is included in the initial network.
(6) Do as step (1) in the new network.

3.4 Application of the Solution

Now we are going to translate the problem of determination of cruise route into Maximum Flow problem.

Firstly, obtaining information above, terrain and environment of the different search area, in order to gain the allocation of rescue resources and search order for distinctive area according to the varying degree of searching difficulty, we decides the area into six districts shown below. We assume that the following figure is just the searching region, with a radius of 87.18 n miles (Fig. 2).

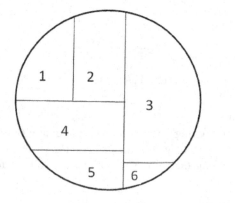
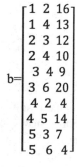

$$b = \begin{bmatrix} 1 & 2 & 16 \\ 1 & 4 & 13 \\ 2 & 3 & 12 \\ 2 & 4 & 10 \\ 3 & 4 & 9 \\ 3 & 6 & 20 \\ 4 & 2 & 4 \\ 4 & 5 & 14 \\ 5 & 3 & 7 \\ 5 & 6 & 4 \end{bmatrix}$$

Fig. 2. Searching Region

Next, we make a stipulation: the maximal area we have traverse before we arrive at region j: the maximal value of path *le(i, j)* is equal to 100:1 and region i is corresponded to node i area in Network Topology Mode.

Then, the connection between different regions reflected by the figure below can be expressed in matrix, which is b. b is stated above. The first column is corresponded to start nodes. The second column is corresponded to sink nodes and the third column is corresponded to maximum value of path *le(i, j)*.

If we transform the connections into network model, it can be expressed as Fig. 3. In this way, we translate the determination problem of cruise route into Maximum Flow problem. The result shows in Fig. 4.

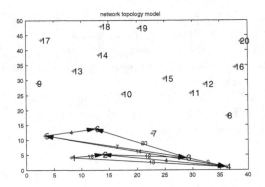

Fig. 3. Initial Network Topology of MF

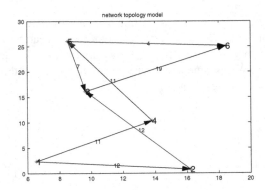

Fig. 4. Ultimate Network Topology of MF

Here are the results of our simulation.

The result shows that, in the searching region above, there are 6 objective searched-areas. The capacity of the path is as Fig. 4, which can be transformed into the allocation of search planes warships along the path. The optimal cruise is as follows.

(1) Path *e(1,2)*: allocate 12 search planes or warships along it.
(2) Path *e(1,4)*: allocate 11 search planes or warships along it.

(3) Path $e(2,3)$: after searching along path $e(1,2)$, allocate 12 search planes or warships along it.

(4) Path $e(4,5)$: after searching along path $e(1,4)$, allocate 11 search planes or warships along it.

(5) Path $e(5,3)$: after searching along path $e(4,5)$, allocate 7 from 11 search planes or warships along it.

(6) Node3: 12 search planes or warships from node2 and 7 search planes or warships from node5 gather at node3.

(7) Path $e(3,6)$: allocate all the 19 search planes or warships gathering at node3 along it.

(8) Path $e(5,6)$: after searching along path $e(4,5)$, allocate 4 from 11 search planes or warships along it.

(9) Node6: 19 search planes or warships from node3 and 4 search planes or warships from node5 gather at node6.

In real searching process, we need to number all the nodes and input the true nodes matrix. Since the matrix depends on the situations, here we use a simulate matrix to verify the feasibility of BFS in cruise route planning. If we would like to use this algorithm program in real searching process, we need to change the b matrix into true matrix in it. Note that in this section, $le(i,j)$ obtained in the ultimate solution is the sum of search planes and warships.

4 Conclusion

The article builds a generic mathematical model that could help to made a useful plan to search for a lost plane that have crashed in open water on the basis of big data through stimulation. In the process, we use different models and find a new rescue method. Firstly, we use the Neural Network Model to solve the problem about area classification. Secondly, as to the determination of cruise route, we choose Maximum Flow Model as to solve the problem.

Appendix

Neural Network Model SOM Classification of Search Planes

```
[xdata,textdata] = xlsread('sjfj.xlsx');xdata = xdata';
aircraft = textdata(2:end 1);
net = newsom(xdata,[3 1]);
plotsom(net.layers{1}.positions)
net.trainParam.epochs = 100;
net = train(net,xdata);
y = sim(net,xdata);
classid = vec2ind(y);
aircraft(classid ==1)
aircraft(classid ==2)
aircraft(classid ==3)
plotsomtop(net)
plotsomnd(net)
plotsomhits(net,xdata)
```

Table of Search Warships (right)

Maximum Flow Model Shortest direct path

zdlzxz.m

```
clear all;close all;clc
b=[1 2 16;1 4 13; 2 3 12;2 4 10;3 4
9; 3 6 20;4 2 4;4 5 14;5 3 7;5 6 4];
m=max(max(b(:,1:2)));
A=compresstable2matrix1(b);
netplot4(A,1);
maxflow=zeros(m,m);
while 1
    flag=[];flag=[flag          1];
head=1;tail=1;queue=[];queue(head)=1
; head=head+1;
    pa=zeros(1,m); pa(1)=1;
    while tail~=head
        i=queue(tail);
        for j=1:m
            if A(i,j)>0 && isempty(find(flag==j,1))
                queue(head)=j;    head=head+1;    flag=[flag        j];
pa(j)=i;
            end
        end
        tail=tail+1;
    end
    if pa(m)==0
        break;
    end
    path=[]; i=m; k=0;
    while i~=1
        path=[path;pa(i) i A(pa(i),i)];i=pa(i);k=k+1;
    end
    Mi=min(path(:,3));
    for i=1:k
        A(path(i,1),path(i,2))=A(path(i,1),path(i,2))-Mi;
maxflow(path(i,1),path(i,2))=maxflow(path(i,1),path(i,2))+Mi;
    end
end
figure;
netplot4(maxflow,1)
```

No.	Initial distance (n mile)	Max speed(n mile /h	Range ^{2}(n mile ^{2})
a	0	8	9
b	21	10	12
c	22	33	50
d	25	12	24
e	26	31	56
f	69	12	21
g	75	21	42
h	77	17	25
i	87	16	21
j	88	13	24
k	92	15	19
l	93	16	27
m	95	21	47
n	97	22	58
o	99	23	62

Reference

1. Kohonen, T., Honkela, T.: Kohonen network. Scholarpedia (2011). Retrieved 2012-09-24

An Informatics Approach for Smart Evaluation of Water Quality Related Ecosystem Services

Weigang Yan[1(✉)], Mike Hutchins[1], Steven Loiselle[2], and Charlotte Hall[2]

[1] NERC Centre for Ecology & Hydrology,
Maclean Building, Wallingford, Oxfordshire, UK
{Weigang.Yan, Michael.Hutchins}@ceh.ac.uk
[2] Earthwatch Institute,
Mayfield House, 256 Banbury Road, Oxford, Oxfordshire, UK
{sloiselle, chall}@earthwatch.org.uk

Abstract. Understanding the relationship between water quality and ecosystem services valuation requires a broad range of approaches and methods from the domains of environmental science, ecology, physics and mathematics. The fundamental challenge is to decode the association between 'ecosystem services geography' with water quality distribution in time and in space. This demands the acquisition and integration of vast amounts of data from various domains in many formats and types. Here we present our system development concept to support the research in this field. We outline a technological approach that harnesses the power of data with scientific analytics and technology advancement in the evolution of a data ecosystem to evaluate water quality. The framework integrates the mobile applications and web technology into citizen science, environmental simulation and visualization. We describe a schematic design that links water quality monitoring and technical advances via collection by citizen scientists and professionals to support ecosystem services evaluation. These would be synthesized into big data analytics to be used for assessing ecosystem services related to water quality. Finally, the paper identifies technical barriers and opportunities, in respect of big data ecosystem, for valuating water quality in ecosystem services assessment.

1 Informatics View for Smart Water Monitoring

Informatics has played a substantial role to improve the interactions between human beings and machines. The information generated from various disciplines is the rosetta stone to bridge our understanding to the world and the engineering of computational methods. In environmental sciences, these data are growing at an exponential rate from various monitoring networks. Together with an explosive growth of mobile applications, cloud computing and big data systems have been introduced to be a potential technology for many aspects of scientific research [2, 4, 6, 7, 10]. Moreover, citizen science, also known as crowd science, is burgeoning in many scientific disciplines beyond conservation ecology [3, 5, 9, 14, 16, 17]. It brings scientists, technologists and

© Springer International Publishing Switzerland 2015
C. Zhang et al. (Eds.): ICDS 2015, LNCS 9208, pp. 178–185, 2015.
DOI: 10.1007/978-3-319-24474-7_24

educators together to share scientific knowledge and data. The application of modern technology such as smartphone, sensors and big data tools has enabled the engagement of citizen scientists into the digital world [4–6, 10]. More importantly, the technical breakthrough in storing colossal datasets provides a new horizon for scientific communities to re-examine the current framework, digital infrastructure, analytic methods and future development trend for water monitoring as a whole.

In water research, accessibility of primary data influences researchers addressing the growing water crisis and improves the clarity of view of decision makers [1, 2, 13, 15]. Although there are fast growing platforms and tools to facilitate data collection and population in the area of monitoring aided by citizen science, for example, iSpot (www.ispotnature.org), there remains a need to orchestrate the technical components in order to deliver the information generated from primary data to end users efficiently and effectively. This is due to the growing volume of data sets and types as well as the increasing analytical capability in the internet [2, 4, 7]. Mashing up the technologies of mobile computing, big data systems and internet accessibility into a harmonized digital data ecosystem will enable the access of these data in an integrated way so that scientists would be able to carry out complex analyses [2].

Moreover, applying informatics approach in citizen science to enhance water monitoring can potentially result in a considerable shift in the way research concerning water resources is conducted and reported. In this way, advances in the measurement of environmental variables using novel sensors, the relaying of information via smartphones and the storage, analytics and visualization of such data on the internet present great potential for increased involvement of citizen scientists in scientific research [2, 4, 10]. The examples of citizen science in a recent review represent in the areas of mathematics, biology, informatics, genetics, biochemistry and astronomy [3]. None of them involves water related challenges, which indicates a gap to bridge between citizen science and water resource management. In this respect Earthwatch Institute's Fresh-Water Watch programme, IBM's Smart Water Management are some of only a few initiatives that are pioneering to link public participation in water resource monitoring and scientific research. In practice, online crowdsourcing of data from citizen science fosters an open collaborative environment for scientific research and provides open sharing of intermediate inputs for a wider audience, therefore it can facilitate scaling up of regional research [3, 5, 16].

Finally, informatics eases upscaling of monitoring activities. The process of collating field data collected by citizen scientists and researchers via advanced computing programmes will help diminish the barriers of high uncertainty and lack of appropriate data in exercises of water quality valuation [5, 6, 9, 16]. For example, the application of mobile technology will support environmental professionals to quickly assess water quality, log data in the phone and transfer data for further analysis, all in a short time. Due to increased accessibility of water quality data, environmental professionals would be able to improve the resolution of monitoring points and enhance the quality and accuracy of data for water resource management and decision making. Furthermore, the application which can populate field data into web-based databases enables support of further modelling and analytical assessment [2, 10, 11].

Whilst we acknowledge that water resource data vary widely, both in format and in purpose, for the purpose of this article we assume that our case study is digital based and comprises only water quality data. Here we propose the informatics system for engaging citizen science projects and other technologies in water monitoring research. The design of the information system is composed of mobile technology, Database Management Systems and big data system. The motivation for such informatics system is multi-faceted. First, increasing public interest and participation in scientific monitoring of water bodies would help to develop a wider understanding of their function and generate a wealth of scientific data [2, 5, 10]. Therefore, it would enhance the knowledge we could build on the baseline data collected by contributors and create new knowledge to advance science. The large flow of data and information assimilated from citizen scientists collection can provide new thinking for evidence based policy practice and influence decision makers. Secondly, getting the right information from and to the right place and people in the right format at the right place and time is crucial for economic opportunity and decision making. In UK, for example, lacking information for detailed cause and effect relationships between urban growth and the quality of rivers and their flow regimes makes optimal planning of future developments difficult [11, 20]. Worse, there are delays in the delivery of such information from the research output [13]. Hence it is imperative to seek solutions technically to keep data provenance and ensure the delivery of derived scientific results to policy and management decisions effectively.

2   A Framework for Smart Water Quality Valuation

We propose a technical framework for monitoring water quality, using the current research affiliated with citizen science project as an example. The informatics system under the framework aims to support water quality valuation and its related services. It attempts to synthesize information from water resource research from both researchers and citizen scientists, in order to meld research and social economics insight into a productive relationship. To maximize the synergies between disciplines, the framework uses the data to bond each component and links to the changes in water quality via environmental model assessments.

2.1   Overview of Conceptual Design

The system we propose supports the collection and aggregation of the data throughout the monitoring activities, both in scientific research and citizen science activities (Fig. 1 shows macro-structure of the system discussed below including pros and cons).

(a) The system is the carrier of data to build connection between functionalities. Data is able to converge on the central data storage system. Research and citizen science activities provide the resource pool of the informatics system. The interface between data storage system and data sources covers activities of data ingestion and process throughout the workflow pipeline in the machine-to-machine environment. For example, smartphone application will automate the collection of data into central databases. The data can be stored into databases systems such as NOSQL databases before they are further analyzed in analytical

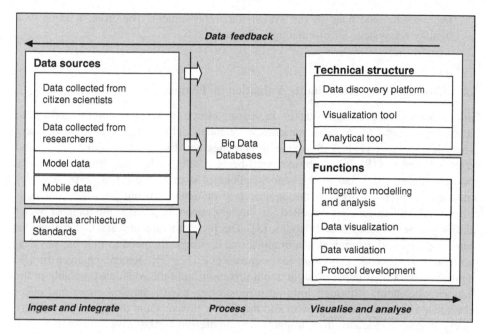

Fig. 1. The outline of smart water monitoring ecosystem. The system aims to (a) distribute the data into functional modules to deliver the features and functions; (b) integrate the data into web accessible status; (c) provide two way communications between users and data.

platform or mash up with other data sources for new aggregation and visualization for decision making. The web services will facilitate the communication between databases and end users.

(b) It is common to evaluate water quality via bio-physical models in water resources management. While water quality data and other relevant physical, biological data are generated from various sources, an important enabler for data exploration is increasing web access for end users. Many models are not always accessible for decision makers and the public. It is viable technically to integrate the web technology and distributed models to increase the accessibility of model outputs and improve the management decision.

(c) The system improves machine-people interaction and enables two-way interactions. An essential facet of the data sources is the need for users, (be they scientists, concerned public or policy makers) to discover the relations between the results of data analysis and primary data. Traditionally, data collectors know about the data they collect but have limited knowledge about the data others collect. After data collectors store the data into the databases they seldom know how their data can be aggregated with the data from other collectors. The informatics system allows data collectors to input data from web forms or allow the data users to participate in data visualization via visualization tools. In this way, data format can be unified into digital and subsequently reduce the cost of storage and data processing. The interaction of data users and machines also offers opportunities for users to feed back to the system for improvement. Therefore, it leads to a healthy ecosystem for circulating information.

2.2 Case Study: Water Quality Valuation in Thames

Global population growth is placing increasing stress on water resources, aside from increasing demand for portable supplies, accelerated deforestation for agriculture and urban development [18]. Anthropogenic activities negatively affect water quality and water availability [19]. In turn human well-being is affected by changing water quality and subsequently the cost to relevant beneficiaries such as breweries. Typically, elevated export of nutrients into the aquatic environment from human waste and agricultural intensification has resulted in eutrophication becoming the biggest water quality problem facing society today [8]. The problems are universal, damaging to water supplies and ecological health alike, and highlight the need to link bio-physical modelling to rigorous economic assessments [11, 12, 20]. Recent changes in UK population has for example brought about urbanisation in the south-east, notably in the Thames catchment. Although long-term monitoring exists, detailed cause and effect relationships between urban growth and the quality of rivers and their flow regimes are poorly known, especially how impacts are manifested further downstream [11, 20]. This makes optimal planning of future development difficult, hence the research project POLL-CURB seeks to better understand the urban natural environment and over the pitfalls of uniformed future development. As one of the academic partners, we works under the network of urban water research projects by the Earthwatch Institute to engage citizen scientists in data collection for water quality research.

As collection of water quality data is becoming increasingly possible in situ using handheld probes without recourse to laboratory analysis the involvement of citizen science can assist the upscaling of the research in the field. Affordable sensors linked to smartphones would potentially allow for much more extensive and detailed surveys of water quality (and its dynamics, such as river nitrogen sinks) to be carried out than is feasible by professional science alone. Therefore we apply the above framework to value water quality (Fig. 1). We engage citizen scientists to collect water quality data from mobile app and handheld sensors to assist water quality valuation.

Through the integration of mobile data input, handheld sensor data input and citizen science data (Table 1), we build a data ecosystem that users can interact with the data storage for depositing data and through SQL queries the data are visualized in the Google maps. Figure 2 gives the example of visualization of data collected by citizen science. The data can be further combined with predictive model to predict water quality status locally or in a larger scale.

3 Pitfalls and Future Work

The system we propose combines technological innovation and citizen science thereby progressing traditional research in response to the challenge on diminishing the barriers of high uncertainty, heterogeneity and unavailability of appropriate data in water

Table 1. Data sources underlying the data ecosystem.

Data source	Utilization
Citizen science probe data: water quality essential parameters	The vital data such as nitrate, ammonium, DOC, chloride, optical DO from monitoring probes can provide feedback for planners or managers to leverage their decisions and are inputs of models to predict environmental conditions
Researcher probe data: water quality essential parameters	As above
Citizen science mobile data: waterbody features	Basic features of rivers such as water colour, morphology, georeferenced locations can be used to help with predictive models for estimating the pollution source when joined with water quality parameters, land use classification and history information

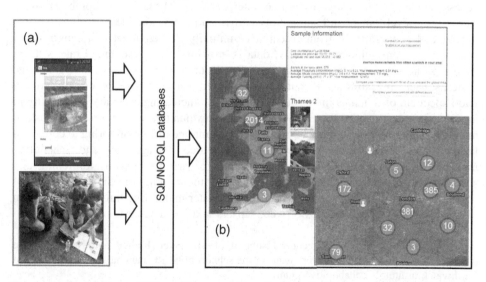

Fig. 2. Data input from mobile application and handheld probes (a) are populated in databases before they are visualized in the web (b), which forms part of the data ecosystem. Each sample containing the essential water quality parameters is available from the internet for further analysis such as modelling or statistical analysis.

quality valuation. However, to build a data ecosystem that brings together relevant data from a wide range of types and sources would create big challenges especially in accurately and efficiently measuring and interpreting the results. These difficulties can arise in various forms.

Attempts are often made to overcome difficulties presented by the dispersed status of data in a water monitoring programme. The efforts of streaming data into databases have been fragmented. This subsequently affects the connectivity between components in the data ecosystem to achieve certain functions, e.g. analytics. This system is limited in terms of functions in data logistics, distribution and predictive analytics for supporting data intensive scientific research. Besides, it is already a challenge to value water quality changes in spatial context and link it to bio-physical and economic models. The efforts of collecting the data for models will be in danger of becoming insurmountable without a holistic system. This also leads to problems of information delay between the processes of linking information from different components [9, 13].

In terms of BIG DATA, the data ecosystem under this approach enables a development niche to host high volume of structured and unstructured data from various data sources including citizen science data, as well as to leverage big data to support large scale data analysis. To meet up social and cultural change challenge addressed in researches, the system can facilitate and encourage local communities to devise their own research questions and hypotheses that might be tested by them. By facilitating community-driven research, it substantially changes the nature of engagement in research and public opinion will move towards emphasizing the value of natural assets. It will create a means to present water quality and ecosystem services research in open access formats with easily accessible interpretation. Through the combination of technology development and community participation, new knowledge will be derived jointly and cooperatively from research community, linked local communities and conservation communities. Secondly, data is growing at an exponential rate with no exception in water resource management. Big Data systems such as NoSQL storage systems, Hadoop Map-Reduce, data analytics platforms address needs for data across a wide spectrum of domains in various formats. With increasing scale and complexity in monitoring water quality for ecosystem services evaluation, it is not a trivial task to manage the Big Data system that connects each components in monitoring to cope with failures and performance problems. New resource management and scheduling mechanisms are also needed for such systems, as are mechanisms for tuning and support from platform layers. To conclude, while the system is in the earlier stage of development it has the potentials to upscaling in water monitoring through combination of the technological advantages of web, sensors and big data system.

Acknowledgments. We thank technical support of Mr. Biren Rathod and Neil Bailey in developing web platforms. This work is under the support of NERC national capability fund and Earthwatch Institute's collaborative grant.

References

1. Bateman, I.J., Mace, G.M., Fezzi, C., Atkinson, G., Turner, K.: Economic analysis for ecosystem service assessments. Environ. Resour. Econ. **50**, 365–387 (2010)
2. Buytaert, W., Baez, S., Bustamante, M., Dewulf, A.: Web-based environmental scientific modeling and decision-making. Environ. Sci. Technol. **46**, 1971–1976 (2012)
3. Franzoni, C., Sauermann, H.: Crowd science: the organization of scientific research in open collaborative projects. Res. Policy **43**, 1–20 (2014)
4. Gannon, D., Fay, D., Green, D., Takeda, K., Yi, W.: Science in the cloud: lessons from three years of research projects on microsoft azure. In: Proceedings of the 5th ACM Workshop on Scientific Cloud Computing, pp. 1–8 (2014)

5. Goodchild, M.F.: Citizens as sensors: the world of volunteered geography. GeoJournal **69**, 211–221 (2007)
6. Graham, E.A., Henderson, S., Schloss, A.: Using mobile phones to engage citizen scientists in research. EOS **92**, 313–315 (2011)
7. Hendawi, A.M., Hazel, D., Larson, J., Li, Y., Trummert, D., Ali, M., Teredesai, A.: AMADEUS: a system for monitoring water quality parameters and predicting contaminant paths. IEMSS 2014 (2014)
8. Hilton, J., O'Hare, M., Bowes, M.J., Jones, J.I.: How green is my river? A new paradigm of eutrophication in rivers. Sci. Total Environ. **365**, 66–83 (2006)
9. Hochachka, W.M., Fink, D., Hutchinson, R.A., Sheldon, D., Wong, W., Kelling, S.: Data-intensive science applied to broad–scale citizen science. Trends Ecol. Evol. **27**, 130–137 (2012)
10. Hope, R., Foster, T., Money, A., Rouse, M.: Harnessing mobile communications innovations for water security. Glob. Policy **3**, 433–442 (2012)
11. Hutchins, M.G., Johnson, A.C., Deflandre-Vlandas, A., Comber, S., Posen, P., Boorman, D.: Which offers more scope to surpress river phytoplankton blooms: Reducing nutrient pollution or riparian shading? Sci. Total Environ. **408**, 5065–5077 (2010)
12. Keeler, B.L., Polasky, S., Brauman, K.A., Johnson, K.A., Finlay, J.C., O'Neill, A., Kovacs, K., Dalzell, B.: Linking water quality and well-being for improved assessment and valuation of ecosystem services. Proc. Natl. Acad. Sci. **109**, 18619–18624 (2012)
13. Michener, W.K., Jones, M.B.: Ecoinformatics: supporting ecology as a data-intensive science. Trends Ecl. Evol. **27**, 85–93 (2012)
14. Miller-Rushing, A., Primack, R., Bonney, R.: The history of public participation in ecological research. Front. Ecol. Environ. **10**, 285–290 (2012)
15. Qiu, J., Turner, M.G.: Spatial interactions among ecosystem services in an urbanizing agricultural watershed. Proc. Natl. Acad. Sci. **110**, 12149–12154 (2013)
16. Silvertown, J.: A new dawn for citizen science. Trends Ecol. Evol. **24**, 467–471 (2009)
17. Tulloch, A.I.T., Possingham, H.P., Joseph, L.N., Szabo, J., Martin, T.G.: Realising the full potential of citizen science monitoring programs. Biol. Conserv. **165**, 128–138 (2013)
18. United Nations: The Millennium Development Goals Report 2012
19. Vitousek, P.M., Mooney, H.A., Lubchenco, J., Melillo, J.M.: Human domination of Earth's ecosystems. Science **277**, 494–499 (1997)
20. Waylett, A.J., Hutchins, M.G., Johnson, A.C., Bowes, M.J., Loewenthal, M.: Physico-chemiscal factors alone cannot simulate phytoplankton behavior in a lowland river. J. Hydrol. **497**, 223–233 (2013)

Credit Risk Evaluation Based on Improved Trust Evaluation Method Under Network Transaction

Lai Hui[1]([✉]), Huang Yumeng[2], and Zhou Zongfang[1]

[1] School of Management and Economics, UESTC, Chengdu 610054, China
laihui98923@163.com
[2] School of Accounting, SWUFE, Chengdu 611130, China

Abstract. Information asymmetry makes network transaction at risk, and trust is the foundation of network transactions. Under network transactions environment, the trust evaluation is important to predict the trust object's credit risk. Therefore, on the basis of analyzing the influential factors of trust, we proposed an improved trust evaluation model based on cloud model; further, credit risk evaluation methodology was proposed based on the trust evaluation model. Taking C2C as an example to do the numerical experiment, results show that the trust evaluation model and credit risk evaluation method proposed in this paper, can make a reasonable evaluation and interpretation of the credit risk under network transactions.

1 Introduction

Network transaction brings a great convenience to people's lives and work. However, there exists a serious information asymmetry between both parties in network transactions [1], so the risk is obvious. On January 23th, the official website of SAIC of China released the "the directional monitoring results of network transaction commodity in second half of 2014", shows that the total rate of qualified commodity is 58.7 percent, illustrating a big problem, so the credit issues of the transaction is particularly prominent. How to describe credit risk of network transactions reasonably and develop credit risk evaluation mechanisms, have become a hot issue in the current study.

A large number of studies have shown, trust influences the willingness to trade under network transaction environment. From the perspectives of McKnight [2] and BABA [3], trust is the prerequisite and the key to network trading, while the breakout of credit risk is always a direct result of network transactions. Therefore, under the network trading environment, the trust network evaluation has played an important role in predicting the credit risk of the network transaction. How to reasonably characterize

This research has been supported by National Natural Science Foundation of China (No.71271043 and No.71473031), the special research Foundation of Ph.D program of China(No.20110185110021) and SiChuan Province Science and technology support project (No.2012SZ0001).

C. Zhang et al. (Eds.): ICDS 2015, LNCS 9208, pp. 186–192, 2015.
DOI: 10.1007/978-3-319-24474-7_25

and evaluate the trust based on analyzing the influential factors, will become the core of credit risk evaluation under the network transaction environment.

2 Literature Review

Scholars from different network scenarios analyzed the influential factors of trust [4, 5]. Summarizing the above studies, we can find that the influential factors of trust can be specific dig out from the three aspects of trust subject, trust object and interaction. As to the study of trust model established based on trust factors [6–8], there exists the following problems. First, the influential factors considered in trust model are not comprehensive enough. Second, few literature conducts the characterization the quantitative relationship between the trust and credit risk. While the traditional methods for quantitative credit risk evaluation [9, 10], cannot be directly applied into quantitative trust evaluation, for the influential factors of trust in network transactions are always not numerical. Therefore, an improved cloud model is introduced into quantitative trust evaluation under network transactions in this paper.

3 Research Model and Hypotheses

3.1 The Basic Theory of the Cloud Model

According to the theory of cloud model [11], the following describes the improved cloud model.

Definition 1: (Attribute weights and Time decay factor) $X_1, X_2, \ldots, X_m$ is trust evaluation attribute, the attribute weight is ω_i, $\sum_{i=1}^{m} \omega_i = 1$; Assuming that there are T evaluation periods, the *jth* evaluation period of the *ith* attribute is X_{ij}, given a time weight t_{ij}, in order to eliminate the effects of time on the trust evaluation, t_{ij} meets the condition: $0 < t_{ik} < t_{il}, 1 \leq k < l \leq T, \sum_{j=1}^{T} t_{ij} = 1$. The time weight t_{ij} is called time decay factor.

Definition 2: (Trust cloud Similarity) Enter $TC_1(E_{x_1}, E_{n_1}, H_{e_1})$ and $TC_2(E_{x_2}, E_{n_2}, H_{e_2})$. Get vector $\overrightarrow{TC_1}(E_{x_1}, E_{n_1}, H_{e_1})$ and $\overrightarrow{TC_2}(E_{x_2}, E_{n_2}, H_{e_2})$, the cosine angle between TC_1 and TC_2 is called cloud similarity

$$sim(TC_1, TC_2) = \cos(\overrightarrow{TC_1}, \overrightarrow{TC_2}) = \frac{\overrightarrow{TC_1} \cdot \overrightarrow{TC_2}}{\left\| \overrightarrow{TC_1} \right\| \cdot \left\| \overrightarrow{TC_2} \right\|} \tag{1}$$

Definition 3: (Conversion of trust evaluation value) The trust evaluation grades are divided into n grades, the corresponding interval of *ith* grade score is $[R_i^{min}, R_i^{max}]$, thus the evaluation value of the interval is

$$TrustEvaluation = R_i^{\min} + \beta\left(R_i^{\max} - R_i^{\min}\right) \qquad (2)$$

If $i \geq {}^n\!/_2$, β is the percentage of higher than or equal ith grade; if $i < {}^n\!/_2$, β is the percentage of lower than ith grade, $i = 1, 2, \ldots n$.

3.2   Research Hypothesis

Hypothesis 1: Under the C2C trading environment, assuming that the main factors affecting buyer's trust are the buyer's trust propensity, the seller's historical credit score, match degree of commodity description, seller's delivery speed and seller's service attitude.

Hypothesis 2: Under C2C trading environment, the main factors affecting the credit risk is the buyer's trust and commodity price.

4   Research Design

4.1   Procedure of Trust Evaluation Based on Cloud Model

The procedure of trust evaluation based on cloud model is shown in Fig. 1.

Figure 1 shows the procedure of trust evaluation based on cloud model, combined with the Hypothesis 1.

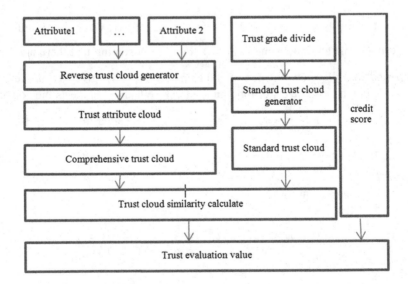

Fig. 1. Procedure of trust evaluation based on cloud model

4.2 Design for Trust Evaluation Based on Cloud Model

4.2.1 Trust Grade Divide

Assuming that the effectiveness domain of the evaluation language set (match degree of commodity description, delivery speed and service attitude) $U = [0, 10]$, and is divided into 5 grades. According to the experience of literature [1], $[0, 10]$ is divided into extremely mistrust([0,1.5]), mistrust ([1.5,3.5]), low mistrust([3.5,6.5]), common trust ([6.5,8.5]), high trust([8.5,10]).

4.2.2 Standard Trust Cloud

Enter the 5 intervals mentioned in Sect. 4.2.1, export *(Standard Trust Cloud)* STC_i (E_{Xi}, En_i, He_i). Calculate the $(E_{X_i}, F_{n_i}, H_{e_i})$, and generate correspondingly Standard cloud: extremely mistrust($STC_1(0, 0.5, 0.2)$), mistrust($STC_2(2.5, 0.67, 0.2)$), low mistrust($STC_3(5, 1.33, 0.2)$), common trust($STC_4(7.5, 0.67, 0.2)$), high trust($STC_5(10, 0.5, 0.2)$), to describe the evaluation vector of n grades {"very bad", "bad", "common", "good", "very good"}.

4.2.3 Qualitative and Quantitative Conversion

Assuming that the language evaluation of a certain attribute is S, the evaluation vector {"very bad", "bad", "common", "good", "very good"}. We use standard trust cloud to do the qualitative and quantitative conversion. Enter the corresponding $(E_{X_i}, E_{n_i}, H_{e_i})$, export a random cloud droplets X, generating a random $E'_n = NORM(E_n, H_e^2)$, and distribution $X = N(E_x, E'^2_n)$, and calculate $\mu(X) = e^{-\frac{(x-E_X)^2}{2(E'_n)^2}}$, thus generating a cloud droplets X with trust membership $\mu(X)$.

4.2.4 Improved Reverse Trust Cloud Generator

Enter sample points $X_i(X_{i1}, X_{i2}, \ldots, X_{im})$ $i = 1, 2, \ldots n$; and time decay factor $t_{ij}(X_{i1}, X_{i2}, \ldots, X_{iT}), j = 1, 2, \ldots, T$, we take the equal ratio decline method to describe the time decay [12] in this paper, $\frac{t_{i(j-1)}}{t_{ij}} = \frac{t_{ij}}{t_{i(j+1)}}, 2 \leq j \leq T - 1, i = 1, 2, \ldots n,$ $j = 1, 2, \ldots, T$. Export the features of X_i $(E_{x_1}, E_{x_1}, \ldots, E_{x_m}; E_{n_1}, E_{n_2}, \ldots, E_{n_m}; He_1, He_2, \ldots, He_m)$. Considering the time decay factor, the expectations, entropy, and ultra-entropy should be adjusted with reference to literature [8].

4.2.5 Comprehensive Trust Cloud

We need to consider corresponding weights of the trust attribute to calculate the expectations, entropy, and ultra-entropy of a new comprehensive trust cloud:

$$E_x = \sum_{i=1}^{m} (E_{x_i} \omega_i) \quad E_n = \sqrt{\sum_{i=1}^{m} \left(E_{n_i}^2 \omega_i \right)} \quad H_e = \sum_{i=1}^{m} (E_{e_i} \omega_i) \tag{3}$$

4.2.6 Trust Cloud Similarity and Trust Evaluation Value Calculate

Assuming the trust propensity is λ, the extent of trust in seller's historical credit score; $1 - \lambda$ is the extent that trust in the result of trust evaluation, so the final trust value is

$$TrustValue = \lambda CreditRating + (1 - \lambda)TrustEvaluation, \lambda \in [0, 1] \qquad (4)$$

4.3 Credit Risk Evaluation Approach Based on Trust Evaluation

4.3.1 Credit Risk Evaluation Process

Figure 2 shows the procedure that the credit risk evaluation model is established on the basis of the result of trust evaluation, with taking the price factor into account.

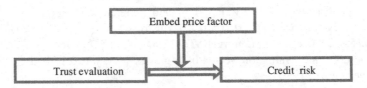

Fig. 2. Procedure of credit risk evaluation based on trust evaluation

4.3.2 Credit Risk Evaluation Model Based on Trust Evaluation

Assuming that $P(j)$ is the commodity price in the *jth* evaluation period, $P_A(j - 1)$ is average price in $j - 1$ evaluation periods. $Trust_j value$ is the trust value in *jth* evaluation period. According to literature [12]. Formula for calculating credit risk under network transactions is as follows:

$$RiskValue = \begin{cases} \dfrac{P(i)}{P_A(j-1)} \times \left(1 - \dfrac{TrustValue_j}{10}\right), 1 < j \leq T \\ 1 - \dfrac{TrustValue_j}{10}, j = 1 \end{cases} \qquad (5)$$

5 Numerical Experiment and Discussion

5.1 Trust Evaluation Attribute

In this paper, we randomly chose a business of Taobao, and collect recent 3 months (3 evaluation periods) 500 transactions with records, to do the numerical experiment. We set the weight of the three attributes (match degree of commodity description, seller's service attitude, seller's delivery speed) as 0.4, 0.3, 0.3.

5.2 Trust Evaluation Procedure

Divide the 3 attributes into 5 grades, from Sect. 4.2.3 we obtained the value for each evaluation attribute, as shown in Table 1.

Table 1. Score of the evaluation attribute interval

Grade interval	Very bad	Bad	Common	Good	Very good
Interval score	[0, 2]	[2, 4]	[4, 6]	[6, 8]	[8, 10]
Match degree of commodity description	1.9	3.6	5.6	6.6	8.2
Seller's service attitude	1.8	3.5	5.5	6.6	8.2
Seller's delivery speed	1.9	3.8	5.8	6.8	8.3

Assuming that the time weight of 3 evaluation periods decay with the rate 0.5, by reverse cloud generator, we got comprehensive trust cloud $TC(5.3, 1, 0.4)$, and similarity between comprehensive trust cloud and standard trust cloud was obtained as in Table 2.

Table 2. Similarity between comprehensive trust cloud and standard trust cloud

Standard trust cloud	Extremely mistrust cloud	Mistrust cloud	Low mistrust cloud	Common trust cloud	High trust cloud
Similarity	0.0012	0.1508	0.7356	0.0548	0.0003

Table 2 shows that, similarity between comprehensive trust cloud and Low mistrust cloud is highest, so that the business trust grade is in low credibility, which is consistent with credit rating in Taobao's (Blue Diamond), the effectiveness of the proposed trust evaluation model is versified.

According to Definition 6, the overall cloud droplets higher than low trust occupied the whole cloud droplets 79 %, according to formula (3), $TrustEvaluation_3 = 3.5 + (6.5 - 3.5) \times 0.79 \approx 5.9$; Taobao's grades are divided into 20 grades, simply set that the grade interval is 0.5, with normalization method we gain the historical credit score is 5.75 (credit score 35233 in Taobao website). So the trust value is

$$TrustValue = 5.75\lambda + 5.9 \cdot (1 - \lambda), \lambda \in [0, 1] \qquad (6)$$

5.3   Credit Risk Evaluation

Use the same method, the credit risk evaluation value can be obtained as Table 3.

Table 3 shows that, credit risk evaluation value decreases with the increase of the $TrustEvaluation_j$; while increase with the increase of the price volatility; which is consistent with the reality situation in practice Taobao business. In general, the higher trust the buyers to the sellers, the better evaluation the sellers will get, makes the seller's credit rating higher and the credit risk lower. If the sellers through price changes, especially to increase the trading volume markdowns and trading volume, it is easy to form a credit fraud.

Table 3. Credit risk evaluation value

$TrustEvaluation_j$	7.2	6.4	5.9
$\dfrac{P_{(j)}}{P_{A(j-1)}}$	1	0.92	0.88
$RiskValue$	$0.28 + 0.027\lambda$	$0.331 + 0.017\lambda$	$0.361 + 0.013\lambda$

6 Conclusions

Through taking the C2C network environment to do the numerical experiment, the effectiveness of the proposed trust evaluation model and credit risk evaluation method based on the trust was verified. In this paper, the trust factors considering in the trust model were too simple, no further consideration of the interaction between factors; the relationship between trust and credit risks was also simplified. How to study further of the interaction between the influential factors of trust, and interaction mechanism between trust and credit risk, is the direction of future research.

References

1. Zhang, S., Xu, C., An, Y.: Study on the risk evaluation approach based on cloud model. J. Univ. Electron. Technol. China **42**(1), 92–104 (2013)
2. McKnight, D.H., Choud Hury, V., Kacmar, C.: The impact of initial consumer on intentions to transact with a web site; a trust building model. J. Strateg. Inf. Syst. **11**(5), 297–323 (2002)
3. Baba, M.L.: Dangerous liaisons: trust, distrust, and information technology in the American work organizations. Hum. Organ. **58**(3), 331–346 (1999)
4. Lu, Y., Zhou, T.: An empirical analysis of factors influencing consumers' initial trust under B2C environment. Nankai Bus. Rev. **8**(6), 96–101 (2005)
5. Ma, Q., ZhaoJia, Z.Y., Hao, J.: A research on the formation mechanism of customers' initial trust under C2C environment: the moderation effect of network shopping experience. Manage. Rev. **24**(7), 70–81 (2012)
6. Ganeriwal, S., Sarivastava, M.: Reputation-based framework for high integrity sensor networks. In: Proceedings of the 2nd ACM Workshop on Security of Ad hoc and Senor Networks, pp. 66–77 (2004)
7. Kim, T.K., Seo, H.S.: A trust model using fuzzy logic in wireless sensor network. In: Proceedings of World Academy of Science, Engineering and Technology, pp. 63–66 (2008)
8. Wang, S., Zhang, L., Li, H.: Evaluation approach of subjective trust based on cloud model. J. Softw. **21**(6), 1341–1352 (2010)
9. Min, X., Zongfang, Z., Lin, C.: A study on the frequency of related party transactions by listed Chinese enterprise groups. Manag. Rev. **23**(7), 124–130 (2011)
10. Shi, Y., Peng, Y., Xu, W.X., Tang, X.W.: Data mining via multiple criteria linear programming: applications in credit card portfolio management. Int. J. Inf. Technol. Decis. Making **1**(1), 131–151 (2002)
11. Chen, J., Zhang, S.: Study on trust evaluation model based on cloud model and trust chain. Appl. Res. Comput. **32**(1), 249–253 (2015)
12. Ruixuan, L., Chang, G., Xiwu, G., Zhengding, L.: Research on credit counting and risk evaluation for C2C e-commerce. J. Commun. **30**(7), 76–85 (2009)

Author Index

Printed in the United States
By Bookmasters